# THE FLY HATCHES

# THE FLY HATCHES

## David Richey

*Illustrations by Darlene Fahlan*

HAWTHORN BOOKS

*A division of Elsevier-Dutton*

NEW YORK

To
Pat Madigan,
a dedicated fly-fisherman, and a favorite companion of mine. He introduced me to fly-fishing for Quebec brook trout on a certain secret lake on a day that shall stand forever in my memory as one of the best ever.

THE FLY HATCHES

**Library of Congress Cataloging in Publication Data**

Richey, David, 1939-
  The fly hatches.

  Bibliography: p.
  1. Trout fishing—United States. 2. Trout
fishing—Canada. 3. Insects, Aquatic—United States.
4. Insects, Aquatic—Canada. 5. Flies, Artificial.
I. Title. II. Title: Hatches.
SH687.R48  1980     799.1'755     80-70
ISBN 0-8015-2686-8

1  2  3  4  5  6  7  8  9  10

# Contents

Preface                                                    vi

Acknowledgments                                            ix


PART ONE
## What's in a Hatch?

1 Why Study Hatches?                                       3

2 How Trout Respond to Fly Hatches                        12

3 Altitude and Latitude are Important                     24

4 Which Fly Is Best?                                      31

5 Dry-Fly Fishing by the Tables                           38


PART TWO
## The Hatches

6 Northeast Hatches                                       51

7 Southeastern Hatches                                    76

8 Southern Hatches                                       133

9 Midwest Hatches                                        146

10 Western Hatches                                       180

11 Canadian Hatches                                      231

Recommended Reading                                      268

Index                                                    273

# Preface

Why write a book on fly hatches? Because logic, sometimes an elusive quality with me, dictates that the world does need another book—a definitive book—on the subject of insect emergence dates for North America. Fly-fishermen have a host of volumes available to tell them how to tie flies to imitate hatches. But to imitate a hatch requires knowing *what hatch* is on. And given the wide-ranging nature of the fly-fishing fraternity, what is required is not a book dealing with two or three regional areas with the same information and dates for each location, but a down-to-earth book detailing all the most important hatches, the dates of emergence, the duration of each hatch, when the peak of activity occurs, and the best (if from a somewhat biased point of view) imitating fly that will work.

This book contains hatch information for every state and every Canadian province or territory. Compiling this information has been an undertaking that staggers the imagination. Between two covers is the sum total of all the important insects found in every state or province. This book allows anglers to plan trips with some certainty of hitting one, two, three, or more hatches. It tells them which hatches are due and what to look for when each insect hatches in order to better plan a fishing day. It also gives data on which imitations to use.

Critics may claim, somewhat self-righteously, that much of this knowledge has been presented before. That is somewhat true, but never in depth. Ernest Schwiebert's *Matching the Hatch* has gone through many printings without substantial change. It's recognized as a classic, and rightfully so, but it is so much more modest in scope than this volume. Other books down through the years have put in an appearance, have been accepted as contributing to the basic knowledge on various hatches, but none has been complete in its coverage of mayflies, caddis flies, and stoneflies. Some are skimpy in their coverage of a particular area or of some of the hatches.

This book, unlike any other, informs fishermen of insect activity in areas that are not well known but that contain trout. Take Ohio for example; it has some decent trout fishing, but who has ever written and outlined the hatches in that state? Or Arkansas? How about Virginia and West Virginia? Or the Carolinas? Where would an angler turn to dig up emergence data for Tennessee or Maryland? The answer: Heretofore, none was available.

When I had all the research information for *The Fly Hatches* compiled, spread throughout my office and all over the living room floor, I was overwhelmed at the possibilities of putting together the book on emerging insects, especially those that apply most directly to trout. Halfway through correlating the research I had a sobering thought: If I put everything on hatches into this book, trying to carry the book would give me and the reader a double hernia. Somewhere, something had to be left out. So I undertook a systematic chopping out of "nondescript" insects that only entomologists have heard of, and of insects that have little or no value as trout food in lakes or streams (except in southern areas where trout are rare, I've tried to provide hatch information important to fly-rodding action there), and, slowly but surely, the book took form.

Readers with an eagle eye for typos may find what they feel to be evidence against the author's claim to intelligence. The same words are spelled differently in various parts of the book. But what I have done is follow local usage. For instance, *Stenonema fuscum*, is commonly designated either as Grey Fox or Gray Fox. Another tidbit I turned up was the common name for *Epeorus pleuralis*. Some areas call this insect the Gordon Quill, while in other regions it's Quill Gordon. Such are the things one turns up in research. I've deferred to the local spelling or name in each case.

The idea for this book came on a trip I made to Tennessee's Cherokee National Forest. Here the Hiwassee River and its tributaries hold a remarkable horde of browns and rainbows. I looked through books and dug through all the information I had at my disposal, but remained without a clue as to which duns and spinners I'd find the second week in June. The fact that I carried two fishing vests cluttered with too many fly boxes is immaterial. Sure, I did catch fish, and I did learn that Yellow Quill, Blue-Winged Olive, Pale Sulphur Dun, Brown Quill, Little Sulphur Quill, and several others were the flies to match. But I didn't know it before I packed up and left home.

I assumed that if such knowledge was lacking to outdoor writers, then it was probable that only a handful of people know what to take along in the line of artificials. So the idea for this book was born, more out of a sense of delivering useful information than as a project for making hordes of money.

The research for this project has required nearly three years of persistent digging. I spent countless hours poring over dusty treatises on insects, months of slugging through a dreary master's thesis, and correlated literally years of on-stream observation in forty-two states and every Canadian province and territory. I found it was still impossible for one man to acquire all the necessary material, so I conned (even if that's not a nice word) several friends into helping with the exhumation of more information. A one-man job it wasn't!

Now the job of research is over. As I go about the task of putting facts down on paper I find I go to sleep with ghostly hatches bobbing over trout streams like sheep over a fence. It's been a horrendous task to assemble this material, but one I'm grateful for undertaking.

You, the angler, can now plan your fishing trip, determine which week, month, or day you'll be fishing, and stand a better-than-average chance of making the connection between a surface-feeding trout (or one of several other species) and an imitating fly. A quick glance at the applicable state table in the pages that follow will pinpoint the hatch activity for that specific time and place.

And that, my friends, is half the battle for a fly-fisherman.

# Acknowledgments

Where does one start to acknowledge assistance in putting together a book of this magnitude? The list could be virtually endless; I've spent thousands of hours writing letters, asking, and even begging for information, made and received long-distance phone calls at all hours of the day and night, and even received help from librarians whose names were never ventured or asked for. I owe a lot to a lot of people.

Pat Madigan of Ottawa, Ontario, was one of the biggest sources of information, particularly for all the Canadian provinces and territories. Pat also dug up little-known insect data for many western states as well.

Jim McGuire, a talented fly-fisherman and author, compiled a list of southern and southeastern hatches that was unbelievable. A native of Dayton, Ohio, Jim practices fly-fishing as a science, and is intensely interested in hatch data.

David O'Connor is a fly-fisherman and personal, outdoor writer friend of mine. His statement when I asked for help was, "You want hatching data for all the important hatches in the Northeast? You've got to be nuts." Several times during the compilation and writing of this book I had to agree with Dave's comment.

Darlene Fahlan of Big Lake, Minnesota, a talented artist friend, graciously consented to complete the drawings that are featured in this book. Darlene's sense of pride and dedication to a cause she believed in resulted in her doing most of these drawings after crushing one hand in an accident. I'm proud of her work, and proud of how she completed her job while in the hospital and during painful periods of physical rehabilitation.

I'd also like to thank John Pinto, David Moeller of Entomological Reprint Specialists, Dr. Vincent Ringrose, Bob Leeman, Terry Mingo, Simeon J. Yaruta, Robert Rifchin, V. John Brennan, Don Ecker, Andrew Gennard, Art Flick, George Harvey, John Harder, David B. Ledlie, and Tom Wendelburg.

A special vote of thanks to my wife, Kay. She researched material from various states and Canada, dug for information, and urged me on when I felt the job was too complex for anyone to pull together.

I also owe thanks to Air Canada, QuebecAir, Bransons Lodge, Air New Zealand, Wanigas Rod Company, Lou Razek for research into old books on hatching insects from his personal collection, and more people and companies than is possible to list here.

To each and every person, mentioned or not, thank you for the giving of your time and knowledge.

David Richey
Buckley, Michigan
June, 1979

# Part One

---

# What's in a Hatch?

# 1

# Why Study Fly Hatches?

There was once a small boy, age about eleven or twelve, who waded into the mainstream of Michigan's AuSable River. It was Easter vacation and a warm breeze had brought a midafternoon hatch to the river.

The boy, equipped with a pair of leaky waders and a makeshift fly rod, diligently flailed the air and water. Husky brown trout tipped up to sip flies off the surface within twenty feet of the youngster, and then settled back into their feeding lane.

Two flies, both No. 12 Adams, comprised the boy's selection of artificials. One was lost to an overhanging cedar limb, the other was sinking badly, and the trout totally ignored the offering. The young lad talked, even pleaded, to the god of fishes, but no trout rose in answer.

Before long, the hatch, which he later was to define as the classic Hendrickson (Ephemerella subvaria), was slowing to a halt. Only a few spent spinners floated downstream. The hatch was nearly over, he knew that, but he wanted a brown trout to take home. He painfully laid out a near-perfect cast and buried the barb in a cedar sweeper tip. The point broke off and the boy wept with frustration along the River of Sands.

A gruff voice broke through the sobbing and said, "Boy, stop that blubbering and tie on this fly. Hurry now, because the Hendrickson flight is nearly over." The boy snatched the fly, muttered an inaudible "thank you" and knotted the Red Quill Spinner to his leader.

The voice continued behind him. "Easy lad, move slow, lengthen line, and give the fly a dead drift to that brown that's still feeding. Make your first cast your best." The boy, with fumbling fingers, was trying to do everything right.

Someone other than the unseen man must have laid his hand on the rod and guided the cast. The leader rolled over as it had never done before, the No. 14 fly drifted downstream without drag, and the brown came to it in a blur of golden brown. "Set easy!" the man hollered as the brown dimpled the surface. The hook was set, not too firm and not too soft, and the battle was joined.

The brown swept down past the boy and tried to work back under the sweeper to safety. The now-gentle voice prodded the boy along, giving instructions, and within a minute or two the boy laid a 14-inch trout over the wooden hoop of his new friend's net. "Damn good fish, boy," he said. "Try that other brownie over there," he pointed. The sight of the netful of fish spurred him on. Two casts, and drag set in and skated the fly across the surface and put the rising trout down for good.

That incident happened nearly thirty years ago and it's etched vividly in my mind as one of the happiest moments of my life. It also accomplished two other things: it made me a student of hatches and a student of trout behavior.

One of the salvations of trout fishing as we know it today is the ability of an angler to limit his kill. There may be some terribly important things in life, but for me, killing trout isn't one of them. To me the point of fly-fishing, particularly dry-fly fishing, is the pitting of one's skills against a wild trout. The challenge is one that is difficult to pass up, and once it's been accepted, nothing in trout fishing really matters except the artful presentation of fly to a wily fish. Once the trout is fooled, and hooked, the battle for me is anticlimactic.

I do not share the opinion of big-fish specialists, meat-hungry sportsmen, and who I call slob fishermen, that a trout doesn't matter, that it's just a fish the state has planted for anyone's enjoyment. Apparently, these people's main pleasure is to kill their limit every time out. It's an ego trip, a macho point of view that does little for the sport, and nothing for the trout or its environment.

It required some time for me to make the progression from that first trout on a fly, through the most trout I could legally catch, on to the biggest trout of my lifetime. Now I'm back at the beginning. The challenge of taking trout on flies is every bit as frustrating and rewarding as it was back when a gruff voice told me to quit blubbering and go fishing. The difference now is that I've learned to slow the pace, study fly hatches and nature, and take with a glad hand anything I'm fortunate enough to hook and land. Now the challenge lies in learning enough about fly hatches to make a reasoned decision on the emergence at hand and to know which fly I should use. Then skill in casting takes over. If the combination is perfect, and the gods smile, the beauty of a day on a trout stream can be something that will live forever in my memory.

Why would anyone want to study fly hatches? Well, the ephemeral qualities of a good spinner flight make me wonder what goes on underwater to bring off so many insects. An outdoor writer must be like any other reporter: He must have an inquisitive mind and be able to spot things happening and then learn as much about what's going on as possible. This was one of the reasons I eased into a study of fly hatches. I wanted to learn as much as possible about insects and figured it was a shortcut to better trout catches. I did the first, and accomplished the second. It took many years, and I'm still learning.

My first step was to study a common insect on the streams near my home in northern Michigan. My first choice (because I was still caught up in stage two of my fishing life where big fish were a major focal point) was the *Hexagenia limbata* hatch. (This insect is commonly and wrongly called a caddis fly. This is not true, for it belongs to a family of burrowing mayflies. The "caddis" label was pinned on it many years ago, and it has stuck.)

The heavy mating flights of Hexes normally occur from dusk until about midnight. A dark, overcast day can bring them off somewhat earlier, but seldom before eight o'clock in the evening. Peak activity usually occurs in mid-June in my area. A typical hatch can place literally thousands of these large mayflies in the air at once. Big trout go wild as they slurp, sip, and dimple the water to feed. I've seen big rainbows and browns literally leap into the air and take the insects on the way down.

I learned these flies weren't caddis flies, but mayflies. They burrow in silt beds along quiet stretches of a river. I also learned these large insects are extremely common in many Michigan lakes. Periods of maximum emergence, when millions of Hexes hatch, have caused some roads and businesses to close until the mess could be cleaned up.

Mating flights of *Hexagenia limbata* along lakes usually occur near the edge of the water and above shoreline vegetation. These mayflies often mate over rivers at a height of thirty or forty feet. The male approaches a swarm of females and other males, performs an intricate

*Hexagenia limbata*—female spinner

up-and-down flight, and then copulates with the female, flying in a horizontal fashion. Mating continues in flight although the pair loses altitude until the insects separate.

The females often dive onto the water, although some fly back and forth over the surface before lying spent on the water with wings spread out. The tail is raised and the female releases the eggs. Some females dip into the water to release their eggs. The best fishing occurs either as the nymphs rise from the silt beds to the surface—as they slip their nymphal shuck and emerge as duns (subimagoes)—or during the spinner (imago) fall after copulation has taken place. Heavy feeding occurs on the spent-winged adults as they drift downstream with the current.

The same basic mating flight of spinners occurs on lakes with large populations of *Hexagenia limbata*. The spinnerfall can create a frenzy of feeding activity for all types of lake fish, including trout. I've seen some lakes where windrows of *limbata* nymphs have washed ashore during a heavy hatch. Large rafts of dead nymphs will litter the lake surface for three or four days.

When a large mating flight takes place, with the females falling to the surface of a lake, one can still find brown trout literally gorged with these large mayflies three days later.

This is, at best, a thumbnail sketch. Students interested in entomology can go farther and learn the length of time a Hex nymph is at home in a silt bed, water temperatures at the time of hatch, other preexisting weather conditions, etc. But it isn't necessary. The purpose of this book is to give anglers the basic information necessary to set out with a reasonable indication of which hatches are due to emerge at certain days, weeks, or months of the year; time of day the best action should be found if the insect hatches on schedule; the duration of the hatch, both daily and weekly (or monthly); and which fly would make a good imitation.

Some anglers who purchase this book will be totally ignorant of the various families of insects covered in these pages. Each family consists of numerous closely related insects. This book will cover primarily mayflies, caddis flies, and stoneflies.

## MAYFLIES

This broad-based family contains more than five hundred recognized species. They travel under common names known to anglers, as well as uncommon Latin names. (My high school Latin teacher kicked me out of class two weeks after it began, reasoning that I would be hopeless as a student of the language. She was probably correct, because I still have difficulty pronouncing some of the Latin names for insects. Some I've rolled around my tongue enough times to get the pronunciation about correct, but a reference to the common, angler-known name has been sufficient to get me past this problem.)

Mayflies are common throughout the United States and Canada, and elsewhere in the world, for that matter. They reside in large rivers, streams, small creeks, backwoods beaver ponds, and farm ponds, but they do not fare well in polluted waters. Some states I've queried indicate that mayfly populations are going slowly down because of water pollution. So much for man's progress.

The majority of mayflies have three tails, although some only have two. The average length of a mayfly runs from one and one-half inches for large spinners like *Hexagenia limbata* down to only about one-eighth of an inch for smaller mayflies such as *Tricorythodes minutus* (Pale Olive Dun).

In the nymphal stage, the insect lives underwater for varying periods of time. Maturation to the next step involves the nymph swimming to the surface, shedding the nymphal shuck, and emerging as a dun. This last phase is the true hatch, but it is often confused with the spinner flight which is when much of the dry-fly fishing takes place. After emerging as a dun, the insect usually flies to shoreline brush, grass, or leaves, and waits patiently for the final molting of its skeleton.

This molting takes place usually within twenty-four hours and a spinner (adult, or imago) emerges. Mating is then ready to take place over a stream or lake. After mating, the spent insects often fall to the water's surface to release the fertilized eggs, which fall to the stream or lake beds, and the cycle is completed.

There are many families of mayflies, all of which are further broken down into subfamilies. This breakdown goes one step farther to specify the individual insects by genera. The most common mayfly families include: *Siphlonuridae, Metretopodidae, Siphlaenigmatidae, Ametropodidae, Baetidae, Oligoneuriidae, Heptageniidae, Leptophlebiidae, Ephemerellidae, Tricorythidae, Neoephemeridae, Caenidae, Baetiscidae, Prosopistomatidae, Behningiidae, Potamanthidae, Euthyplociidae, Ephemeridae, Palingeniidae,* and *Polymitarcyidae.*

## CADDIS FLIES

The caddis fly is another widespread insect of major importance to trout and other game fish. Nearly 1,000 caddis flies exist in the New World and many are imitated by artificial flies. This group of insects hasn't gained the acceptance of anglers to the extent of mayflies, but some of the caddis flies rate highly on a trout's diet. Some of the more popular are the Grannom *(Brachycentrus numerosus),* American Sedge *(Brachycentrus americanus),* and White Miller *(Leptocella albida).*

The uninitiated may confuse caddis flies with mayflies. The similarity ends with their appearance over a lake. Caddis flies fly in a much different manner than mayflies. The former have a more erratic flight—they seem to bounce through the air instead of flying like mayflies.

A close examination of a caddis fly will show two sets of wings that function in flight. These wings are folded backward over the body when the insect is not flying; a mayfly's wings are usually held in an upright position.

A caddis fly undergoes four stages of development. First is the egg stage which lasts for varying lengths of time, partly depending upon water temperature. The second stage is as a larva. In the larval stage most caddis flies build a protective case from pebbles, sand, and other bottom debris, or from twigs. A secretion cements these particles together to form a case around the larva. The caddis fly larva feeds heavily during this stage and builds a new case as it outgrows the older one. Some caddis flies build nets and a few are completely free-living without a dependency on protective devices.

Caddis fly larva undergo a second change during pupation. The larva ceases to eat or grow and enters a hibernationlike stage during which it transforms into an adult. When maturity arrives the pupa leaves the case and ascends rapidly to the water's surface. Those in some families do not swim to the surface but crawl out onto stream-side rocks or bushes. During the period of emergence of the adult, many similar caddis flies can be seen resting on tree branches, leaves, bushes, or flying high over the river.

Caddis flies mate over land and often mate two or three times. They do not die immediately thereafter like mayflies, but may live for ten or more days. The female caddis fly will deposit her eggs on or under the water surface—a few species anchor their eggs to rocks underwater. This is the prime period for anglers to be fishing caddis fly imitations.

Because caddis flies are not as well known to anglers as mayflies, there is a decided lack in common names to describe the many caddis fly species. Approximately 18 families of caddis flies exist in North America, and many more in other parts of the world. These families are made up of nearly 1,300 species, many of which could be important to fishermen. The important families in this country are *Brachycentridae, Goermdae, Helicopsychidae, Hydropsychidae, Lepidostomatidae, Leptoceridae, Limnephilidae, Odonticeridae, Philopotamidae, Phryganeidae, Polycentropidae,* and *Rhyacophilidae.* Caddis flies may be found in swift streams, quiet pools, boggy areas, low elevations, high elevations, riffles, rocky areas, or quiet ponds.

## STONEFLIES

This grouping of insects includes almost four hundred species and most constitute a surprisingly large portion of a trout's diet. Stoneflies are present year round and are actively preyed on by game fish. The best hatches occur during summer months, but winter, spring, and fall also show some major activity.

The insects lay eggs in streams or along gravel areas in northern lakes. The female dips her lower abdomen into the water while in flight to lay her eggs.

The eggs hatch and the nymphs remain in a dormant state for some months. A nymph will undergo several molts before becoming an adult. This process normally takes from one to two years, depending on species.

At the point of maturity nymphs crawl from the water to rest on a rock, boulder, tree, or branch. The nymphal shuck is discarded and the adult rests as wings dry. Emergence can occur any time during day or night. Mating takes places any time other than in flight, which makes these insects different in that respect from mayflies or caddis flies.

Stoneflies are habitually weak flyers. They can vary in length from one-eighth inch to two inches. The most common coloration is brown or gray, but some species are yellow and others green.

One of the hottest hatches for western anglers to hit is the *Pteronarcys californica* (western salmon fly). This giant gray or black stonefly makes its appearance in late spring and big trout gorge themselves on adults or emerging nymphs. I've known anglers to drive 2,000 miles to fish the salmon fly hatch. I've hit it several times in Montana, Wyoming, and Oregon. The sport with big browns and rainbows can be exceptional, the best of the season.

This large group of insects is second only to mayflies in importance to fly-fishermen. Among the most critical families for anglers are *Nemouridae*, *Pteronarcidae*, *Peltoperlidae*, *Perlidae*, *Perlodidae*, and *Chloroperlidae*. Each family has subfamilies. This may seem as clear as mud, but anglers can refer to *McClane's Standard Fishing Encyclopedia* as a good reference for sorting out distinctions. Al McClane has broken down the families into their subfamilies and noted distinguishing characteristics to each that will aid anglers in differentiating between the various species.

The preceding summaries are intended as background information to give readers an insight into the basic characteristics of mayflies, caddis flies, and stoneflies. If you understand the basic life history of these insects, the rest of the book will be more worthwhile and easier to follow.

One point to remember about hatches is that these families of insects, like people, do not all mature at one time. It might seem that way when you witness a blanket hatch for the first time, but the truth is that all insects hatch over a period of days, weeks, or months. In the charts that follow, this information will be listed under specific hatches as "duration of hatch." Also indicated is the time of year that a hatch is most apt to occur.

The "peak of activity" section of the hatch charts indicates when the major emergence or spinner flight should take place. Weather conditions can cause this to vary somewhat, so I always make it a point to fish one hour before a hatch is scheduled to begin, and one hour after the peak activity is supposed to be over. This gives a fisherman several hours each day when insects should be emerging or mating.

Part of studying fly hatches is learning the nymphal and adult characteristics of the most common insects on each body of water. Some nymphs prefer various types of bottom habitat or current speeds. During the hatch some nymphs swim rapidly for the surface, some crawl out, some ascend slowly. In some cases I've noted these preferences in order to better familiarize the reader with a specific insect's behavior.

Studying hatches can lead to other knowledge. All the information absorbed, when pieced together, can form a whole that can then be applied with stream-side logic. For example, this information helps an angler decide whether to offer a feeding trout the male or female imitation of the hatching insect. Some fish will prefer to feed on egg-carrying females and will pass up males until the spinnerfall is nearly over.

It's been my pleasure to have fished over most of the world and I've found that a study of fly hatches and the knowledge that comes of such observation have made me a far better trout fisherman.

# 2

# How Trout Respond to Fly Hatches

Trout are not the only fish to feed on fly hatches, and you will note that further on I've indicated the importance of hatches for anglers after other gamefish. But trout are the prime fish species to come to mind when talking of hatches and matching them, so I've oriented most of the material in this book to trout-fishing situations.

To cover thoroughly the manner in which trout rise to hatching insects would require almost a book in itself. Riseforms differ from one trout species to another, and a riseform can vary according to the intensity of the hatch.

My experience during the past thirty years of trout fishing is that trout vary their attempts to capture hatching duns in a number of ways. Some are most dramatic. In other instances, it's a case of a sipping riseform that gradually widens out in concentric circles before disappearing into the full thrust of river currents.

One rising brown I remember all too well was holding forth along the edge of a riverbank on Montana's Madison River. It was late July and the pale mayfly *Ephemerella inermis* was hatching. The brown was sipping this small insect from the surface of a quiet pool. The fish was in a feeding lane at the edge of an eddy and at intervals darted two feet either way to waylay a struggling dun.

My experience with this particular hatch was spotty, but the No. 12 or No. 14 Pale Olive Quill seemed a logical choice to imitate the pale olive yellow fly. As I attached my dry fly to the fishing line, the trout continued to suck naturals from the surface with amazing regularity. I watched it rise up from its holding position, drift downstream and to one side, and make a dainty riseform as it sipped a mayfly from the surface. It seemed easy to duplicate the path of the natural because the current, what there was of it, was slow, and drag didn't appear to be a problem.

I stationed myself downstream and to one side of the fish, shook loose my fly line, false cast once, and laid the imitation about ten feet above the stationary fish. It rose immediately, followed the fly downstream, and then returned to its feeding lane. Cast after cast followed, but none were accepted although the fly traveled without drag.

I snipped off a No. 12 and replaced it with a No. 14 and tried that. The trout responded in predictable fashion; it followed for several feet, made a half turn, and then called off the critical inspection.

My next cast proved to be the one that ultimately turned the trick. As the trout left his feeding station, I gave the imitation a slight pull to cause the hackle tips to reflect light, and the trout struck with a dainty sip that pulled the fly under the surface.

The fish completed his turn and headed for home. As the line came tight, it snugged the fly into the corner of the trout's mouth. The brown, a fish I guessed to weigh about four pounds, made a strong run for some cover along the bank. My 5X tippet was singing across the surface as the trout made a panicked upstream run.

The fish gave a terrific account of itself, including a short downstream run that made me wonder whether I should have cut the tippet back to a heavier leader. I gave line and kept steady pressure on the fish until it began sulking in midstream. A downstream move and sideways pressure on the fish upset its balance and it had to continue fighting. Ten minutes later the brown was in close for netting. After a brief moment of admiration, I twisted the fly out.

That day proved one very important thing to me: If trout are rising naturally, but refuse a fly that is presented imitating the hatching natural, a slight bit of movement to simulate a dun emerging from the nymphal shuck may do the trick. It doesn't always work, but it works often enough to be included in any angler's repertoire.

Anglers including Vince Marinaro, Ernest Schwiebert, G. E. M. Skues, and others have broken some of the ground in regard to describing various riseforms. The importance of understanding how trout rise to a natural is important when utilizing the information that follows. Riseforms can follow a general pattern or reflect the singularity of an individual trout's behavior. I've spent many days and weeks observing trout during peak and marginal hatches and have concluded that there are trout that have personalities all their own. This has great bearing on how any individual trout will respond to either an imitation or a natural fished on the surface.

Here are some of the various riseforms that are common on trout streams. Study the text, then study wild trout. You'll probably learn that some trout obviously haven't read the books and consequently do not perform according to set patterns, but this is what makes fly-fishing so interesting.

## THE SIMPLE RISE

This is the most common of all the possible rises. It normally occurs during peak activity of any hatch. Duns struggling to shed their nymphal shuck create some commotion on or just under the surface and this allows feeding trout to home in on an easy meal. It also allows fly-fishermen who can imitate hatching duns to take some trout.

The simple rise takes place with a trout holding position in an area where drifting insects are brought over his vision window. This type of rise is a deliberate upstream-and-downstream drift with the current. The trout is nose-up and drifting down with the natural or imitation. Drag on an imitation at this point can make feeding trout reject the offering. If all appears well with the drifting fly, the trout will continue his upward movement and take the fly off the surface. The beginning of the riseform will be triangular in shape and then finish outward to make the circular pattern that is so familiar to fly-fishermen.

One important thing that even many experienced fly-fishermen do not know is that a riseform is *always* downstream from the trout's holding position in the river. This is because trout will drift downstream from their feeding station for one to several feet before taking a natural. Cast above the riseform, and you'll have better success with rising trout.

## THE DOUBLE (Compound) RISE

This riseform takes about twice as long for a trout to perform as the simple rise. The fish rises from a feeding lane and drifts downstream to inspect the fly. A certain suspicion that all is not right will cause the fish to hesitate. In doing so, the fish will turn sideways in the current while maintaining a near-vertical position and drift down with the fly.

Close scrutiny follows as the trout moves in under the imitation and studies it. A drag-free float is necessary. If the fly suits the trout's fancy, it will then move up to the surface and complete the double rise. If not, the trout will refuse the offering somewhere between the first and second rise and return to the feeding lane.

## THE SIPPING RISE

A tiny sound or a rolling splash often accompanies rises. The combination of both sight (riseforms) and sound triggers interest in many anglers. The combination of the two may be the first clue an angler has that fish are feeding in a certain location.

Such is not the case with the sipping rise. This is a soundless, almost slow-motion tip-up of the fish followed by a methodical upward rise. The fish approaches the insect or artificial, closes to within an inch or two, and with jaws open sips the fly from the surface. This is a very quiet riseform with very little surface disturbance. By the time an angler has seen the circles spreading, the fish may be moving to still another position to feed on the next insect.

Trout that perform this type of rise are often feeding on small mayflies such as the various *Baetis* species. The insects themselves can be difficult to spot in the surface film, and the rises are equally hard to see.

## THE SUCKING RISE

This type of rise is one that any fly-fisherman can recognize. It is an audible rise accompanied by a sucking sound as the trout pulls the insect or fly from the surface film. The noise involved usually leaves one or more bubbles floating on the surface in indication of the exact location of the riseform.

This type of rise is usually created by a larger-than-average trout. I've seen twelve-inchers perform this riseform, and I've seen six-pounders do the same. But it's usually accomplished by some of the largest trout in any stream.

## THE HEAD-AND-TAIL RISE

This type of rise has been duly recorded by writers down through many years of angling literature. Roderick Haig-Brown, British Columbia magistrate and author of many fine books on fly-fishing sport, is one who has made mention of this rise in many of his works.

The head-and-tail rise is characteristically made by large trout. It is accomplished by the fish moving up and back with the fly and then taking it from the subsurface or surface in a classy showing of head, then back, and then tail as the trout turns and heads for bottom.

## THE BULGE RISE

In this type of rise, the fish moves to waylay a nymph on its way to the surface to emerge. The insect is taken somewhere in the mid-to-upper layer of water, and the water surface is bulged by the trout's back as it turns back to the bottom with the nymph. This riseform is often confused with an actual surface rise. One needs to look closely to spot the difference.

## THE SWIRL RISE

This method of taking naturals or imitations off the surface is one of the most dramatic riseforms. It is certainly audible to nearby anglers, and often attracts the attention of fishermen looking for better-than-average fish. The riseform is characterized by a swirl of the fish at or near the surface, often within sight of an observing angler. It is usually the end result of the trout's scrutiny of its prey. It usually comes as a nymph heads for the surface, or it can take place with a dun or spinner on the surface. The presence of air bubbles would indicate active surface feeding. The lack of bubbles on the surface would tell us that the trout is feeding on nymphs.

## THE FLASH OR "GLITTER" RISE

This is fairly common during heavy insect emergences. The fish shows itself curious and interested in a fly but does not take insects off the surface. However, the flash or glitter of sunlight and water passing along the side of the fish indicates its presence.

I've used several variant or spider patterns to locate feeding fish. A flash rise can pinpoint the approximate area of the trout's feeding station. My best success with fish located this way has come when I've rested the fish and then tried a smaller fly. When a fish investigates a larger pattern but is reluctant to strike, using the same pattern in a smaller size will often turn the trick.

There are other lesser-known rises, but detailing all of them will only serve to confuse beginning fly-fishermen. The trick is to learn the most common riseforms, how trout behave during each, and then to imitate the natural that feeding fish are most apt to strike.

Riseforms of themselves actually tell fly-fishermen very little about the specifics of what trout are feeding on. All they tell an angler is where the death of an insect took place. Anglers should be aware that trout are constantly rising to the surface to check out drifting bits of wood, leaves, and a myriad of other items. The same fish is always catching and rejecting, or accepting, insects and other things of a foreign nature along the bottom and at mid-depth levels.

Trout are most adept at zeroing in on the beginning of a hatch. As solitary nymphs begin moving toward the surface to hatch into sub-imagoes or duns, this minor movement means little to a fish. If it feels the need to feed, it can do so with little problem. It's when a major activity occurs and thousands of nymphs begin their upward swim to the surface that trout begin feeding either near bottom or somewhere between the bottom and the surface. The primary feeding movement is not on the surface; it's usually under water.

Some duns are airborne within seconds after reaching the surface. Others may require several minutes before leaving their nymphal shuck and taking wing. These floating insects require more work on the part of feeding trout who must leave the security of the bottom, rise through moving currents while maintaining the proper perspective with the insect, take the natural off the surface, and swim back to their feeding station. This can be considerable work for a feeding trout, especially in fast water.

It makes little difference to a trout whether it inhabits a freestone or limestone stream, or fast or slow water. The tip-up, rise to the surface, and ultimate acceptance or rejection of the insect follows a period of brief or somewhat longer inspection.

Some insects, such as *Ephemera guttulata* (Green Drake) or *Hexagenia limbata* (Michigan Caddis), prompt superb action with big trout during a spinnerfall. The temporary abundance of spent-wing flies on the surface after mating and egg-laying has caused the demise of some of our larger stream trout. These insects represent an appetizing mouthful to otherwise wary fish. When there are decreasing numbers of insects on the water after a short time of plenty, this often brings about cases of competition among trout. I've seen big browns and rainbows throw caution aside and behave like hatchery plants in their eagerness to nail a drifting insect. This, of course, offers encouragement to fly-fishermen.

The key to understanding the purpose of this book and its information lies in understanding that trout can be very selective. Any trout that rises to a natural is almost insistent upon an artificial that is approximately the same size, presents the same basic silhouette, and is somewhat the same color. What perplexes many anglers is that the female and male of the same insect may vary greatly in size and color. *Siphlonurus quebecensis* (Brown Quill) offers a good example. The male spinner (imago) is best represented by a No. 14 Red Quill Spinner, while the egg-laden female is best imitated by a No. 12 Brown Quill Spinner. The same holds true for many other insect species, as you will note in the pages that follow.

Many anglers have seen days when egg-carrying females are commonly the first choice of rising trout. Fish biologists and some fishing writers advance the theory that females are full of protein, at least more so than males, because of the heavy load of eggs. This may or may not be true, but it is true that trout often feed exclusively on females during a spinnerfall. Only after many females have been consumed will trout begin a systematic gorging on male insects. As with many other things, this holds true much of the time, but not always. There is always an element of chance with anything relating to fly-fishing and fly hatches.

Many neophyte anglers are confused by the fly hatches themselves. It's common in many areas for one or more hatches to be in progress at the same time. Another possibility is a hatch at ten A.M. that continues until noon, only to be replaced by a similar appearing insect that begins hatching then and continues on until three or four P.M. Which of these insects should one fish?

The proper answer is to fish the insect that is being fed on most heavily by the trout at that time. This is more easily said than done, as only by careful examination can a fisherman discover which fly is actually producing the most action. I've solved this to some extent by determining the two most populous hatches occuring at any one time, then trying both male and female imitations of both species in one or two sizes until I hit the proper combination. But this works only part of the time. I've also spent many fruitless hours trying to decide what I'm doing wrong. At best, it's a hit-or-miss proposition.

Whatever the situation, a study of stream or lake entomology, and the resulting fly hatches, can be an important first step in allowing a fly-fisherman an insight into which imitations he should use. Any fly selected should appeal to a trout's selectivity. Anything less will usually cause the fish to reject the offering.

Several types of hatches occur and anglers must learn to understand how trout respond to each. Some prompt a noticeable, sustained feeding response; others, while providing some food, may not occasion heavy feeding behavior.

## BLANKET HATCH

This means different things to different people. Some anglers may consider a blanket hatch to denote that period when massive numbers of nymphs are emerging as duns. Thousands of insects are on the surface for varying lengths of time, and this can be a good time to fish. However, most commonly we speak of a blanket hatch coming after the duns emerge, perform the necessary maturation process, and begin mating, and then fall spent-winged to the surface. This time of egg-laying and ultimate death for all trout flies can produce the most spectacular fishing of all. It is called the spinnerfall, when hordes of mated spinners fall to the surface. Trout come to dinner the way humans do on Thanksgiving Day.

## INTERMITTENT HATCH

This type of hatch is characterized by intermittent periods of activity and inactivity. Certain insect species, such as the green drake or great red spinner (Ephemerella grandis), can deliver intermittent periods where large numbers of insects may be present. Trout relish these insects and often feed actively whenever they make an appearance.

## MINOR HATCHES

Many minor hatches occur each season on trout streams throughout North America. They can be important to trout and to anglers, or they can represent very little of importance to man or fish. This is where a study of fly hatches will offer an insight for fishermen.

Some species of insects are so small at hatching that it requires a trained eye to witness an emergence or spinnerfall. Numerous hatches of *Tricorythodes* are common during summer months, but only occasionally will anglers hang big fish on imitations of these, because peak activity often coincides with "hatches" of terrestrials such as grasshoppers.

I have hit minor hatches of *Tricorythodes stygiatus* or *attratus* (Dark Brown Spinner) and taken some good fish. These insects are best matched by flies tied on No. 24 and 26 hooks, which necessitate long wispy leaders tapered to 5X or 6X. My largest catch to date on this offering was a wildly acrobatic rainbow that measured 18½ inches in length and weighed 3½ pounds.

Although I do not intend to present a fly-fishing instruction section in this book, there are a few points especially to keep in mind when casting to trout.

One very important factor involved with dry-fly fishing is drag. This is a word used by fly-fishermen to denote an unnatural resistance to the current by fly, leader, or fly line. Rising trout are accustomed to seeing insects drifting downstream in the surface film without drag. Drag can literally pull an imitation away from a rising fish. Also the drag of a fly moving sideways in the current may spook the trout. Sometimes it won't, but it certainly will not hook the fish.

Trout, as they rise to the surface, often study an insect and make calculations or adjustments in swimming speed so they can cope with the current speed to arrive at the surface in time to intercept the insect with a minimum of expended energy. The flies that trout feed on are usually small, and a fish cannot use up too much body energy in its search for food, or all is in vain. What happens when a trout comes for an imitation and drag pulls it away, is that the fish has used up some energy going for an apparent insect that has gotten away. Your next cast, even though it may be drag-free, may be ignored by the trout because of a dim recall that a similar-appearing insect got away.

So the first culprit anglers must learn to contend with, and to overcome, is drag on their fly line. I know of no angler who isn't bothered with it at times, and I fight this battle nearly every time I fish. Many are the anglers that can cast a longer line than I, and many of these same fishermen have more drag-free floats than I can achieve. I lay no claims to being a world-beater with a fly rod, but I'm convinced it's better to make shorter casts, which in themselves are more conducive to freedom from drag, than to make a beautiful cast and then try to cope with several conflicting currents which will all induce some degree of drag.

My preference in fly-fishing with dry flies is to make short casts. I seldom cast over thirty feet and catch many fish on twenty-foot throws. But this means that besides some degree of proficiency in casting, the angler must also be able to wade into position without spooking fish. I learned the concept of close approach while fishing for spawning trout and salmon in Michigan. Large runs of these fish move upstream from the Great Lakes and spawn on shallow, exposed gravel bars. Overhead tree branches and brushy shorelines pose a problem to fly-fishermen, so I learned how to move as close as possible to the fish before making a cast. A roll cast will work wonders in positioning the fly in the proper place in close quarters, and it also eliminates the flash of the rod while false casting.

Learn to move slowly, take advantage of all cover, stop often, and make the first cast the best one possible. Trout rising to hatching duns or spent spinners can often be approached quite closely because they are intent on filling an empty belly. I've taken thousands of trout (the majority were released) by casting no more than twenty feet. This works well on eastern and midwestern streams as well as in the West. But again, it does call for some skill in wading to achieve close-at-hand fishing.

The ability to place a fly in the proper place to cover a rising fish is of utmost importance. This necessitates studying current flows to decide the best avenue of approach so the fly will pass over the trout's window of vision without the fish spotting the fly line or fisherman's shadow. Currents are never a single steady flow; they include small or large flows of varying speed, eddies, deflections around submerged or partially submerged logs or sweepers, or around grasses in some limestone streams, and other obstructions. It behooves the angler to study the current and decide which type of cast will provide a drag-free float. This, too, is easier said than done, and usually best learned by experience. A reader can study fishing literature to learn something about it, but on-the-stream experience will provide better knowledge of this aspect of fly-fishing.

The various types of casts needed to fish a dry fly could easily fill a book of this size. Anglers should especially be aware that a cast that produces on a swift freestone stream will probably scare the wits out of trout on a slow moving, clear, limestone stream. Different situations call for different presentations.

A limestone stream has slow currents that meander between submerged islands of weeds. The conflicting currents found on a limestone stream are as different as night and day when compared to a freestone stream. The shifting of currents and varying conditions posed by weed beds can cause trout to face downstream although they are really facing into the current. The first time I fished Pennsylvania's Letort River I was totally confused. The fish seemed, in many places, to be facing directly downstream. It was apparent that a change in casting methods was called for to take these sophisticated trout.

We'll assume that you can learn to read water and the currents, so the next important thing is to get the fly to the trout without drag. One of the most useful casts on a limestone stream is the "puddle" cast. I've always called it my slop cast because when the line falls to the water in a sort of mess, it looks like the end result of an inept angler trying to make a forward cast. However, the results this cast can produce far outweigh its apparent lack of form.

The puddle cast is made by false casting once or twice and then making a soft, high delivery on the forward cast. The rod tip is stopped at a ten or eleven o'clock position and the fly line and leader tend to fall in loose coils. The current will literally pick out the fly at the end of the leader and start it floating downstream to the fish. As more leader uncoils, the tension on the fly and leader will cause the fly line to uncoil and this can give a long, drag-free cast. The angler should be above, or above and slightly to one side of, the fish for this cast.

Other more traditional methods of casting to rising fish will produce on freestone and on limestone streams. One of the best ways is to fish upstream. Locate a rising trout and work up within casting distance. I prefer to stand below and slightly to one side of the fish and cast above the trout. If the angle is good, one should be able to obtain a relatively drag-free float by simply stripping in line as the fly drifts down to the fish. This places the fly line and most of the leader to one side of the riser and in an area where it won't pass over the trout. It is slightly more difficult detecting the riseform and hooking a fish when the line is coming down to you, but it works!

I've found it far easier to be slightly upstream from the fish and cast across and above the fish. This involves mending the line once or even several times in order to create a drag-free float. Many anglers have heard of or tried mending the line (rolling a small loop up or downstream to decrease drag) but a lot of them use far too much force when they mend their line. It's very easy to mend too much line, or mend with too much force, and the result is that you move the fly and create an artificial drag. In most cases a line mend should be a soft, delicate upstream or downstream movement of the line belly, just enough to eliminate the effects of the current on the fly line.

Every fly-fisherman wants to hit a hatch during the peak of activity, encounter the best of the spinnerfall, and enjoy solitude while fishing. Taking one or two nice trout on a well-placed cast is important as well. But without a knowledge of insects, their hatching times, and the necessary imitations, one may experience the first three items listed above and yet seldom have the exquisite pleasure of knowing the fourth.

The point of these brief remarks on casting to trout is to illustrate the importance of understanding the feeding habits of these fish in response to a hatch, and of being able to fool the fish into thinking your artificial is part of the natural hatch. Refer to books recommended at the end of this book if you desire more detailed information.

# 3

## Altitude and Latitude Are Important

I'd been fishing a sporadic hatch of *Epeorus pleuralis* (Quill Gordon) on an unnamed spring creek in southern Wisconsin. Spinner flights had been disappointing, but reasonably productive. Two browns, one 16 inches and another crowding 20 inches, had been duped into taking my No. 12 or No. 14 Quill Gordon.

The next step was to move north about one hundred fifty miles and hope to hit the quill gordon hatch on one of the streams near Sturgeon Bay. I knew it was too early in the season for much insect activity on the Brule—my favorite—but I figured that a bit farther south might show some activity.

I was fishing a stretch of the upper Kewaunee River and nothing was happening—no dun emergences, no swarms of spinners, nothing. I sat for an hour, watching the river and discussing the inactivity with another angler, when a third fisherman happened along.

The third angler carried spinning gear. Noting our fly tackle, he queried us on our success. It had been a dry run, we said, and he nodded in agreement. I told him we had hoped to hit the quill gordon, but the hatches were still to come.

He sat for a moment while pondering the statement. His reaction was one that has changed my thinking on fly hatches to a marked degree. "I've fly-fished this stream for years, and still do, even though I'm spinning right now, and I've studied fly hatches for my entire life. It's too early for the Quill Gordon hatch, and I'll tell you why," he ventured.

Sensing a captive audience he began to elaborate. "The two key factors toward timing an approximate hatch are altitude and latitude. Wisconsin anglers worry little about altitude because there is little change in elevation from one area to another in this state. The same is not true for fly-fishermen working the blue ribbon streams of mountain states such as Montana and Wyoming. I've seen hatches and spinner flights delayed for weeks in states with some mountains, such as West Virginia or even upper New York.

"Latitude is important for flatlanders, especially in the northern tier of states, or in Canada. The difference of one hundred fifty to two hundred miles is enough to delay hatches up to two weeks. I've fished grayling in northern Saskatchewan during peak hatches and then moved to the Northwest Territories. The same hatch may be as much as four weeks later, the farther north you go.

"Charts of fly hatches, at best, offer anglers and readers an *approximate* starting point. God gave man the ability to think, and to reason out such things, but it's surprising how few fishermen take the time to consider a difference in hatching dates from one area to another. You guys might as well go home and forget the gordons. They won't come," he said. He proved to be right, because we didn't catch a fish.

That incident happened many years ago and every year it's confirmed again: The higher in elevation a body of water lays, and the farther north an angler goes, the later a hatch will come off.

It's another basic fact that the farther north one fishes, say in the Northwest Territories, the more apt that fisherman is of finding three, four, or even a half-dozen hatches in progress at one time. Nature has a way of seeing to it that all insects hatch, even if they must do so at the same time.

The hatch tables that follow in subsequent chapters are approximate. They do not purport to give exact dates, although some of my correspondents have marked dates as being the *average* date when certain duns begin emerging. The reader that follows through this text and gets to the hatching charts would be wise to remember that I'm offering some advice on about when a hatch should occur, but cannot absolutely guarantee that it will fall within that time period.

Weather is a major influencing factor on hatching times, regardless of where they occur. I live in northern Michigan and for the last two years we've had an extremely late spring. In 1977 snow was still present in my neighborhood on the seventh day of May. In 1979 we had a snowstorm on May 6 and another a week later. The effect this type of weather condition has on hatches is incredible. Our Hendrickson hatches were two weeks late and somewhat sporadic.

A late spring with cold rains or snow will lower both air and water temperatures and have a pronounced effect on fly hatches. I've seen some reports that say insects hatch according to the amount of available sunlight, with hatches increasing as days grow longer, but there are entomologists and anglers who question this theory in its entirety. I seriously question the validity of this statement as well. It's been my experience on too many occasions to see hatches develop as weather warms. The first appearance of duns may be two weeks later than the previous year—or two weeks earlier. I'm a firm believer that water and air temperature play a much more important role in insect development than is commonly accepted. I would like to see some serious entomological studies made on hatching times in correlation to the warming of the water and air.

Another point that should be kept in mind is that two streams, separated by just a few miles but at the same elevation and latitude, may still vary as much as ten days in hatching time for certain insects. Fly hatches are fraught with such inconsistencies.

How much can elevation (altitude) mean to an emerging insect? My travels, particularly in the mountainous West, indicate that if a hatch is tentatively scheduled to occur in the foothills on June 1, it may be June 15 for an emergence 2,000 feet higher. It may well be June 21 or 28 for the same hatch to occur at a 4,000-foot increase over foothill streams.

On the other hand, if the weather warms quickly and in an unpredictable manner, a hatch may be two weeks ahead of schedule in the foothills and two weeks earlier than normal at higher elevations, too. The amount of snowpack in the mountains, and resulting spring runoffs, can also seriously affect the quantity and quality of any given hatch.

The difference in elevation is equally important in many eastern states. New York and Pennsylvania's mountainous regions fall prey to the same inequities. Hatch time for the same insect may occur as much as two weeks later in the Catskills, Adirondacks, or the Green Mountains as it does in lower-lying areas.

What the angler who refers to the tables does have going for him is a probable range of activity, or duration of hatch, if you prefer. This applies almost anywhere an angler will find hatching insects and fish that feed on them. Seldom is a hatch of one-day duration, and many will and can last up to a month or more. This gives fishermen a spread

**Stream research**

of time during which they can reasonably expect to find one or more insects in mating activity. Spinner flights turn on more anglers than anything. The average emerging hatch swarm and resulting spinnerfall may occur the same day, or at most, within three or four days of each other. This allows the angler to pinpoint an approximate time span in which he can expect to find some activity. It may not always be the insect he has in mind, but some activity is better than none.

The higher one goes to pursue his sport, the more apt he is to find a heavy hatch whenever all conditions are right. I've seen countless cases where insects like *Ephemerella subvaria* (Hendrickson or Red Quill) will seemingly pop from the water en masse. The hatch may be of brief duration, but the quantity of insects available, and the quality of trout fishing to be had at such times is enough to send any sportsman into ecstasy. These same insects, when found at lower elevations, may have a hatch time that continues sporadically for several days, or as long as two weeks. Hatches may be shorter in mountainous areas, but they are often the sweetest of the year.

Hatches in western states are more difficult to pin down to specific time schedules than northeastern, midwestern, southern, or southeastern hatches. Canadian hatches are equally difficult to describe for much the same reasons. One has to deal with the varying weather patterns in each area, plot the hatch courses for flatland or mountainous areas, and cope with the difference in latitude in some cases. This involves some theory, experiences on various waters in each state or province, and trying to second-guess the weather. Any or all of these factors can blow holes in any hatch chart for the West or Canada. The best one can hope for is to know in advance which hatches *should* occur, and which might occur, and plan accordingly.

Latitude is difficult to explain, for many reasons. Again, weather is the major factor in the presence or absence of successful hatch in any area. The greater likelihood of a late snow, freezing rain, or just cold weather at high elevations has been explained, but moving 200 miles north, or 400 miles, or 1,000 miles, can also seriously crimp any sportsman's plans. Anglers are on shaky ground if they expect the same insect that hatches on a Pennsylvania limestone stream to be popping from the surface on Ontario's Bighead River on about the same date. This may be an extreme case, but the opening anecdote in this chapter showed what can happen when a fisherman moves only one hundred fifty to two hundred miles to the north. Hatches are always later the farther north one travels. Be prepared for this possibility.

The thing that puzzles some anglers is, for example, an expectation that a hatch of *Hexagenia limbata* (Michigan Caddis) on Michigan's Au Sable River will be occurring at the same time on the middle branch of the Ontonagon about four hundred miles to the northwest. The peak period for hatches of this trout-getter on the AuSable, Pine, or other Lower Michigan streams is the second or third week of June, sometimes later, depending on the prevailing weather conditions. Hexes hatch on the middle branch of the Ontonagon about July 4 and as late as mid-July during cold years.

This kind of variation is also the case between southern New York streams and those in upstate New York. The same holds true in southern versus northern Maine. Unless a state is small, with little variation in latitude (or altitude) between the northern and southern portions, fishermen can expect a change of one to three weeks between peaks of activity in each area.

Southern states, where conditions are moderate, offer anglers a better chance of hitting hatches somewhat on schedule. But there is a big difference between southern Georgia and northern Georgia, both in terrain and in air and water temperatures. Anglers in that state would be wise to judge the weather, examine long-range forecasts, and seek up-to-date information before heading for the trout streams northeast of Atlanta. If they live near Macon, or even farther south, these changes will be dramatic.

Altitude (elevation) and latitude are indeed important, but other factors join hands to throw a fly-fisherman off course.

Many insects hatch only on sunny days, and often during the peak of sunshine—about noon. If the weather is stormy, skies are overcast, or the day turns cold with rain or snow in the early season, this will upset the timetable of the insects and my hatching charts. However, given solid bluebird weather, chances are good that trout will feed both on emerging duns and on fallen spinners roughly "on schedule." These same insects will, on occasion, hatch late in the afternoon or in early evening if the sun comes out after a long spell of overcast skies. This forces anglers into a mode of flexibility; demanding they stay for longer periods than planned in hopes that a flight occurs. Sometimes it does, and sometimes it doesn't. . . .

Some insects are programmed to hatch at sundown. Yet if the sun suddenly passes behind cloud cover at midday, and the temperature drops, they may be fooled into early emergence. I've seen flights of *Ephemera guttulata* (Green Drake) begin swarming at midday. The peak abundance of spinners is still usually in the evening, at which time big trout go on a heavy feeding spree. *Isonychia bicolor* (Slate Drake) offers another classic example of this behavior: They are prone to daytime hatches and spinner flights when the weather is unstable, meaning dark and overcast long before sundown. Dusk is still the principal time for heavy activity, but they can and will swarm earlier in the day if the conditions are ripe for such activity.

An angler may think that rainfall has little effect on spinnerfalls, but he'd be wrong. Although spinners may fall spent to the surface during a rainstorm, many will not have mated and completed their life cycle. A drop of rain striking a mayfly, caddis fly, or stonefly squarely during the spinner flight can stun the insect and prevent copulation. It's been my experience, both in the East, Midwest, and West, that a long-term spell of bad weather will cause insects that rest in trees or bushes to hold off the mating flight until conditions reach an optimum level. This may be three or four days. When ideal weather arrives, the insects take full advantage of the lull, and spinner flights and subsequent spinnerfalls can deliver a most spectacular brand of fishing.

Heavy winds can raise the devil with spinner flights that are in progress. Insects are blown into the water, either from the air or from nearby bushes and trees. This can give one the false impression of an active spinnerfall, but I feel the feeding trout can sense the difference. Fallen insects who have been unable to complete mating often struggle mightily to rise from the water's surface only to be swatted down again by the wind. A genuine spinnerfall is a spectacle to see—and to fish. Spent insects by the thousands can drift downstream into the waiting mouths of feeding fish. Their life complete, the spinners are destined to become either food for a trout or some other species, or to wind up piled in windrows along a river or lake shore.

A trout feeding during a fall of spinners can be mighty selective. He may feed heavily in the shallows, in swirling eddies, or in the main thrust of the current. One seldom knows in advance where the best fishing will take place, and if we knew, it would take away some of the challenge.

It is important that you understand the points made in this chapter. You don't want to plan a summer vacation around one specific hatch and then be one or two weeks too early or late for it. Hatches can be plotted, up to a certain point, but too many variables exist that can throw even the best calculations off.

Plan for hatches to make the best use of all available fishing time, but do so with some thought in mind of elevation and latitude. It may save you some valuable fishing time.

# 4

# Which Fly Is Best?

Choosing the proper fly to use at the proper time is similar to choosing your in-laws. It can be done, but some peril is involved. In either case, if the wrong choice is made, it can seriously affect the outcome of your success.

Many years ago my selection of flies left something to be desired: Japanese imports with loose heads, wings that fell off if I pushed my cast too hard, or dull hooks with cheap materials. I made do with this type of equipment because I could afford nothing more.

My next step was to acquire a fishing vest stocked with more pockets than Macy's has shelves. Before long, each pocket was filled to the brim with flies—dries, wets, nymphs, streamers, bucktails, steelhead patterns, and the odd Atlantic Salmon Fly picked up in my travels through the Maritime Provinces. I was a walking fly shop, and more than a little stooped over from the weight. Seasons later it dawned on me that I hadn't fished with most of the flies for years, some had never seen the light of day since the time of purchase, and it always seemed that I fell back on some old favorites that produced an occasional trout for me.

An article in a well-known outdoor magazine by a famous fly-fisherman turned my thinking around. It said that many anglers are so caught up in fly-fishing on a certain level of acquisition that they go overboard in the number of flies they carry in their vest. I knew the feeling because I'd just taken a header in a swift western stream, emerged like a *Hexagenia* dun, and crawled onto the bank to dry my wings, so to speak. Every fly box dripped water and all flies were thoroughly soaked. I was scheduled to leave in three hours for an extended trip back East, so I cased my rod, packed my bags, and headed out for business. My tackle was shipped home. By the time my business trip was finished, and I'd returned home, every fly I owned was terribly rusted, and many had to be thrown away.

I remembered the magazine article and decided that I would forget weighting myself down unnecessarily with fly boxes, and concentrate only on imitations that had proved their worth. I've never been happier.

There is no pat answer to the question of which fly is best. An angler must determine from experience which flies he wishes to carry for his immediate area. It's when a fisherman branches out and begins working new waters that the need for new flies productive for that region becomes evident.

As a youngster, the only fly I carried was an Adams. Obviously, I missed out on some fine fishing. I now have my fly vests (I own two) stocked with flies to meet most conditions. One vest is stocked for western fly-fishing, the other for eastern action. This allows me to take one vest, and leave the other home, and I'm usually prepared for almost any eventuality.

I will admit that on occasion my vests have not contained the proper fly. In such cases, because I'm usually fishing with a local, I bum one or two hot flies from him. It's in reaction to a situation like this that the average person falls into the trap of too many flies to choose from.

There is a basic procedure to follow in making your fly selection. First, an in-depth study of entomology in your particular area will pinpoint the major hatches that occur. The next step is to study coloration of both the male and female, in both dun and spinner form. Then you should determine size, because this is nearly as critical as coloration. You will need, of course, to determine whether the insect is a mayfly, caddis fly, or stonefly. Each has a different basic appearance and holds its wings in a different manner.

Mayfly imitations range in size from those tied on a No. 4 or No. 6 hook to diminutive flies used with a No. 24 or No. 26 hook. The various members of this widespread family possess most of the colors of the rainbow. Any one stream can show hatches during one season of mayflies in brown, black, cream, white, pale blue, dark blue, dark red, dark green, bluish gray, ginger, gray, sulphur, olive, and so on.

Hatching caddis fly imitations are available throughout the United States and Canada in sizes from No. 6 to No. 22. Many caddis fly species are similar in appearance. About the only differences between these insects are color and size. Caddis flies are commonly found in grayish black, brown, brownish gray, light yellow, yellowish green (olive), dark green, bright green, kelly green, black, pale green, cream, brownish yellow, slate gray, orange brown, brownish tan, reddish brown, and tan.

Stoneflies and their imitations are often similar in appearance to caddis flies. There are differences between the two, but both caddis fly and stonefly imitations are tied in basically the same way. Stoneflies, members of the order *Plecoptera*, are usually tied on No. 12 and No. 14 hooks, although some larger and smaller members are found in North America. These insects, like caddis flies, are often best represented by imitations that reproduce the basic coloration of the naturals. One finds a range of colors: pale yellow, dark brown, black, green, yellow, pale orange, and other variations in these flies.

Any book that deals with hatches must necessarily talk about two primary phases—the dun emergence and the spinner flight and fall. These two events mean more to a dry-fly man than any other. This is not to say that nymph fishing or fly-fishing emerging pupae are not fun, but in this book we are primarily concerned with hatches. This means a thorough discussion of duns and their importance to dry-fly anglers, and of the exciting and demanding spinnerfall.

The fisherman must decide which of these two dry-fly periods is most important to him to fish. I've had the best success fishing during a spinnerfall. Others dislike the indifference trout often show to their imitations during the spinnerfall, and much prefer fishing during an emergence of the dun.

Mayflies, in particular—but the same applies to caddis flies and stoneflies as well—are judged according to the period of time they spend on the surface during the emergent stage. Some duns lift immediately into the air and thus provide feeding fish with little opportunity to grab a quick meal. Other duns may tarry for several minutes while drying their wings. This type of behavior is preferred by fly-fishermen because it gives them a chance to imitate the dun, and then present it to a feeding trout.

Another point worth considering when deciding whether to fish duns or spinnerfall or flights is the peak of activity. The duns of some species may emerge in a rather sporadic manner, thus giving anglers only a brief pass at matching the hatching insect. But spinners of the same species often hold off mating flights until an optimum time, and then the air and water are full of flying, mating, or dying insects. This offers anglers a much better chance at tying into trout on spinner imitations.

Fishing emerging duns is a more contemplative sport than working the spinnerfalls. I often find myself tense as mayflies swarm at treetop level to begin mating, and then as females dip to the surface to lay their eggs. My heart starts beating fast, both hands are thumbs-only, and I can't seem to get tracking straight. I've been known to miss guides while threading my fly line, fail to knot the tippet properly, and in general, become so shook that I fish poorly.

One time on Pennsylvania's Penn's Creek when the Green Drake hatch was in the offing, I spent a patient hour watching swarming insects overhead. As time passed I became more excited and began trembling in anticipation. Every angler was waiting for the fall to begin, knowing full well that it would trigger a massive feeding spree.

I had tied a No. 10 Coffin Fly to my 4X tippet well ahead of the fall. Past experience had taught me not to wait until the last minute. The line was threaded properly, for a change, and the knot well tied.

The fall began and that portion of Penn's Creek came alive with dimples, as if a soft summer rainstorm were passing overhead. Seemingly thousands of trout were on the prowl as we took up casting positions.

I singled out one fish that was slashing at spinners on the surface. My first cast quickly put the fish down for a few minutes when the fly line dropped across his feeding station. My next choice was a golden brown, maybe 16 inches long, that was feeding near a tongue of current sweeping past a half-submerged log. It was necessary to cast slightly above the log to obtain a proper drift. My first cast neatly anchored the barb in the log and it promptly broke off.

That was when the anxiety set in, something that always happens during a major spinnerfall. I had difficulty tying on a new tippet, and then the fly. It seemed to take twenty minutes to do it correctly.

The fall was nearly over by the time I finally settled down and laid the fly out properly. The brown nosed up, drifted downstream with the imitation for three feet, and slashed upward in a firm take.

Hooked, the brown rampaged downstream for twenty feet, circled quickly against the pull of the line, and headed back up, punching hard in an attempt to work in under the log. I placed as much pressure as possible on the fish and succeeded in turning it back out into the current. We slugged it out for a few minutes before it tried a last-ditch jump that didn't quite come off. The trout rolled on the surface and went belly up and I landed it.

My companions, both far better fly-fishermen than I, had landed five fish during this fall of Green Drake. I'm always somewhat reluctant to tell fellow anglers that I get shook up during a blanket spinnerfall. But the truth is that when the day comes that I fail to get excited at such times, I'll hang up my graphite rod, give away my collection of fishing books and other related material, and take up croquet.

Duns are seldom on the water in blanket proportions and the trout seem to sense this. Slow deliberate rises are more common during an emergence, the quality of fishing (to me at least) is far superior, because the angler can often select one specific trout in a certain stretch of water, and cast imitating duns in his direction. If the approach is quiet, the cast is made with skill, and the angler is finely attuned to the nature of that specific hatch, he'll probably find the kind of action around which fishing dreams are born.

Emerging duns that linger for short periods on the surface are of more interest to anglers than those duns that immediately take flight upon emergence. Insects that rest for a brief moment can trigger some of the most selective feeding by trout I've ever seen. Many anglers feel that trout rising to a spinnerfall are more highly selective, but I've witnessed many cases where the greatest onus on an angler is to imitate perfectly a hatching dun. If the imitation is somewhat off color, the cast is poorly made, or some shiver of movement is not given the fly to imitate a dun drying its wings, the trout may not strike. Fishing duns offers a quality of sport that goes far above many others in calling for a deft presentation and a jeweler's eye in noting certain details about the hatching insect.

Spinnerfalls—although trout can be mighty particular about presentation and proper attention to detail—often provoke such a heavy feeding spree that any imitation that is close to the proper size and color may take fish. But there are other times when trout are so selective, or feeding on some insect floating in the surface film that is totally different from the one you are fishing, that even the best fly-fisherman will have difficulty taking fish.

As trout, the major game fish sought after by fly-fishermen, will feed heavily during either the emergence of duns or during the egg-laying flight or the spinnerfall, it's up to the individual angler to decide which of the two times best meets his needs.

I've known anglers so finely attuned to upcoming hatches that the best fishing they could find took place just as the nymphs rose from the bottom and shed their nymphal shuck on the surface. This, to them, was the epitome of fly-fishing. Obviously it demands that the angler know when and where the nymphs are most likely to emerge. Study of the research and hatch charts in this book will indicate that some nymphs will hatch from certain waters and not from others. Some require fast water, some slow, while some will hatch almost anywhere if the water quality is good.

*Taeniopteryx faciata* (Early Brown Stonefly) is common to many eastern streams. It hatches from fast water over a bed of rocks. *Leptophlebia cupida* (Black Quill) hatches from slow water and swims freely wherever the water suits its fancy. This illustrates why the angler must know something about the hatch due to emerge before he can decide which fly is best suited for his purposes. Incidentally, the two insects noted above have been known to hatch on the same streams at the same time. But anglers would look for the stonefly to emerge in fast-water stretches and the Black Quill fly to pop out from slower areas.

One of the fascinating things about studying trout-stream entomology is the transition of an insect from emerging dun to a vibrant, soon-to-reproduce spinner. This transformation is one item that anglers should be somewhat knowledgeable about, for it involves knowing which fly should be used at a particular time on any stream. There can be subtle, or even drastic changes in coloration, between a newly emerged dun and a spinner. These color changes dictate which flies to use during either the dun or spinner phase. It is possible to take trout on flies which imitate the dun phase during a spinner flight or fall, and the reverse is true, but it's still best to determine which type of fishing you wish to participate in and to stock your fly boxes accordingly.

Three years ago I attended a convention of outdoor writers in Snowmass, Colorado. The Frying Pan River flows nearby and it is a predictable stream for insect activity, and is a steady producer of good trout. It was here that my notions on coloration of imitations and the relative importance of dun or spinner fishing were reestablished.

A good hatch of *Ephemerella doddsi* (Western Green Drake) started coming off about noon on one of my free days. I caught and released several trout on a No. 10 Green Drake imitation. The hatch ended but some fish were still searching for duns and I continued to have half-hearted passes at my fly, but they wouldn't take.

I went into town and grabbed a hamburger and Coke and headed back to the river. The Green Drake pattern had worked so well I decided to leave it on to determine the results during a spinner flight and fall.

The flight started and I was treated to one of the best spectacles in all fly-fishing—a massive blanket spinnerfall. The imitation that had worked for me early in the day was now failing miserably. Trout were rising steadily and taking spinners from the surface. I covered fish after fish, but each ignored my offering to sip a natural off the water.

It required but little time for me to understand that some excellent fishing was going to waste because of my experimentation. It was obvious the trout weren't interested in the dun imitation. I snipped off the fly and replaced it with a No. 10 Great Red Spinner to imitate the color phase of the spinners.

I was fishing downstream from the Footbridge Pool. Both rainbows and browns were feeding heavily as far as the eye could see. My first cast dropped the imitation two feet above an active fish and it rose eagerly and sipped my fly off the surface. I gently eased the rod tip up and made my set. That fish responded in typical rainbow fashion; it jumped, not once, but three times in rapid succession before settling down to a hard-paced scrap. It required five minutes of exquisite pleasure before I could lay the fish over the lip of my net. A quick glance indicated it would weigh about three pounds, a husky trout for that water.

Five minutes later I was hooked up to a bulldogging brown that showed himself in a blur of brown and gold as he took the imitation. We slugged it out on my 5X tippet for several minutes before he took me downstream and wound the leader around an obstruction and broke off. That fish would have weighed five pounds.

This anecdote proves the importance of knowing the various colorations of duns and spinners. Fish, especially trout, feed in response to visual stimuli. They have pretty fair eyesight and although it's questionable whether they can see colors, I'm certain that different colors show up in varying light intensities. A dun may actually appear different in color than a spinner of the same species. You have to realize this when selecting your imitation. Trout respond or choose to ignore anything that doesn't appear natural to them.

Learning which fly to choose to meet the existing conditions is one of the biggest challenges a fly-fisherman can run across, but it's also one of the most rewarding. Decide whether to fish the dun or spinner stage, know the colorations of each, which hook size is most appropriate, and you're well on the way to increased enjoyment.

# 5

# Dry-Fly Fishing by the Tables

Dry-fly fishing is a sport that is addictive. It involves the angler in tradition, prompts a gentleness of mind and action, and satisfies a deep-seated need for at least occasional solitude. It is you alone against one trout. I've been a dry-fly fisherman for three-fourths of my lifetime, long enough to have some thoughts on the sport and its techniques.

An inquisitive mind and a sharp eye are things all anglers should possess, but this is doubly true for anglers that fish tiny bits of fluff and feathers on the surface in the hope of fooling wary trout (or other game fish). These fishermen need to watch not only the water, but overhead trees and shoreline bushes to learn exactly what trout are feeding on. Is it a dun or glassy-winged spinner? And color is important, but only as long as you realize that the view from the vantage point of a feeding trout under water is radically different than a top view. To fool trout on a consistent basis you must possess some stream-fishing savvy, know how to read rivers, and learn everything possible about the hatching insects.

Last year I flew Air New Zealand from Los Angeles to Honolulu and then nonstop to Auckland. Two days later I was shin-deep in a private stretch of the Waikato River, a tributary of trout-rich Lake Rotorua. An ardent angler had talked the landowner into allowing me access to this tiny stream which was in many places less than fifteen feet wide.

The water was gin clear and twisted through a miniature gorge. One bank was festooned with impenetrable berry bushes. The opposite side was more open, prompting extreme wariness in trout there. The river had received an overnight run of rainbows and browns, fresh from the lake. These fish were the wildest I've seen—many were spooked by a bird flying over the river. The only way to fish was to kneel behind or beside any cover and lay a cast accurately above the fish.

I spotted two burly rainbows feeding below a tiny island. The current washed down from above, split around the bit of grass in midstream, and then funneled drifting spinners down to the fish. The flies were reddish in color, and small—about a No. 18. The trout were feeding on these insects.

I had purchased a local fly—the Red Spinner—for just this eventuality. It represents the spinner phase of this particular mayfly. New Zealand, incidentally, has only twenty species of mayfly available, but those generate heavy feeding response from trout in most streams.

I'd tied the fly on to a 5X tippet, twelve feet in length. Overhead bushes prevented a proper backcast so I shook out enough line and roll cast the fly about four feet above the lower fish. I mended the line twice and the fly drifted down. The trout rose, I held my breath, but it sipped a natural from alongside my imitation. He wasn't spooked—yet.

I cast again, quartering across and upstream, and the No. 18 imitation cocked itself on its tail and hackle tips and began drifting naturally downstream. The fish rose from the bottom, tipped up, and began drifting downstream directly under the fly. Drag was about to set in when the rainbow nosed up to my fly and sucked it under. There was a characteristic tail movement as the fish turned back toward bottom. The fly line and leader came tight and the hook was set.

That fish leaped from the water in a burst of spray, gills widespread and rattling like a baby tarpon, and smashed down into the tiny stream. I was afraid it would fall on shore, or fall so close it would hang my line in nearby brush. But I was safe. I began feeding slack line through my guides in order to cope with the run and to prevent it tangling and popping the tippet. I soon had the fish on the reel, something I prefer not to do when fishing with a light tippet, but I wanted the line free of any obstructions in the river or on shore.

I entered the stream and my movement caused the rainbow to streak upstream away from me. That ten-yard run ended with a beautiful head-over-tail jump. The fish turned and headed my way with the speed of a runaway locomotive. This required delicate handling in the small stream. As the fish approached within ten feet of me I splashed water with my foot and the trout turned and headed back upstream. He jumped again and then settled into fighting a hard battle in one of the deepest holes along that stretch.

The end came when the trout finally had fought his heart out and rolled to the surface for netting. It was a beautiful male with a bright crimson stripe down his side. He had fire in his eyes and unfortunately had fought so long he was unable to recover. I kept that five-pounder for dinner that evening.

Several days later I was fishing the Lochy River, a South Island stream of some note. It has some of the finest brown and rainbow fishing in the world. About dusk I found a small hatch of *Coloburiscus humeralis* (Twilight Beauty) coming off. Trout were rising to the duns and some spent-wing spinners were drifting down with the current.

Geoff McDonald, an affable young guide from Queenstown, suggested I try a No. 14 Twilight Beauty, a fly tied locally in New Zealand. One brown, which I judged to be four pounds, was rising steadily at the edge of a deep run. Large lombardy poplars towered over the run and the setting sun cast a golden glow through them at twilight. The fish continued to rise as I worked into casting position.

My first cast was taken by a fish in a smooth head-to-tail rise. I jolted the hook home and was pleasantly surprised when the fish boiled to the surface, rolled heavily, and headed downstream for the safety of Lake Wakatipu. I was using a heavier tippet and leaned on the fish as much as my tackle would stand; the trout turned back upstream. He rolled again in midstream before coming back up to his original feeding station. We settled into a hard-fought tug of war. The fish tried nosing under a submerged log, and I was just as stubborn about keeping him in the open. The rod pressure finally wore him down and he surfaced just inches from Geoff's waiting net. One scoop and he was in the bag. That fish, a silvery brown obviously fresh up from the lake, scaled just over six pounds. We admired him briefly and then turned him back.

Although I was in a strange land, fishing strange waters, my background in studying fly hatch data enabled me consistently to take trout. It worked for me, and can work for any fly-fisherman.

Dry-fly fishing by the tables enables anglers to determine which phase of surface activity they wish to fish (hatching duns or spinner-falls), when hatches are expected to come off, how to cope with an overlapping of hatches, and it will, with additional study, alert fishermen to how they can differentiate between one hatching insect and another.

In order for an angler to decide which hatching duns or spinnerfalls to fish, he must be alert to the possibility of simultaneous emergences or of two insects being on the surface at one time in the form of spent spinners. It does little good to be fishing the duns of one species while trout are feeding on spent spinners of another.

I've seen cases where two and even three insects were hatching or falling to the surface as spinners. Invariably, trout will feed on one insect exclusively. The way to work this situation is to forget about fishing for several minutes and watch closely to determine whether the fish are feeding on duns or spinners, and in the case of a simultaneous hatch or spinnerfall, which insect is being taken.

This is where the hatch tables come in handy, because they can pinpoint which hatches would be occurring within the same time span. They also indicate which artificials stand the best chance of success.

A common occurrence is for one insect to hatch in the afternoon, only to be followed by a spinnerfall of another insect in the early evening. The tables again explain the best times to fish each. If studied closely, the hatch tables can remove most of the doubt from an angler's mind. You should be able to check with the charts, study briefly the size, shape, and coloration of the insects, and determine which fly to use. It sounds easy, and it is, in most situations.

I have run across cases where a specific insect was scheduled to hatch at a certain time, but hit the river and found a totally different insect coming off. The tables in this book outline the best hatches. Some streams can produce very showy hatches, but these often mean little to feeding trout. Stick with the tables, allow for a weather pattern difference of one or two weeks in either direction, and chances are you'll find one or two hatches or spinnerfalls available that will deliver good sport.

Trout in streams are selective and wary. They may choose to feed actively on the smallest of a dual hatch, or they may feed heavily on the largest insect coming off the water. Awareness of this selectivity is crucial to the angler and cannot be stressed often enough. Trout do not always play by the rules. They may feed heavily on duns for ten minutes and then pursue spent spinners or another insect. Or they may feed on the spinnerfall of one insect and switch to hatching duns of another species. Their wariness is important to understand when deciding which imitating fly to use. A fly of an off color, or a hook size too large or too small, may turn the fish right off. They may continue to feed, but they will feed on naturals of the proper size, color, and silhouette. This means you must learn your duns and spinners, their relative size and color, and then be able to imitate the exact insect trout are using for food.

It's important to analyze all phases of a fly hatch, with the nagging thought in the back of your mind that trout can and will throw a monkey wrench into your best laid plans. Feeding is a stimulated response in stream trout. You have to realize that the key to unlocking fly rod action is to understand hatches and how a trout will move and feed during a hatch. Through a thorough study of stream-side entomology you can take advantage of a trout's selectivity, but only if you prepare yourself properly and use the appropriate flies. This is why throughout this book I nag at readers to determine whether trout are feeding on hatching duns or spent spinners, and having done this, discover which fly (insect) is involved.

It requires some rather lengthy periods of both stream-side observation and book research to pin down certain hatches. The angler willing to expend some effort along both lines will be able with this book to transport himself anywhere in North America and stand a better-than-average chance of meeting and fishing a hatch.

A friend of mine who stopped by and thumbed through the paperwork involved for this book, studied the original manuscript for thirty minutes, then made the comment I most wanted to hear. He said, "A person could pick up this book, study it, and be able to fish anywhere on this continent, knowing exactly which hatch was due to come off. I think that even I [he's not a fly-fisherman] could catch trout on flies with this vast amount of knowledge."

It's my fondest wish that my fellow fly-fishermen greet this work with the same type of enthusiasm.

## PLANNING YOUR FISHING TRIP AROUND THE TABLES

Vacationing fishermen take many trips every year, and plan those trips in intricate detail. A sportsman may pore over maps, quiz fisheries departments on latest trends in fishing in those areas, as well as attend to such mundane projects as tuning up the family vehicle. Letters are written and phone calls made to various individuals tending to last-minute details. The purchase of new lures or flies is taken care of, as is checking on all reels and rods to ensure they are ready for action.

The one thing that many fly-fishermen forget about—or have never thought of because such a thing hasn't been available before in more than limited form—are insect emergence tables. Many are the anglers who buzz off on a fly-fishing trip without any thought of the insects due to hatch while they are on vacation. This is a sorry sort of pretrip planning, and one I hope to rectify in these pages.

The majority of us seldom can leave on a fishing trip on short notice. The trend is for anglers to put in for vacation time two to six months in advance. And most fishermen take off during summer months. That means they'll be on stream during a period when there is likely to be a hatch or spinnerfall.

A study of the hatch tables for the state or province to be visited can reveal something about the general trend of emergences in that area. So armed, the fisherman can plan his vacation time to hit one or several hatches with some background knowledge of what's likely to be happening, and where. He can learn peak periods of activity, and in some cases obtain an overall view on what types of water to look for when searching out good hatches. I've been on fly-fishing trips where I was without a clue as to what was hatching. This is a common problem for anglers and one I felt compelled to alleviate. I wanted a standard source of information available for every specific area so that fishermen could plan their activities to coincide with peak hatches. I realize that this is a lofty goal, and one full of risks. A fisherman who plans a trip to Yellowstone National Park in July with full expectations of hitting good hatches on the Madison, Firehole, and other streams may still find that a late spring or extended periods of cold weather can shoot those expectations down in a hurry. Readers can benefit greatly by the tables in this book, but they must realize that all things, including hatches, are subject to change on sudden notice. Any other thought is pure foolishness.

As a well-traveled outdoor writer I've found it immensely important to plan ahead. Without good background information and solid pictures, I'd be hard pressed to sell my books or magazine articles. So I try to cover all angles, sometimes try to second-guess the weather, and check with whatever public or private agencies are needed to secure the most timely information possible. This can be good advice for fly-fishermen planning a trip. One problem exists: Whom should anglers contact for information?

When I go on a trout-fishing trip, I want the most current information available. I want to know about stream conditions, water levels, how the trout wintered, and other data. And I want to know what the trout are going to be feeding on. Now I will carry this book with me whenever I plan to fish an area with which I am not familiar—whether it is in the United States or Canada.

It is true that one or more hatches have been omitted from the tables, but this is for a reason—the hatch is irregular in schedule or of minimal interest to feeding game fish. The tables that are presented are current and based on both experience and countless months of research. These tables are also given with the premise that insects mentioned will undoubtedly hatch for many future years.

The research here gives fly-fishermen a distinct advantage over those anglers who are not knowledgeable about hatches, peaks of abundance, or which flies to use. It eliminates the otherwise pressing need for anglers to check ahead with fly shops or other sources at a distance to determine which insects may be coming off during the period of their visit.

These tables, studied during winter or other non-vacation months, can pinpoint approximate times when you should find good insect activity. It allows for enough time to tie a box of artificials to cover all likely hatches at your destination. But when doing so, make sure to tie up a variety of flies to imitate any hatches that ordinarily occur just before or just after your planned vacation. If a hatch is late in coming off, you may hit it on the nose, while another hatch you hoped to hit may be one or two weeks late, depending on weather patterns at the time. It pays to cover all possibilities, and this is where the tables can help plan a fishing vacation. Incidentally, you will note that in the tables the hatches are arranged in a rough chronological order, i.e., April hatches before May hatches, May before June, etc.

When planning a fly-fishing trip, double check with the Fish and Game Department, Department of Natural Resource, or Ministry of Industry and Tourism in the state or province of destination to ascertain whether they expect good hatches during the time period planned for a trip. It might also pay to check with the professor of the entomology department in a state university in that area for an update of insect patterns. Address a polite, written request for information on a specific hatch, or series of hatches, and ask if they foresee any acute changes for the coming season. A self-addressed, stamped envelope should be enclosed with your letter for a reply. Very few people will refuse to answer such a letter if you enclose a stamped envelope. But they may refuse it if you don't show the courtesy of furnishing the stamp and envelope. Don't ask a thousand questions; keep your questions brief and easily answered. I've found it best to word questions that can be answered by a yes or no. Give these people at least a month to answer the letter so they aren't rushed. Preplanning such letters well ahead of time can save you a lot of money and frustration.

If the fishing trip is to a remote Canadian area, or to a high western mountain lake or stream, be aware that weather conditions can change within twelve hours, often less. A trip in August to northern Quebec, Northwest Territories, Yukon Territory, or even northern British Columbia can result in heavy snowfall which can knock fly hatches all to pieces. High altitude or northern latitude areas have unstable weather patterns. Plan on such eventualities.

In a nutshell, planning ahead is the key to hitting good periods when plenty of insects are on the water. I've gone to areas several times in the last two or three years and hit fantastic fishing simply because I planned for the hatches there. I bided my time, watched the weather, and arrived at the stream one or two hours before the hatches were due, or before the spinner flights occurred. This gave me a chance to size up the water conditions, prepare my tackle, and to observe prehatch insect activity.

One trip particularly stands out in my mind. A magazine had given me an assignment to interview a man in northern Pennsylvania. The trip had been planned for two months. I made the trip, completed the interview, and then had two days available to fish before heading home. I consulted my tables (many of them were completed years ago) and discovered that the Loyalsock had good hatches of *Ephemerella subvaria* (Hendrickson) in late April. The river was only twenty miles away, so I headed out hoping to hit the peak of activity.

My tables also revealed that *Epeorus pleuralis* (Quill Gordon) hatches take place just slightly earlier than the Hendrickson fly. This meant that one or both insects should be on the water and offering good sport. For once I felt confident of hitting a hatch or spinnerfall in progress.

I stopped at a stretch of the Sock and climbed into waders, threaded fly line through the guides, and knotted on a tippet of 5X material. As I studied the stream, several Quill Gordons fell to the surface and were hastily consumed by trout. That settled the question of which fly I'd use—it would be a No. 12 Red Quill Spinner. If that failed to produce, I'd switch to a No. 12 Quill Gordon to imitate the dun instead of a spinner.

My first cast neatly covered a rising brown. The fish dimpled the water and I set fast and too hard, expecting a smaller trout. This had been a two-pound trout and my forcefulness left the fly in its lip.

I tied on another fly and sought another rising trout. This fish had set up a feeding station in smooth current in midstream. The fall of *Epeorus pleuralis* was getting heavier, and my excitement mounted as insects drifted by in the current. I cast the fly across and downstream to the fish, mended line to ensure a drag-free float, and saw the trout rise and suck a natural from the surface just ahead of my fly. I timed its rises and laid my fly out again, allowing just enough time for it to drift down to it. The trout rose without waiting and intercepted the imitation. The line tightened as it turned to head back to its feeding station.

That fish seemed dumbfounded that it had been fooled. It paused in midstream for an instant and then sizzled across and downstream on a hard run. My fly line peeled from the reel and I was nearly down into my backing before the fish turned and headed back upstream. I cranked furiously on the reel and then began stripping in line in an attempt to keep the trout under control. It looked to be three pounds or a bit better.

It was a delicious battle, one that I shall always remember. This brown threw all the tricks at me—including one beautiful jump that arched part way across the river. It sawed back and forth near bottom, head both up and downstream on hard rushes, and it required nearly fifteen minutes to break the trout's spirit. I led it close, grasped the bedraggled fly after a moment of admiration, and quickly twisted it loose. The fish hovered near my leg for long seconds and then finned slowly under a submerged log to safety.

Two more browns, one 14 inches long and the other 17 inches, fell to my flies that afternoon. I hooked and lost two other fish, one to a weakened tippet and the other when I tried to force the trout away from an obstruction.

I went back the next day to the same stretch. It was early afternoon and the hendrickson flies were emerging. I landed one nice trout on a No. 14 Red Quill tied to imitate the male dun. The hatch appeared short-lived, but I waited around and hoped the spinner flight would take place that afternoon.

It was nearly five P.M. when the first Hendricksons and Red Quills (the females and males of the E. subvaria species) began their flight. The tension built inside me and was almost to a fever pitch when the first female hit the surface. Another and another fell and soon the air and the water were blanketed with egg-laying females and dying males. The trout showed up, as is predictable, and laid in at the feeding trough.

It would be a sin to state how many trout I hooked, played, and released that day. I released all but one—a sleek, red-spotted brown that measured 15 inches. I kept it because it had engulfed the fly and was bleeding heavily from the gills. That fish made a wonderful meal that evening.

Such trips are not only possible, but can be common if a fisherman studies hatch tables and uses a little common sense. I expected the Hendricksons to be available, but had given only cursory thought to the Quill Gordon hatch, figuring it would probably be over. But I had the proper imitations available and found the type of fishing that anglers always hope to find.

Idaho's Henry's Fork is a classic stream with bountiful hatches. I fished it several years ago. Weed beds were in profusion and it reminded me of some of the fine Pennsylvania limestoners I've fished.

On this particular day, at about two P.M., a blizzard of Dark Brown Duns (*Baetis parvus*) had emerged and trout were feeding everywhere. It was impossible to cast a No. 20 Dark Brown Dun anywhere without drifting the fly over six or eight fish. I landed and released three fish and then I tangled with a big fish for thirty minutes but was never able to see it closely enough to identify. It's just a guess, but I figure that trout must have weighed in excess of ten pounds.

My trip from Michigan to Yellowstone, and then on to the Henry's Fork area, had been planned for several weeks. I'd heard casual reference to the Dark Brown Dun hatch but could find little or no scientific reference to it. This diminuitive insect creates a feeding orgy that must be seen to be appreciated. It is a difficult hatch to hit, in my experience, and I was reluctant to mention it in the hatch tables for Idaho simply because I've made two other trips to the area since then, and at approximately the same time, and failed to connect either time.

However, anyone planning a late June trip to this classic Idaho stream should bear the brown dun fly hatch in mind and stock up on some imitations. But, if you don't hit it, don't blame me because I've been down that trail myself. But if your timing is correct, and these insects hatch, you'll find fly-fishing of the caliber only a chosen few ever experience.

The above anecdote makes an important point. If some knowledge of a hatch can improve your pleasure while fly-fishing, more knowledge can be even more beneficial. I've tried to track down more information on the Dark Brown Dun and cannot seem to find anyone that really knows this insect. Here, then, is a challenge for readers. Look, study, and observe while fishing, and make notes. Perhaps you'll find a clue to unravel some other hatch information in your state and thereby be able to do a favor to other anglers.

The foregoing remarks about the Dark Brown Duns also point out an obvious hazard to this book, or any book that attempts to simplify hatch tables. In trout-fishing areas, some insects are left out simply because they do not figure significantly in the feeding habits of trout. Other insects are not included in the tables because of irregular emergences. And some hatches that may figure importantly in some locations are simply unknown to me so far. There are many hatches in many states or provinces that I have not fished. This points the finger of blame at me. I willingly accept any blame for omitted hatches, but rest my case on the knowledge that the data delivered in this book is by far the most complete of any that has been presented to date.

Furthermore, if an angler consults this book of hatch tables and cannot increase his catch of trout after giving it a fair piece of study and practice, then I will feel I have failed. However, I feel that as this book lists most known and widely accepted insect species important to fly-fishermen in each state and province and gives accurate dates of emergence, that it should help anyone to better plan a fishing trip . . . anywhere.

# Part Two

## The Hatches

# 6

# Northeast Hatches

The northeastern region of the United States is steeped in fly-fishing history. It was on some of the waters in this region that much of what we know today about fly hatches was first uncovered. Here some of the angling greats of yesteryear made their debut, and their eternal mark on the sport.

Some of the northeastern hatches are legendary—the green drake fly, the hendrickson fly, the quill gordon fly, all are world famous among fly-fishermen. The complete list will be covered in the pages that follow.

The Northeast was once home to the native brook trout. Now most of its former native waters have been usurped by rainbows and browns, although a few brookies still thrive in remote areas and in most of Maine. It's the browns and rainbows that turn anglers' knees to jelly during a spinnerfall. Some of the hatches which follow assume blanket proportions and some truly great fishing can take place at these times.

The states covered in this regional chapter are Connecticut, Delaware, Maine, Maryland, Massachusetts, New Hampshire, New Jersey, New York, Pennsylvania, Rhode Island, and Vermont. The topography and water quality varies from state to state, and even within a particular state. This means that hatches that are productive in, say, New York may not be the same as for those in Massachusetts.

## CONNECTICUT

This small Atlantic Seaboard state may be tiny in comparison with other states in the Northeast region, but it does have some good hatches and produces brook, rainbow, and brown trout. Connecticut hosts some three hundred hatchery-stocked streams and about one hundred sixty ponds and lakes, some of which contain trout. This offers anglers living in this urban area the opportunity to match wits and flies with both stocked and wild carryover trout.

*Tricorythodes fasciata* (Early Brown Stonefly)
 Hatch begins about March 15
 Duration is 30 days
 Peak activity occurs at midday for about 4 hours
 *Note:* Important during a cold winter and late spring.
 Best imitating fly—Early Brown Stonefly

*Iron Fraudator* (Quill Gordon)
 Hatch begins about March 15
 Duration is 30 days
 Peak activity occurs for 4 hours at midday
 *Note:* Important to anglers only during cold, late spring.
 Best imitating fly—Quill Gordon, No. 12 & 14

*Ephemerella subvaria* (Hendrickson or Red Quill)
 Hatch begins about April 25
 Duration is 15 days
 Peak activity occurs at midday for 2 hours
 *Note:* A very important early season hatch on Connecticut streams.
 Best imitating fly—Red Quill or Hendrickson, No. 14

*Ephemerella attenuata* (Blue-Wing Olive)
 Hatch begins about May 10
 Duration is 15 days
 Peak activity occurs all day in a sporadic fashion
 *Note:* Another very important early spring fly.
 Best imitating fly—Blue-Wing Olive, No. 18

*Paraleptophlebia adoptiva* (Blue Quill)
 Hatch begins about May 5
 Duration is 3 weeks
 Peak activity occurs sporadically all day
 Best imitating fly—Blue Quill or Dark Brown Spinner, No. 18

*Stenonema vicarium* (March Brown)
 Hatch begins about May 10
 Duration is 3 weeks
 Peak activity occurs in late afternoon and evening
 *Note:* Many anglers consider this the most important hatch of the year.
 Best imitating flies—American March Brown or Great Red Spinner, No. 10 & 12

*Stenonema fuscum* (Grey Fox)
  Hatch begins about May 20
  Duration is 10 days
  Peak activity occurs in late afternoon and evening
  Best imitating fly—Ginger Quill Spinner, No. 12

*Stenacron canadense* (Light Cahill)
  Hatch begins about June 1
  Duration is 3 weeks
  Peak activity occurs in the evening
  *Note:* A very important hatch.
  Best imitating fly—Trico Dun or Trico Spinner, No. 24

*C. tricorythides* (Trike or Trico)
  Hatch begins about July 15
  Duration is 6 weeks
  Peak activity occurs at daybreak
  Best imitating fly—Trico Dun or Trico Spinner, No. 24

*Ephoron leukon* (Spook or White Mayfly)
  Hatch begins about August 15
  Duration is 30 days
  Peak activity occurs in the evening
  Best imitating fly—White Mayfly or Cream Variant, No. 12 or 14

The best trout fishing on streams occurs on the Housatonic, West Branch Farmington, East Branch Salmon, Fenton, Mt. Hope, or Farmington rivers and Bigelow Brook. Some good trout action can be had on Ball, West Hill, and Mohawk ponds and on Twin, Highland, Crystal, Gardner, East Twin, and Mashapaug lakes.

*Stenonema vicarium*—male dun

## DELAWARE

There is little trout fishing in Delaware, but a handful of streams have been stocked. Rainbows and browns are planted on a put-and-take basis but a few carry-over fish exist and develop wild characteristics. These semi-wild trout are of prime interest to local anglers who cannot get away for a fishing trip to a more productive location.

Because of the lack of interest in fly hatches, very little research has been done on this subject.

*Baetis vagans* (Tiny Blue Wing Olive)
    Hatch occurs in mid-March
    Duration is through late fall
    Peak activity occurs sporadically through day
    Best imitating fly—Tiny Blue Wing Olive, No. 18

*Epeorus pleuralis* (Quill Gordon)
    Hatch begins in mid-April
    Duration is 4 weeks
    Peak activity occurs in early-to-late afternoon
    Best imitating fly—Quill Gordon, No. 12

*Stenonema vicarium* (March Brown)
    Hatch begins in mid-May
    Duration is 4 weeks
    Peak activity occurs in late morning and through afternoon
    Best imitating fly—March Brown or American March Brown, No. 12

*Paraleptophlebia adoptiva* (Mahogany Dun or Iron Blue Dun)
    Hatch occurs in mid-April
    Duration is 4 weeks
    Peak activity occurs in late morning until 2 P.M.
    Best imitating fly—Dark Brown Spinner, No. 18

*Stenonema fuscum* (Grey Fox)
    Hatch begins in late May
    Duration is 4 weeks
    Peak activity occurs in early evening
    Best imitating fly—Ginger Quill Spinner, No. 12

*Stenacron canadense* (Light Cahill)
    Hatch begins in mid-June
    Duration is through early August
    Peak activity occurs in late afternoon and early evening
    Best imitating fly—Light Cahill, No. 12

*Tricorythodes* (Trico)
    Hatch begins in July
    Duration is until first killing frost
    Peak activity occurs in early morning to early afternoon
    Best imitating fly—Trico Spinner, No. 22, 24, & 26

*Isonychia bicolor* (Dun Variant)
    Hatch begins in June or July
    Duration is through August
    Peak activity occurs at dusk
    Best imitating fly—Dun Variant, No. 12

The best bets for trout fishing and matching fly hatches in Delaware would come on White Clay Creek, Pike Creek, and Mill Creek.

## MAINE

This state,with its more than 5,000 streams and about 2,500 lakes or ponds, has some of the best native brook trout fishing left in the continental United States.

Brook, brown, rainbow, lake trout, landlocked salmon, and a smattering of Atlantic salmon offer fly-rodders an opportunity to match an emerging insect and try to tempt the fish.

Air and water temperatures can vary from one portion of Maine to another. The northern region, north of an east-west line drawn through Bangor, will find insects hatching about seven days later than the southern region. The dates provided in the table here are fixed on the southern portion. Add one week when planning a trip to the north.

A stream inventory is being completed now (early 1979) by the Department of Entomology of the University of Maine at Orono. When these surveys are complete, anglers in that state will have a much better idea of which insects are available and when hatch times occur.

*Leptophlebia cupida* (Black Quill)
    Hatch begins about May 6
    Duration is 4 weeks
    Peak activity occurs about 2 P.M.
    Best imitating flies—Black Quill or Whirling Dun, No. 14 & 12

*Siphloplecton basale*
    Hatch begins about May 12
    Duration is unknown
    Peak activity during daylight hours

*Siphlonurus quebecensis* (Grey Drake)
    Hatch begins about May 25
    Duration is 11 days
    Peak activity occurs in late afternoon and early evening
    Best imitating fly—Grey Drake or Brown Quill Spinner, No. 16

*Brachycentrus fuliginosus* (Grannom)
    Hatch begins about May 27
    Duration is 6 weeks
    Duration is from 3 to 7 P.M.
    Best imitating fly—Grannom, No. 14

*Taenioteryx faciata* (Early Brown Stonefly)
    Hatch begins in late May
    Duration is sporadic
    Peak activity occurs in the afternoon
    Best imitating fly—Early Brown Stonefly, No. 12 & 14

*Heptagenia aphrodite* (Pale Evening Dun)
    Hatch begins about June 21
    Duration is 9 weeks
    Peak activity occurs about 8 P.M.
    Best imitating flies—Red Quill or Hendrickson, No. 10 & 14

*Ephemerella subvaria* (Hendrickson)
    Hatch begins about June 21
    Duration is about 7 weeks
    Peak activity occurs afternoons and early evenings
    Best imitating flies—Little Rusty Spinner or Female Hendrickson, No. 12
        & 14

*Baetis vagans* (Tiny Blue-Wing Olive)
    Hatch begins about June 21
    Duration is about 14 weeks
    Peak activity occurs from early morning until about 6 P.M.

*Hydropsych slossanae* (Spotted Sedge)
    Hatch begins about June 25
    Duration is 5 weeks
    Peak activity occurs from early to late afternoon
    Best imitating fly—Spotted Sedge, No. 14 or 16

Other hatches occur sporadically but have yet to be studied and set to specific schedules.

Streams with good hatches of some (or all) of the above insects include the Narraguagus, Allagash, Spencer, Kennebago, Kennebec,

Penobscot, Moose, and Fish rivers. Good trout and landlocked salmon fishing occurs on Fish River, Chesuncook, Moosehead, Gangeley, Sebago, Green, Branch, Phillips, Alligator, East and West Grand, West Musquash, Kennebago, and other lakes or ponds.

## MARYLAND

Maryland, an eastern seaboard state, produces far better trout fishing and fly hatches than many anglers might suspect. Brook, rainbow, and brown trout are hatchery-planted in about fifty inland streams. Some carryover exists and some surprisingly big trout are taken in this state, primarily in the western regions.

Hatches are pretty short-lived, many lasting only fifteen days. The bulk of the insect activity is over by the end of July.

*Paraleptophlebia adoptiva* (Dark Brown Spinner)
    Hatch begins about April 15
    Duration is 15 days
    Peak activity occurs in early-to-late afternoon
    Best imitating fly—Dark Brown Spinner or Blue Quill, No. 18

*Iron Fraudator*
    Hatch begins about April 15
    Duration is 15 days
    Peak activity occurs after 2 P.M.
    Best imitating fly—Dark Gordon Quill, No. 12 & 14

*Ephemerella subvaria* (Hendrickson)
    Hatch begins about April 25
    Duration is 15 days
    Peak activity occurs in early-to-late afternoon
    Best imitating flies—Red Quill or Hendrickson, No. 12 & 14

*Stenonema vicarium* (Great Red Spinner)
    Hatch begins about May 15
    Duration is 10 days
    Peak activity occurs about 8 P.M.
    Best imitating fly—Great Red Spinner, No. 12

*Stenonema fuscum* (Ginger Quill Spinner)
    Hatch begins about May 20
    Duration is 15 days
    Peak activity occurs all day
    Best imitating fly—Gray Fox or Ginger Quill Spinner, No. 12

*Stenonema fuscum*—male dun

*Paraleptophlebia mollis* (Jenny Spinner)
    Hatch begins about May 25
    Duration is 15 days
    Peak activity occurs usually in the evening
    Best imitating flies—Dark Blue Quill or Blue Quill Spinner, No. 18 & 20

*Ephemera guttulata* (Green Drake)
    Hatch begins about May 28
    Duration is 15 days
    Peak activity occurs in the evening
    Best imitating flies—Male Coffin or Female Green Drake, No. 8 & 10

*Ephemerella dorothea* (Pale Evening Dun)
    Hatch begins about May 28
    Duration is 30 days, or slightly longer
    Peak activity occurs in the evening
    Best imitating fly—Pale Evening Dun, No. 16 & 18

*Isonychia bicolor* (Slate Drake)
    Hatch begins about June 1
    Duration is about 30 days
    Peak activity occurs in late afternoon or early evening
    Best imitating fly—Grey Variant, No. 10 & 12

*Stenacron canadense* (Light Cahill)
    Hatch begins about June 15
    Duration is 15 days
    Peak activity occurs in early evening
    Best imitating fly—Light Cahill, No. 12

*Ephemerella attenuata* (Blue Wing Olive Dun)
    Hatch begins about June 15
    Duration is 15 days
    Peak activity occurs sporadically during day and in evening
    Best imitating fly—Blue Wing Olive Dun, No. 14 & 16

*Potamanthus distinctus* (Golden Drake)
    Hatch begins about June 28
    Duration is 30 days
    Peak activity occurs at twilight
    Best imitating flies—Golden Spinner or Paulinskill, No. 10 & 12

Good trout fishing and fly hatches have been found on Maryland's Savage River, Big Hunting Creek, Deer Creek, Morgan Run, Beaver Creek, Principio Creek, and Rock Creek.

## MASSACHUSETTS

The favorite game fish species, rainbow, brown, and brook trout, are available in many streams and brooks. Lake trout have been planted in large Quabbin Reservoir. Other important species that are apt to feed on insects during a hatch include largemouth and smallmouth bass, yellow perch, bluegill, pumpkinseed sunfish, and other fishes on occasion.

This state is small, but delivers good insect activity on many of its smaller streams. The tables listed below denote approximate hatching times in the eastern part of the state. Anglers should add about ten to fourteen days to listed dates for hatches in the Berkshire region. Trico hatches on Cape Cod streams or ponds are approximately thirty days later than those noted below.

*Leptophlebia cupida* (Black Quill)
    Hatch begins about April 15
    Duration is 20 days
    Peak activity occurs from mid-to-late afternoon
    Best imitating flies—Compara Dun and Compara Spinner, No. 12

*Paraleptophlebia adoptiva* (Dark Brown Spinner)
    Hatch begins about May 1
    Duration is 20 days
    Peak activity occurs in late afternoon
    Best imitating flies—Compara Dun and Compara Spinner, No. 18

*Iron Fraudator* (Quill Gordon)
    Hatch begins about April 15 to May 1
    Duration is 15 days
    Peak activity occurs from 11 A.M. to 3 P.M.
    Best imitating fly—Quill Gordon, No. 12

*Ephemerella subvaria* (Hendrickson or Red Quill)
    Hatch begins about May 10
    Duration is 20 days
    Peak activity occurs from 2 to 8 P.M.
    Best imitating flies—Little Rusty Spinner or Female Hendrickson, No. 12
      & 14

*Stenonema vicarium* (March Brown)
    Hatch begins about June 1
    Duration is 20 days
    Peak activity is sporadic, from 10 A.M. to 8 P.M.
    Best imitating fly—American March Brown, No. 10

*Stenonema fuscum* (Grey Fox)
    Hatch begins about June 5
    Duration is 20 days
    Peak activity occurs from 4 to 8:30 P.M., often sporadic
    Best imitating fly—Grey Fox, No. 14 & 16

*Stenonema canadensis* (Light Cahill)
    Hatch begins about June 10
    Duration is 40 days
    Peak activity occurs from 6 to 9 P.M.
    Best imitating fly—Light Cahill, No. 12

*Stenonema ithaca* (Light Cahill)
    Hatch begins about June 10
    Duration is 40 days
    Peak activity occurs from 6 to 9 P.M.
    *Note:* S. *ithaca* and S. *canadensis* often hatch at the same time.
    Best imitating fly—Compara Spinner, No. 14, 16, & 18

*Isonychia bicolor* (Dun Variant)
  Hatch begins about June 20
  Duration is 30 days
  Peak activity occurs from 7 to 8 P.M.
  Best imitating fly—Dun Variant or Slate Wing Dun, No. 12

*Ephemerella attenuata* (Blue Wing Olive)
  Hatch begins about June 15
  Duration is 25 days
  Peak activity is sporadic, both afternoon and evening
  Best imitating fly—Dark Olive Spinner, No. 14 & 16

The best chance an angler has of meeting a hatch and parlaying that into good trout action is on the Deerfield, Farmington, Green, Ware, Quinapoxet, or Konkapot rivers. Good trout action exists on Quabbin Reservoir, Comet Pond, Lake Quinsigamond, Cliff Pond, Lake Cochituate, Lake Quacumquasit, and Lake Mattawa.

## NEW HAMPSHIRE

This state is known principally for its cold-water fisheries. The catch on New Hampshire streams and lakes runs heavy to brook, brown, rainbow, and lake trout, with the odd landlocked salmon thrown in for good measure. Sunapee Lake, once home for the rare and now possibly extinct Sunapee trout, is well known for the other trout and salmon species listed above.

New Hampshire has more than 4,000 miles of running water that contains trout species. Trout are also found in a large number of ponds and lakes, especially in the northern area.

The table that follows is based on the southern New Hampshire streams, and hatches can be as much as fourteen days later in the northern regions, especially those north of the White Mountains.

*Epeorus pleuralis* (Quill Gordon)
  Hatch begins in late April or early May
  Duration is 30 to 40 days
  Peak activity occurs from 1 to 2:30 P.M.
  Best imitating fly—Hare's Ear, No. 12 & 14

*Ephemerella subvaria* (Hendrickson or Whirling Dun)
  Hatch begins about May 1
  Duration is 20 days
  Peak activity occurs from 2 to 4 P.M.
  Best imitating flies—Male or Female Hendrickson or Red Quill, No. 12 & 14

*Hilara femorata* (Black Gnat)
    Hatch begins about May 1
    Duration is 30 days
    Peak activity is sporadic, can occur any time during day
    Best imitating fly—Black Gnat, No. 18, 20, or 22

*Paraleptophlebia adoptiva* (Iron Blue Dun)
    Hatch begins in early May
    Duration is 50 days
    Peak activity occurs in late afternoon or early evening
    Best imitating flies—Dark Blue Quill or Dark Brown Spinner, No. 18

*Epeorus vitrea* (Pale Evening Dun)
    Hatch begins in late May
    Duration is 10 days
    Peak activity occurs in the evening
    Best imitating flies—Pink Cahill or Salmon Spinner, No. 14

*Ephemerella walkeri* (Olive Quill)
    Hatch begins in late May
    Duration is 20 days
    Peak activity occurs sporadically in the evening
    Best imitating fly—Dark Olive Spinner, No. 14

*Ephemera guttulata* (Coffin)
    Hatch begins in late May
    Duration is 20 days
    Peak activity occurs about 8 P.M.
    Best imitating fly—Coffin or Green Drake, No. 8 or 10

*Hexagenia limbata* (Mayfly)
    Hatch begins in mid-to-late June
    Duration is 30 days
    Peak activity occurs on some lakes or ponds and a few rivers at night
    Best imitating fly—Light Michigan Mayfly, No. 6

*Ephemerella dorothea* (Pale Watery Dun)
    Hatch begins in mid-June
    Duration is 1 month
    Peak activity occurs about 8 P.M.
    Best imitating fly—Pale Evening Dun, No. 16 or 18

*Stenonema canadense* (Light Cahill)
    Hatch begins in June
    Duration can last 2 months
    Peak activity occurs usually from 6 to 9 P.M.
    Best imitating fly—Light Cahill, No. 14

*Potamanthus distinctus* (Cream Cahill)
    Hatch begins in late June or early July
    Duration is 20 to 30 days
    Peak activity occurs at twilight
    Best imitating flies—Golden Spinner or Cream Variant, No. 10 & 12

*Ephemerella attenuata* (Blue Wing Olive)
    Hatch begins in late June or early July
    Duration is 20 to 30 days
    Peak activity occurs anytime after 11 A.M. but spinnerfall normally
      occurs in the evening
    Best imitating flies—Blue Quill Spinner or Blue-Winged Olive Dun, No.
      14 & 16

*Leptophlebia cupida* (Whirling Dun)
    Hatch begins in June or early July
    Duration is 25 to 35 days
    Peak activity occurs normally about 2 P.M.
    Best imitating flies—Whirling Dun or Black Quill Spinner, No. 14

*Stenonema vicarium* (March Brown)
    Hatch begins anytime from May through summer
    Duration is sporadic but can cover 4 months
    Peak activity occurs with spinnerfall at about 8 P.M.
    Best imitating flies—Great Red Spinner or American March Brown, No.
      10 & 12

Hatches can be sporadic in nature, depending greatly on the existing weather conditions. Cold weather in northern New Hampshire can actually put an emergence off entirely.

*Leptophlebia cupida*—female spinner

The best streams for trout or salmon fishing during some or all of the above hatches include the Androscoggin, Connecticut, Sugar, Saco, Dead Diamond, Ammonoosuc, Baker, Bearcamp, Smith, Mascoma, Cold, Ashuelot, Dry, Sawyers, and Swift Diamond rivers. Cones Siding Run is another solid bet for fly-fishermen. Lake and pond action can be found at Lake Francis, Second Lake, First Lake, Third Lake, Stratford Bog, Munn Pond, Big Diamond Pond, Sunapee Lake, Scott's Bog, Big Brook Bog, Ashuelot Pond, Little Diamond Pond, Lake Winnipesaukee, Squam Lake, Winnisquam Lake, Newfound Lake, and many others.

## NEW JERSEY

New Jersey may be fairly small in size, and possess limited numbers of trout waters, but it has some excellent hatches and produces some fine trout. Favorite species include rainbow, brown, and brook trout.

The tables listed here are generally good for the entire state but emergence dates may vary from year-to-year depending on a late winter or early spring break-up. The dates shown are *normally* quite reliable from one year to the next.

*Taeniopteryx fasciata* (Early Brown Stonefly)
 Hatch begins about April 9
 Duration is about 20 days
 Peak activity occurs at sporadic intervals
 Best imitating fly—Brown Stonefly, No. 14 & 16

*Paraleptophlebia adoptiva* (Blue Quill)
 Hatch begins about April 13
 Duration is 1 month
 Peak activity occurs from 11 A.M. to 4 P.M.
 Best imitating flies—Blue Dun and Blue Quill, No. 16 & 18

*Epeorus pleuralis* (Quill Gordon)
 Hatch begins about April 13
 Duration is one month
 Peak activity occurs from 1 to 7 P.M., spinnerfall latest
 Best imitating flies—Quill Gordon and Brown Spinner, No. 12 & 14

*Chimarra* (Little Black Caddis or Dark Caddis)
 Hatch begins about April 17
 Duration is 4 months of sporadic activity
 Peak activity occurs sporadically, usually morning is best
 Best imitating flies—Black Caddis or Black Henryville, No. 18 & 20

*Ephemerella subvaria* (Hendrickson)
    Hatch begins about April 26
    Duration is 14 days
    Peak activity occurs in late afternoon
    Best imitating fly—Hendrickson, No. 12

*Brachycentrus fuliginosus* (Grannom or Shad Fly)
    Hatch begins in late April
    Duration is 14 to 21 days
    Peak activity occurs sporadically all day
    Best imitating fly—Wetzel's Grannom, No. 14 & 16

*Ephemerella attenuata* (Blue Wing Olive)
    Hatch begins about June 1
    Duration is 30 days
    Peak activity occurs from 9 A.M. to noon
    Best imitating fly—Blue-Winged Olive, No. 16 & 18

*Stenonema vicarium* (March Brown)
    Hatch begins in mid-May to early June
    Duration is about 14 days
    Peak activity occurs from 10 A.M. to 6 P.M.
    Best imitating fly—March Brown Emerger, No. 12

*Ephemerella dorothea* (Sulphur Dun)
    Hatch begins from mid-May to early June
    Duration is usually 30 days
    Peak activity occurs in late afternoon to early evening
    Best imitating fly—Pale Evening Dun, No. 16

*Ephemerella guttulata* (Green Drake)
    Hatch begins in late May or early June
    Duration is short, often less than 2 weeks
    Peak activity occurs in late afternoon
    Best imitating fly—Green Drake or Coffin, No. 8

*Stenonema ithaca* (Light Cahill)
    Hatch begins in mid-June
    Duration is sporadic but usually lasts for 30 days
    Peak activity normally occurs in late afternoon to evening
    Best imitating fly—Light Cahill, No. 12 & 14

*Rhyacophila lobifera* (Green Caddis)
    Hatch begins in mid-May to early June
    Duration is 30 to 45 days
    Peak activity occurs in the morning
    Best imitating flies—Green Caddis or Green Henryville, No. 14 & 16

*Epeorus vitrea* (Pale Evening Dun)
    Hatch begins in early to mid-June
    Duration is 30 days
    Peak activity occurs in afternoon or early evening
    Best imitating fly—Pale Evening Dun, No. 12

*Potomanthus distinctus* (Yellow Drake)
    Hatch begins in mid-June
    Duration is 1 month
    Peak activity occurs in early evening to twilight
    Best imitating fly—Light Cahill, No. 10

*Tricorythodes* species (White-Winged Black)
    Hatches of this species take place in late June
    Duration is 60 days
    Peak activity usually occurs early in the morning after daybreak
    Best imitating fly—White-Winged Black Spinner, No. 22

Four streams—Big Flat Brook, Musconetcong River, South Branch of the Raritan River, and Paulinskill River—rate as New Jersey's best trout streams. The Wanaque, Manasquan, and Pequest rivers are also good at times and deliver good hatches and decent trout fishing.

## NEW YORK

This state is famous for its infinite variety of hatching insects. Reams of sporting books have been written about fly-fishing these waters.

Streams in southern New York often have hatches beginning one to two weeks ahead of those in mountain areas or in northern New York. The tables here reflect southern emergence dates. Anglers should bear this in mind when planning a trip for trout. The trout species available include brook, brown, rainbow, and lake trout. More than 20,000 miles of trout streams with fly hatches are available and the trout species are found in hundreds of lakes and ponds.

Hatches begin early in the year, and as in many eastern states, most major insect activity is over by July. Only sporadic hatches occur after that date, but this is the time when terrestrials figure significantly in a trout's diet.

*Baetis vagans* (Little Blue Dun)
    Hatch begins about April 1
    Duration is about 3 weeks
    Peak activity occurs from 10 A.M. to 6 P.M.
    Best imitating fly—Rusty Spinner, No. 18

*Taeniopteryx faciata* (Early Brown Stonefly)
    Hatch begins about April 10
    Duration is 30 days or less
    Peak activity occurs in the afternoon
    Best imitating fly—Early Brown Stonefly, No. 14

*Paraleptophlebia adoptiva* (Iron Blue Dun)
    Hatch begins about April 15
    Duration is 30 days
    Peak activity occurs from 2 to 4 P.M., spinnerfall from 4 to 7 P.M.
    Best imitating flies—Dark Blue Quill or Dark Red Quill, No. 18 & 20

*Epeorus pleuralis* (Quill Gordon)
    Hatch begins about April 20
    Duration is 1 month
    Peak activity occurs from 11 A.M. to 3 P.M.
    Best imitating flies—Dark Gordon Quill or Gordon Quill, No. 12 & 14

*Chimarra atterima* (Little Black Caddis)
    Hatch begins about April 25
    Duration is sporadic, often 2 to 4 months
    Peak activity occurs in the morning
    Best imitating fly—Little Black Caddis, No. 16

*Ephemerella subvaria* (Red Quill or Hendrickson)
    Hatch begins in early May
    Duration is 1 week
    Peak activity occurs from 2 to 8 P.M.
    Best imitating fly—Red Quill Spinner or Hendrickson, No. 14

*Isoperla signata* (Light Stonefly)
    Hatch begins in early May
    Duration is 3 weeks
    Peak activity occurs in the afternoon
    Best imitating fly—Light Stonefly, No. 12 or 14

*Stenonema vicarium* (Grey Fox)
    Hatch begins in early May
    Duration is 1 to 2 weeks
    Peak activity occurs from 10 A.M. to 8 P.M.
    Best imitating flies—Great Red Spinner or American March Brown, No.
      10 & 12

*Rhyacophila lobifera* (Green Caddis)
    Hatch begins about May 10
    Duration is about 1 month
    Peak activity occurs from 4 to 9 P.M.
    Best imitating fly—Green Caddis, No. 16 & 18

*Brachycentrus fuliginosus* (Grannom)
    Hatch begins in mid-May
    Duration is about 6 weeks
    Peak activity occurs in late afternoon
    Best imitating fly—Grannom, No. 14 & 16

*Stenonema fuscum* (Grey Fox)
    Hatch begins in mid-May
    Duration is 7 to 10 days
    Peak activity occurs from 4 to 9 P.M.
    Best imitating fly—Ginger Quill Spinner, No. 12

*Hydropsyche slossanae* (Spotted Sedge)
    Hatch begins third week in May
    Duration is sporadic
    Peak activity occurs from 1 to 6 P.M.
    Best imitating fly—Spotted Sedge, No. 14 or 16

*Stenonema ithaca* (Light Cahill)
    Hatch begins in late May
    Duration is about 2 weeks
    Peak activity occurs in the evening
    Best imitating fly—Light Cahill, No. 12

*Stenonema canadensis* (Light Cahill)
    Hatch begins in early June
    Duration is about 10 days to 2 weeks
    Peak activity occurs from 6 to 9 P.M.
    Best imitating fly—Light Cahill, No. 12

*Ephemera guttulata* (Green Drake)
    Hatch begins in early June
    Duration is 1 to 2 weeks
    Peak activity occurs about 8 P.M.
    Best imitating fly—Green Drake or Coffin, No. 10 or 12

*Isonychia bicolor* (Dun Variant)
    Hatch begins in early June
    Duration is 10 to 14 days
    Peak activity occurs from 7 P.M. to dark
    Best imitating fly—Dun Variant, No. 12

*Ephemerella dorothea* (Pale Evening Dun)
    Hatch begins about June 1
    Duration is 2 to 3 weeks
    Peak activity occurs in afternoon and early evening
    Best imitating flies—Pale Evening Dun, No. 16 or 18

*Ephemerella attenuata* (Blue Wing Olive)
   Hatch begins in early June
   Duration is 1 to 2 weeks
   Peak activity occurs during daylight hours
   Best imitating flies—Blue Quill Spinner or Blue-Winged Olive Dun, No.
      14 & 16

*Potomanthus distinctus* (Cream Variant)
   Hatch begins in late June
   Duration is 2 to 3 weeks
   Peak activity occurs about 9 P.M.
   Best imitating flies—Golden Drake and Golden Spinner, No. 12

*Baetis* species (Little Blue Dun)
   Hatch begins in July
   Duration is about 6 weeks
   Peak activity occurs during afternoon and early evening
   Best imitating fly—Rusty Spinner, No. 20

*Tricorythodes stygiatus* (Trico)
   Hatch begins in mid-July
   Duration is about 4 weeks
   Peak activity occurs in early morning
   Best imitating fly—Dark Brown Spinner, No. 24 or 26

Good trout fishing and fly-matching can be had on the Battenkill, Beaverkill, upper Hudson, Ausable, Catherine Creek, Mettawee, Salmon, Delaware, Willowemoc, Kinderhook, Saranac, Fish Creek, Neversink, and Wallkill rivers. Numerous other smaller streams have excellent hatches and delightful fishing. Good lakes for trout include Seneca, Canandaigua, Keuka, Owasco, Cayuga, George, Indian, Lewey, Raquette, and Otsego. Anglers can touch bases with the local fisheries office for up-to-date information on smaller streams.

## PENNSYLVANIA

Two mountain ranges—the Appalachian and Allegheny—and their watersheds, are headwaters for some of Pennsylvania's finest trout fishing. This state is probably the finest fly-fishing state in the Northeast, and one of the best in the continental United States.

The state has nearly 5,000 miles of trout streams and brook, brown, and rainbows are common in most areas. Some lakes offer lake trout and other trout species, but the heart of the fishing lies in the streams.

The following emergence dates are based primarily on southern

Pennsylvania streams. Anglers that fish the mountain streams and those in the northern portion of the state should add one to two weeks to the dates listed below. Although there are some hatches that occur that are not listed in these tables, the emergences listed are considered to be the most important to Pennsylvania anglers.

*Chimarra atterima* (Caddis)
    Hatch begins about April 15
    Duration is for 2 weeks
    Peak activity occurs from 11 A.M. to 2 P.M.
    Best imitating fly—Dark Caddis, No. 14

*Paraleptophlebia adoptiva* (Blue Quill)
    Hatch begins about April 17
    Duration is 3 weeks
    Peak activity occurs from 11 A.M. to 3 P.M.
    Best imitating fly—Blue Quill Spinner, No. 12

*Epeorus pleuralis* (Quill Gordon)
    Hatch begins the end of April
    Duration is 3 weeks
    Peak activity occurs about 1:30 P.M.
    Best imitating fly—Quill Gordon, No. 12

*Ephemerella subvaria* (Red Quill)
    Hatch begins about May 1
    Duration is 3 weeks
    Peak activity occurs about 2 P.M.
    Best imitating fly—Red Spinner or Hendrickson, No. 12

*Stenonema vicarium* (March Brown)
    Hatch begins about May 15
    Duration is 3 weeks
    Peak activity occurs from 10 A.M. to noon and 4 P.M. to twilight
    Best imitating fly—American March Brown, No. 10 & 12

*Stenonema fuscum* (Ginger Quill)
    Hatch begins about May 20
    Duration is 2 weeks
    Peak activity occurs from 10 A.M. to noon and 4 P.M. to twilight
    Best imitating fly—Ginger Quill Spinner, No. 12

*Ephemerella dorothea* (Sulphur)
    Hatch begins May 25
    Duration is 3 weeks
    Peak activity occurs in later afternoon, about 1½ hours before dark
    Best imitating fly—Pale Evening Dun, No. 14

*Isonychia sadleri* (Leadwing Coachman)
    Hatch begins about June 1
    Duration is 3 weeks
    Peak activity occurs in the evening
    Best imitating fly—Slate Drake, No. 12

*Ephemera guttulata* (Green Drake)
    Hatch begins about June 1
    Duration is 3 weeks of sporadic activity
    Peak activity occurs 1 hour before dark
    Best imitating fly—Coffin, No. 8 or 10

*Stenonema canadense* (Light Cahill)
    Hatch begins about June 1
    Duration is 3 to 4 weeks
    Peak activity occurs just before dark
    Best imitating fly—Light Cahill, No. 12

*Tricorythodes atratus* (Trico)
    Hatch begins about July 20
    Duration is 2 months
    Peak activity occurs in the morning, usually 9 to 11 A.M.
    *Note:* This productive hatch is found on limestone streams only.
    Best imitating flies—Pale Olive Dun or Dark Brown Spinner, No. 24 & 26

Some of the East's premier trout streams are found in Pennsylvania. Both limestone and freestone streams abound and fly hatches are common on all streams that contain trout species. Among the favorites are Yellow Breeches Creek, Big Spring Creek, Mountain Creek, Falling Spring Creek, Letort River, Spruce Creek, Honey Creek, Yellow Creek, Stoney Creek, Bushkill Creek, Laurel Hill Creek, Fishing Creek, Lackawaxen River, Brodheads Creek, upper Delaware River, Poncho Creek, Allegheny River, Loyalsock Creek, East Licking Creek, Penns Creek, Elk Creek, Walnut Creek, Trout Run, Raccoon Creek, and many others.

## RHODE ISLAND

America's smallest state is one of the heaviest populated along the Atlantic Seaboard. Some sixty streams contain trout; most are planted annually but some have a carry-over of fish from previous stockings. This offers anglers a chance at some larger rainbow, brown, and brook trout.

Hatches offer anglers a chance at these hatchery and gone-native trout. Some fish are taken every year that pull a scale's peg down to 5 or 6 pounds, a very respectable weight indeed.

*Leptophlebia cupida* (Black Quill)
     Hatch begins in late April
     Duration is 3 weeks
     Peak activity occurs from 10 A.M. to 2 P.M.
     Best imitating fly—Black Quill Spinner, No. 14

*Baetis* species (Blue Wing Olive)
     Hatch begins in mid-to-late April
     Duration is 4 weeks
     Peak activity occurs from 11 A.M. to 3 P.M.
     Best imitating fly—Blue Wing Olive, No. 18

*Epeorus pleuralis* (Blue Quill)
     Hatch begins in early May
     Duration is 2 to 3 weeks
     Peak activity occurs from 1 to 4 P.M.
     Best imitating flies—Quill Gordon or Red Quill Spinner, No. 12 & 14

*Paraleptophlebia adoptiva* (Small Dun Variant)
     Hatch begins in mid-May
     Duration is about 3 weeks
     Peak activity occurs at midday
     Best imitating flies—Dark Red Quill or Dark Blue Quill, No. 18 & 20

*Ephemerella subvaria* (Red Quill or Hendrickson)
     Hatch begins in mid-to-late May
     Duration is 2 to 3 weeks
     Peak activity occurs from 2 to 8 P.M.
     Best imitating flies—Female Hendrickson or Little Rusty Spinner, No. 12 & 14

*Hydropsyche* (Micro Caddis)
     Hatch begins in early May to mid-June
     Duration is sporadic
     Peak activity occurs from 1 to 6 P.M.
     Best imitating fly—Spotted Sedge, No. 14 or 16

*Stenonema vicarium* (March Brown)
     Hatch begins in late May
     Duration is about 2 weeks
     Peak activity occurs from 10 A.M. to 2 P.M.
     Best imitating flies—Great Red Spinner or American March Brown, No.
         10 & 12

*Stenonema fuscum* (Gray Fox)
     Hatch begins in early to mid-June
     Duration is about 2 weeks
     Peak activity occurs from 4 to 8:30 P.M.
     Best imitating flies—Gray Fox or Ginger Quill Spinner, No. 12

*Ephemerella dorothea* (Pale Evening Dun)
    Hatch begins in early to mid-June
    Duration is about 2 weeks
    Peak activity occurs from 7 to 9 P.M.
    Best imitating flies—Little Maryatt or Pale Evening Dun, No. 16 & 18

*Stenonema canadense* (Light Cahill)
    Hatch begins in mid-June to early July
    Duration is 2 weeks
    Peak activity occurs from 4 to 8 P.M.
    Best imitating fly—Light Cahill, No. 12

*Ephemerella attenuata* (Blue Wing Olive)
    Hatch begins in mid-June or early July
    Duration is 2 weeks
    Peak activity occurs from 9 A.M. to noon
    Best imitating fly—Dark Olive Spinner, No. 14 or 16

*Tricorythodes* species (Trico)
    Hatch begins in mid-July
    Duration is 2 months
    Peak activity occurs from 8 A.M. to noon
    Best imitating fly—White Wing Black Spinner, No. 22 & 24

Wood River is probably the best bet for larger carry-over trout. Other streams with fair-to-good trout fishing and hatches include Falls River, Breakheart Brook, Flat River, Paris Brook, and Roaring Brook.

## VERMONT

Vermont offers fly-fishermen some of the better trout action in the northeast region. Cold water, an abundance of trout streams, and fairly moderate weather once spring sets in, team up to produce good hatches.

Rainbows, brookies, browns, lake trout, and landlocked salmon offer anglers a wide choice of fishing activities. All species are known to feed on hatching insects at one time or another.

Spring is usually late in coming to the Green Mountain state, and stable weather seldom is available before early May. Few hatches occur before midMay, but hatches often continue through September. The tables listed here apply to the entire state most of the time.

*Ephemerella subvaria* (Hendrickson or Red Quill)
    Hatch begins about May 18
    Duration is 3 weeks
    Peak activity occurs in midafternoon
    Best imitating fly—Male or Female Hendrickson, No. 14 & 16

*Potamanthus distinctus*—male dun

*Stenonema vicarium* (March Brown)
    Hatch begins about May 22
    Duration is 3 to 4 weeks
    Peak activity occurs from noon to 3 P.M.
    Best imitating fly—American March Brown, No. 10 & 12

*Stenonema fuscum* (Grey Fox)
    Hatch begins about May 25
    Duration is 3 weeks
    Peak activity occurs from noon to 3 P.M.
    Best imitating fly—Grey Fox, No. 12 & 14

*Ephemerella dorothea* (Light Cahill)
    Hatch begins about May 26
    Duration is 3 weeks
    Peak activity occurs in the evening, usually about 8 P.M.
    Best imitating fly—Light Cahill, No. 16 & 18

*Potamanthus distinctus* (Golden Drake)
    Hatch begins about July 3
    Duration is 3 to 4 weeks
    Peak activity occurs at dusk
    Best imitating fly—Golden Drake or Golden Spinner, No. 12

*Tricorythodes stygiatus* (Trico)
    Hatch begins about July 16
    Duration is 3 to 4 weeks
    Peak activity occurs in early morning
    Best imitating fly—Dark Brown Spinner, No. 24 & 26

*Isonychia sadleri* (Dun Variant)
    Hatch begins about July 13
    Duration is about 8 weeks
    Peak activity occurs at dusk
    Best imitating fly—Slate Drake, No. 12

*Ephemerella lata* (Blue Wing Olive)
    Hatch begins about July 27
    Duration is 1 week
    Peak activity occurs at dusk
    Best imitating fly—Blue Wing Olive Quill, No. 18 & 20

*Ephoron leukon* (White Miller)
    Hatch begins about July 21
    Duration is 3 weeks
    Peak activity occurs at dusk
    Best imitating fly—White Mayfly, No. 12 & 14

Top honors for trout fishing and fly hatches go to Deerfield River, Battenkill River, Otter Creek, Big Branch, Furnace Brook, White River, West River, Black River, Williams River, Saxton River, Connecticut River, Winooski River, Lamoille River, Barton River, Clyde River, and Nulhegan River.

# 7

## Southeastern Hatches

Fly-fishermen, unless they live in the southeastern states, seldom consider hatches in the southeast to be of any importance. But some excellent trout fishing takes place in many of the mountainous areas of this region, and there a hatch is of as much importance as in the Northeast, Midwest, or West.

This chapter includes Florida, Georgia, Kentucky, North Carolina, South Carolina, Tennessee, Virginia, and West Virginia. Every state, with the exception of Florida, has some trout fishing. Florida, although it lacks cold water and trout species, makes up the difference with other species.

This region is temperate in climate with warming tendencies the farther south one goes. Average amounts of rainfall, a predictable climate, and well-oxygenated water allows insects to hatch on a regular basis. These factors account for some significant emergences and good top-water fly rod action.

### FLORIDA

This state is 447 miles long and faces the Atlantic Ocean on the east and the Gulf of Mexico on the west. Bordered on the north by Georgia and Alabama, it is too warm for any trout to live. However, other species of game fish do feed on the hatches, some of which go on year round.

The prize-winning game fish for most Florida anglers is the largemouth bass. These game fish can reach weights of ten to fifteen pounds although the average would be much less.

Other highly sought-after species include bluegill, sunfish, redear sunfish (shellcrackers), chain pickerel, shad, crappie, redeye bass, warmouth bass, and catfish. Some or all of these species feed at times on emerging insects.

Although the charts that follow are based on reliable information from sources in the state, the author admits to a limited personal knowledge of Florida's insects and their imitating flies. Although insect species here include species listed in other areas, I am not familiar with popular names in Florida. It's probably a fair bet that you can use imitating flies noted for these species in other lists.

*Ameletus lineatus*
    Hatch occurs in March and April
    Duration is 6 to 8 weeks
    Peak activity occurs at dusk

*Siphlonurus decorus*
    Hatch occurs from April to July
    Duration is from late April on
    Peak activity occurs from late morning to late afternoon

*Siphlonurus luridipennis*
    Hatch occurs from April to July
    Duration is 8 weeks
    Peak activity occurs in the afternoon

*Siphlonurus mirus*
    Hatch occurs from April through July
    Duration is 10 to 12 weeks
    Peak activity occurs in the afternoon

*Siphlonurus quebecensis*
    Hatch occurs from April to July
    Duration is 8 weeks
    Peak activity occurs in late afternoon or early evening

*Isonychia annulata*
    Hatch can occur all year
    Duration is sporadic
    Peak activity occurs at twilight

*Isonychia bicolor*
    Hatch can occur all year during warm weather
    Duration is sporadic
    Swarms normally take place at dusk

*Isonychia georgiae*
    Hatch can occur all year
    Duration is sporadic
    Peak activity occurs at dusk

*Isonychia sadleri*
    Hatch can occur all year in warm weather
    Duration is sporadic in nature
    Peak activity occurs at twilight

*Baetis amplus*
    Hatch occurs during summer months
    Duration is 4 to 8 weeks
    Peak activity occurs during daylight hours

*Baetis australis*
    Hatch occurs during summer months
    Duration is all summer if warm
    Peak activity occurs during daylight hours

*Baetis pallidulus*
    Hatch occurs during summer months
    Duration is all summer if warm
    Peak activity occurs in late morning to early afternoon

*Baetis spinosus*
    Hatch occurs during summer months
    Duration can be all summer
    Peak activity occurs during daylight hours

*Ephemerella attenuata*
    Hatch occurs from May through September
    Duration is 4 months
    Peak activity occurs at dusk

*Ephemerella cornuta*
    Hatch occurs from May through September
    Duration is 4 months or less
    Peak activity occurs at dusk

*Ephemerella lata*
    Hatch occurs from May through September
    Duration is 4 months
    Peak activity occurs at dusk

*Ephemerella tuberculata*
　　Hatch occurs from May through September
　　Duration is 4 months
　　Peak activity occurs at dusk

*Ephemerella walkeri*
　　Hatch occurs from May through September
　　Duration is 4 months
　　Peak activity occurs at dusk

*Epeorus dispar*
　　Hatch occurs in late summer
　　Duration is 4 weeks
　　Peak activity occurs at dusk or other low light level times

*Epeorus pleuralis*
　　Hatch begins in late summer
　　Duration is 4 weeks
　　Peak activity is sporadic, often in midafternoon

*Ephemera guttulata*
　　Hatch occurs May through August
　　Duration is 16 weeks
　　Peak activity occurs at midday, often during overcast periods

*Ephemera simulans*
　　Hatch can occur from May through August
　　Duration is sporadic but up to 16 weeks
　　Peak activity occurs at sunset

*Tricorythodes atratus*
　　Hatch occurs February to October, often late in the season
　　Duration is many months
　　Peak activity occurs after dusk

*Leptophlebia cupida*
　　Hatch occurs February and March, but can appear later
　　Duration is sporadic
　　Peak activity in midafternoon until dark

　　Big lakes with nearby marshes and inflowing streams offer the best habitat. Try lakes Jackson, Kississimmie, George, Tsala Apopka, Eustis, Harris, Hell 'N Blazes, Kerr, Martin, Seminole, Blue Cypress, and Trafford. Good hatches occur on the St. John's, Oklawaha, Suwanee, Homosassa, Crystal, Apalachicola, and Peace rivers.

## GEORGIA

It's been estimated that northern Georgia has some 700 miles of trout streams. It's been my experience fishing these waters that excellent hatches do occur and that trout feed actively at these times.

In addition to these streams, Georgia has a number of natural lakes and impoundments. Such waters deliver good fishing for largemouth bass, white bass, striped bass, bluegill, redear sunfish, crappie, and other game fish.

The tables below are geared to the mountainous Northeast. Anglers anticipating hatches in other low-lying areas should look for earlier insect emergence than shown here.

*Baetis levitans* (Blue Wing Olive)
 Hatch occurs April through November
 Duration of hatch 32 weeks
 Afternoon peak activity
 Best imitating fly—Blue Wing Olive, No. 22 & 24

*Baetis intercalaris* (Brown Quill)
 Hatch occurs April through November
 Duration of hatch 32 weeks
 Peak activity midafternoon
 Best imitating fly—Brown Quill, No. 20 & 22

*Baetis brunneicolor* (Rusty Dun)
 Hatch occurs April through November
 Duration of hatch 32 weeks
 Peak activity midafternoon
 Best imitating fly—Rusty Dun, No. 20 & 22

*Baetis vagans* (Little Iron Blue)
 Hatch occurs April through November
 Duration of hatch 32 weeks
 Peak activity midmorning
 Best imitating fly—Little Iron Blue, No. 18

*Leptophlebia cupida* (Early Blue Quill)
 Hatch occurs in April
 Duration of hatch 4 weeks
 Peak activity midday
 Best imitating fly—Early Blue Quill, No. 12 & 14

*Leptophlebia nebulosa* (Brown Quill)
  Hatch occurs April through May
  Duration of hatch 8 weeks
  Peak activity midday
  Best imitating fly—Brown Quill, No. 12

*Ephemerella invaria* (Pale Evening Dun)
  Hatch occurs April through May
  Duration of hatch 8 weeks
  Peak activity midafternoon
  Best imitating fly—Pale Evening Dun, No. 12 & 14

*Ephemerella subvaria* (Red Quill or Hendrickson)
  Hatch occurs April through June
  Duration of hatch 12 weeks
  Peak activity midafternoon
  Best imitating fly—Red Quill or Hendrickson, No. 10 & 14

*Ephemera guttulata* (Green Drake)
  Hatch occurs in May
  Duration of hatch 4 weeks
  Peak activity evening
  Best imitating fly—Green Drake, No. 6 & 10

*Hexagenia atrocaudata* (Leadwing Drake)
  Hatch occurs in May
  Duration of hatch 4 weeks
  Peak activity twilight
  Best imitating fly—Leadwing Drake, No. 6 & 8

*Hexagenia carolina* (Sulphur Drake)
  Hatch occurs in May
  Duration of hatch 4 weeks
  Peak activity twilight
  Best imitating fly—Sulphur Drake, No. 10 & 12

*Hexagenia marlicanda* (Sulphur Drake)
  Hatch occurs May through June
  Duration of hatch 8 weeks
  Peak activity twilight
  Best imitating fly—Sulphur Drake, No. 10 & 12

*Ephemera simulans* (Brown Drake)
  Hatch occurs in May
  Duration of hatch 4 weeks
  Peak activity twilight
  Best imitating fly—Brown Drake, No. 10 & 12

*Ephemera blanda* (Sulphur Drake)
    Hatch occurs in May
    Duration of hatch 4 weeks
    Peak activity twilight
    Best imitating fly—Sulphur Drake, No. 14

*Ephemera triplex* (Pale Sulphur)
    Hatch occurs in May
    Duration of hatch 4 weeks
    Peak activity twilight
    Best imitating fly—Pale Sulphur, No. 12 & 14

*Siphlonurus quebecensis* (Brown Quill)
    Hatch occurs May through June
    Duration of hatch 8 weeks
    Peak activity midday
    Best imitating fly—Brown Quill, No. 12 & 14

*Callibaetis ferrugineus* (Speckle-Wing Olive)
    Hatch occurs May through October
    Duration of hatch 20 weeks
    Peak activity midday
    Best imitating fly—Speckle-Wing Olive, No. 16 & 18

*Pseudocloeon carolina* (Gray-Winged Brown)
    Hatch occurs May through August
    Duration of hatch 16 weeks
    Peak activity morning
    Best imitating fly—Gray-Winged Brown, No. 22 & 24

*Ephemerella lutulenta* (Yellow Quill)
    Hatch occurs May through June
    Duration of hatch 8 weeks
    Peak activity midday
    Best imitating fly—Yellow Quill, No. 12 & 16

*Ephemerella doris* (Blue-Winged Yellow Quill)
    Hatch occurs May through June
    Duration of hatch 8 weeks
    Peak activity midday
    Best imitating fly—Blue-Winged Yellow Quill, No. 14 & 16

*Ephemerella temporalis* (Yellow Quill)
    Hatch occurs May through June
    Duration of hatch 8 weeks
    Peak activity midday
    Best imitating fly—Yellow Quill, No. 12 & 14

*Ephemerella attenuata* (Blue-Winged Olive)
    Hatch occurs May through June
    Duration of hatch 8 weeks
    Hatch is sporadic
    Best imitating fly—Blue-Winged Olive, No. 14 & 16

*Ephemerella dorothea* (Pale Sulphur Dun)
    Hatch occurs May through June
    Duration of hatch 8 weeks
    Peak activity evening
    Best imitating fly—Pale Sulphur Dun, No. 14 & 16

*Ephemerella rotunda* (Pale Evening Dun)
    Hatch occurs in May
    Duration of hatch 4 weeks
    Peak activity midafternoon
    Best imitating fly—Pale Evening Dun, No. 12 & 14

*Acroneuria nigrita* (Black Willow)
    Hatch occurs May through June
    Duration of hatch 8 weeks
    Peak activity midday
    Best imitating fly—Black Willow, No. 8 & 10

*Pteronarcys dorsata* (Giant Black Stonefly)
    Hatch occurs May through June
    Duration of hatch 8 weeks
    Peak activity twilight
    Best imitating fly—Giant Black Stonefly, No. 1 & 8

*Stenonema heterotarsale* (Pale Gray Fox Quill)
    Hatch occurs June through August
    Duration of hatch 12 weeks
    Peak activity late afternoons and evening
    Best imitating fly—Pale Gary Fox Quill, No. 12 & 14

*Stenonema femoratum* (Light Cahill)
    Hatch occurs June through August
    Duration of hatch 12 weeks
    Peak activity afternoons and evenings
    Best imitating fly—Light Cahill, No. 14 & 16

*Stenonema carolina* (Little Sulphur Cahill)
    Hatch occurs June through July
    Duration of hatch 8 weeks
    Peak activity afternoons and evenings
    Best imitating fly—Little Sulphur Cahill, No. 14 & 16

*Stenonema canadense* (Light Cahill)
    Hatch occurs June through August
    Duration of hatch 12 weeks
    Peak activity afternoons and evenings
    Best imitating fly—Light Cahill, No. 14 & 16

*Stenonema rubrum* (Pale Cahill Quill)
    Hatch occurs June through August
    Duration of hatch 12 weeks
    Peak activity afternoons and evenings
    Best imitating fly—Pale Cahill Quill, No. 14 & 16

*Hexagenia bilineata* (Brown Drake)
    Hatch occurs June through July
    Duration of hatch 8 weeks
    Peak activity twilight
    Best imitating fly—Brown Drake, No. 6 & 8

*Siphlonmirus mirus* (Olive Drake)
    Hatch occurs June through September
    Duration of hatch 16 weeks
    Peak activity midday
    Best imitating fly—Olive Drake, No. 10 & 12

*Potamanthus rufus* (Golden Drake)
    Hatch occurs June through September
    Duration of hatch 16 weeks
    Peak activity twilight
    Best imitating fly—Golden Drake, No. 10 & 12

*Potamanthus distinctus* (Golden Drake)
    Hatch occurs June through August
    Duration of hatch 12 weeks
    Peak activity twilight
    Best imitating fly—Golden Drake, No. 12 & 14

*Isonychia bicolor* (March Brown)
    Hatch occurs in June
    Duration of hatch 4 weeks
    Peak activity evening
    Best imitating fly—March Brown, No. 10 & 12

*Paraleptophlebia debilis* (Dark Blue Quill)
    Hatch occurs June through October
    Duration of hatch 20 weeks
    Peak activity midday
    Best imitating fly—Dark Blue Quill, No. 16 & 18

*Isonychia bicolor*—female spinner


*Neocloeon almance* (Gray-Winged Yellow)
    Hatch occurs June through September
    Duration of hatch 16 weeks
    Peak activity midday
    Best imitating fly—Gray-Winged Yellow, No. 20 & 22

*Epeorus dispar* (Little Yellow Quill)
    Hatch occurs June through July
    Duration of hatch 8 weeks
    Peak activity twilight
    Best imitating fly—Little Yellow Quill, No. 16 & 18

*Ephemerella simplex* (Dark Slate-Winged Olive)
    Hatch occurs June through September
    Duration of hatch 16 weeks
    Peak activity midday
    Best imitating fly—Dark Slate-Winged Olive, No. 14 & 16

*Ephemerella serrate* (Dark Iron-Blue Quill)
    Hatch occurs June through August
    Duration of hatch 12 weeks
    Peak activity midday
    Best imitating fly—Dark Iron-Blue Quill, No. 16 & 18

*Ephemerella deficiens* (Dark Lead-Winged Olive)
    Hatch occurs June through August
    Duration of hatch 12 weeks
    Peak activity midday
    Best imitating fly—Dark Lead-Winged Olive, No. 16 & 18

*Ephemerella lata* (Light Blue-Winged Olive)
    Hatch occurs June
    Duration of hatch 4 weeks
    Peak activity midday
    Best imitating fly—Light Blue-Winged Olive, No. 14 & 16

*Perla immarginata* (Orange Stonefly)
    Hatch occurs in June
    Duration of hatch 4 weeks
    Peak activity midday
    Best imitating fly—Orange Stonefly, No. 8 & 12

*Acroneuria lycoris* (Brown Stonefly)
    Hatch occurs June through July
    Duration of hatch 8 weeks
    Peak activity morning
    Best imitating fly—Brown Stonefly, No. 8 & 12

*Stenonema pollidum* (Little Pale Fox)
    Hatch occurs July through August
    Duration of hatch 8 weeks
    Peak activity afternoon and evening
    Best imitating fly—Little Pale Fox, No. 16 & 18

*Stenonema integrum* (Pale Cahill Quill)
    Hatch occurs July through August
    Duration of hatch 8 weeks
    Peak activity afternoon and evening
    Best imitating fly—Pale Cahill Quill, No. 14 & 16

*Stenonema ithaca* (Light Gray Fox)
    Hatch occurs July through August
    Duration of hatch 8 weeks
    Peak activity afternoon and evening
    Best imitating fly—Light Gray Fox, No. 12 & 14

*Baetisca carolina* (Humpbacked Nymph)
    Hatch occurs in July
    Duration of hatch 4 weeks
    Peak activity afternoon
    Best imitating fly—Humpbacked Nymph, No. 12 & 18

*Baetis spinosus* (Slate-Wing Olive)
    Hatch occurs July through August
    Duration of hatch 8 weeks
    Peak activity midafternoon
    Best imitating fly—Slate-Wing Olive, No. 20 & 22

*Brachycercus nitidus* (White-Wing Red Quill)
 Hatch occurs July through August
 Duration of hatch 8 weeks
 Peak activity early morning
 Best imitating fly—White-Wing Red Quill, No. 16 & 18

*Caenis diminuta* (White-Winged Sulphur)
 Hatch occurs June through September
 Duration of hatch 16 weeks
 Peak activity twilight
 Best imitating fly—White-Winged Sulphur, No. 22 & 24

*Ephemerella cornuta* (Blue-Winged Olive)
 Hatch occurs in July
 Duration of hatch 4 weeks
 Peak activity midday
 Best imitating fly—Blue-Winged Olive, No. 12 & 14

*Leuctra grandis* (Dark Stonefly)
 Hatch occurs July through August
 Duration of hatch 8 weeks
 Peak activity midday
 Best imitating fly—Dark Stonefly, No. 14 & 16

The best bets for trout action occur in the tailwaters of Lake Lanier and in fifteen or twenty heavily wooded trout streams located in the Chattahoochee National Forest north of Atlanta. This area borders on Tennessee and North Carolina. Most trout taken are rainbows, but some brown and brook trout are taken. The streams provide both native and stocked fish populations.

## KENTUCKY

This midsouthern state doesn't offer too much in the way of trout fishing or insect hatches. Largemouth, smallmouth, and Kentucky spotted bass are the favorite game fish species.

Some rainbow trout are found and I keep hearing vague rumors of some delightful brook trout fishing in small jump-across streams in the Cumberland Mountains. Time always seems to be at a premium and chasing possible ghost brookies in Kentucky's mountains always gets placed on the list of "must do, but later" things.

*Leptophlebia nebulosa* (Brown Quill)
 Hatch occurs April through May
 Duration of hatch 8 weeks
 Peak activity midday
 Best imitating fly—Brown Quill, No. 12

*Stenonema femoratum* (Light Cahill)
 Hatch occurs June through August
 Duration of hatch 12 weeks
 Peak activity sporadic
 Best imitating fly—Light Cahill, No. 14 & 16

*Hexagenia bilineata* (Brown Drake)
 Hatch occurs June through July
 Duration of hatch 8 weeks
 Peak activity twilight
 Best imitating fly—Brown Drake, No. 6 & 8

*Centroptilum rufostrigatum* (Red Quill)
 Hatch occurs June through October
 Duration of hatch 20 weeks
 Peak activity midmorning
 Best imitating fly—Red Quill, No. 22 & 24

With the possible exception of the aforementioned brookies, the best trout fishing is found in Cumberland Lake and the Rough River Reservoir.

## NORTH CAROLINA

Approximately 2,000 miles of trout streams beckon anglers in North Carolina. Stream headwaters are often in the Appalachians along the Tennessee-North Carolina border. Brook, brown, and rainbow trout are common catches, with brookies being prevalent in mountainous areas.

The hatching table that follows applies solely to the mountainous areas in the northeastern corner of the state. Any other waters will probably warm earlier and provide exciting hatches about one week ahead of the dates listed below.

*Baetis levitans* (Blue-Wing Olive)
 Hatch occurs April through November
 Duration of hatch 32 weeks
 Peak activity afternoons
 Best imitating fly—Blue-Wing Olive, No. 22 & 24

*Baetis intercalaris* (Brown Quill)
　　Hatch occurs April through November
　　Duration of hatch about 32 weeks
　　Peak activity midafternoon
　　Best imitating fly—Brown Quill, No. 20 & 22

*Baetis brunneicolor* (Rusty Dun)
　　Hatch occurs April through November
　　Duration of hatch 32 weeks
　　Peak activity midafternoon
　　Best imitating fly—Rusty Dun, No. 20 & 22

*Baetis vagans* (Little Iron Blue)
　　Hatch occurs April through November
　　Duration of hatch 32 weeks
　　Peak activity midmorning
　　Best imitating fly—Little Iron Blue, No. 18

*Leptophlebia grandis* (Brown Quill)
　　Hatch occurs April and May
　　Duration of hatch 8 weeks
　　Peak activity midday
　　Best imitating fly—Brown Quill, No. 10 & 12

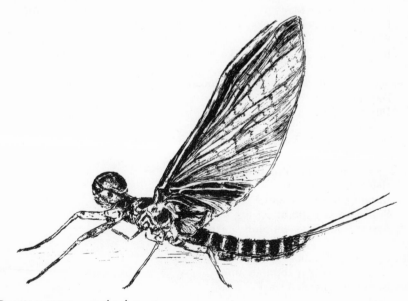

**Baetis vagans—male dun**

*Leptophlebia nebulosa* (Brown Quill)
    Hatch occurs April through May
    Duration of hatch 8 weeks
    Peak activity midday
    Best imitating fly—Brown Quill, No. 12

*Paraleptophelebia adoptive* (Blue Quill)
    Hatch occurs April through May
    Duration of hatch 8 weeks
    Peak activity midday
    Best imitating fly—Blue Quill, No. 14 & 18

*Ephemerella invaria* (Pale Evening Dun)
    Hatch occurs April and May
    Duration of hatch 8 weeks
    Peak activity midafternoon
    Best imitating fly—Pale Evening Dun, No. 12 & 14

*Ephemerella subvaria* (Red Quill & Hendrickson)
    Hatch occurs April through June
    Duration of hatch 12 weeks
    Peak activity midafternoon
    Best imitating fly—Red Quill or Hendrickson, No. 10 & 14

*Ephemera guttulata* (Green Drake)
    Hatch occurs in May
    Duration of hatch 4 weeks
    Peak activity evening
    Best imitating fly—Green Drake, No. 6 & 10

*Hexagenia atrocaudata* (Leadwing Drake)
    Hatch occurs in May
    Duration of hatch 4 weeks
    Peak activity twilight
    Best imitating fly—Leadwing Drake, No. 6 & 8

*Hexagenia carolina* (Sulphur Drake)
    Hatch occurs in May
    Duration of hatch about 4 weeks
    Peak activity twilight
    Best imitating fly—Sulphur Drake, No. 10 & 12

*Hexagenia marlicanda* (Sulphur Drake)
    Hatch occurs May through June
    Duration of hatch 8 weeks
    Peak activity twilight
    Best imitating fly—Sulphur Drake, No. 10 & 12

*Ephemera simulans* (Brown Drake)
    Hatch occurs in May
    Duration of hatch 4 weeks
    Peak activity twilight
    Best imitating fly—Brown Drake, No. 10 & 12

*Ephemera blanda* (Sulphur Drake)
    Hatch occurs in May
    Duration of hatch about 4 weeks
    Peak activity twilight
    Best imitating fly—Sulphur Drake, No. 14

*Ephemera triplex* (Pale Sulphur)
    Hatch occurs in May
    Duration of hatch 4 weeks
    Peak activity twilight
    Best imitating fly—Pale Sulphur, No. 12 & 14

*Callibaetis fluctuans* (Speckle-Wing Dun)
    Hatch occurs May through June
    Duration of hatch 8 weeks
    Peak activity late morning
    Best imitating fly—Speckle-Wing Dun, No. 16 & 18

*Siploplecton signatum* (Olive Quill)
    Hatch occurs May through June
    Duration of hatch 8 weeks
    Peak activity midday
    Best imitating fly—Olive Quill, No. 12 & 14

*Siphlonurus quebecensis* (Brown Quill)
    Hatch occurs May through June
    Duration of hatch 8 weeks
    Peak activity midday
    Best imitating fly—Brown Quill, No. 12 & 14

*Callibaetis ferrugineus* (Speckle-Wing Olive)
    Hatch occurs May through October
    Duration of hatch 24 weeks
    Peak activity midday
    Best imitating fly—Speckle-Wing Olive, No. 16 & 18

*Leptophlebia johnsoni* (Dark Blue Quill)
    Hatch occurs in May
    Duration of hatch 4 weeks
    Peak activity midday
    Best imitating fly—Dark Blue Quill

*Paraleptophlebia mollis*—female dun

*Paraleptophlebia mollis* (Iron Blue Dun)
    Hatch occurs May through June
    Duration of hatch 8 weeks
    Peak activity midday
    Best imitating fly—Iron Blue Dun, No. 16 & 18

*Paraleptophlebia swannanoa* (Iron Blue)
    Hatch occurs May through June
    Duration of hatch 8 weeks
    Peak activity midday
    Best imitating fly—Iron Blue, No. 16 & 18

*Paraleptophlebia assimilis* (Early Blue Quill)
    Hatch occurs May through June
    Duration of hatch 8 weeks
    Peak activity midday
    Best imitating fly—Early Blue Quill, No. 14 & 16

*Pseudocloeon carolina* (Gray-Winged Brown)
    Hatch occurs May through August
    Duration of hatch 16 weeks
    Peak activity morning
    Best imitating fly—Gray-Winged Brown, No. 22 & 24

*Ephemerella lutulenta* (Yellow Quill)
    Hatch occurs May through June
    Duration of hatch 8 weeks
    Peak activity midday
    Best imitating fly—Yellow Quill, No. 12 & 16

*Ephemerella doris* (Blue-Winged Yellow Quill)
  Hatch occurs May through June
  Duration of hatch 8 weeks
  Peak activity midday
  Best imitating fly—Blue-Winged Yellow Quill, No. 14 & 16

*Ephemerella temporalis* (Yellow Quill)
  Hatch occurs May through June
  Duration of hatch 8 weeks
  Peak activity midday
  Best imitating fly—Yellow Quill, No. 12 & 14

*Ephemerella attenuata* (Blue-Winged Olive)
  Hatch occurs May through June
  Duration of hatch 8 weeks
  Peak activity sporadic
  Best imitating fly—Blue-Winged Olive, No. 14 & 16

*Ephemerella dorothea* (Pale Sulphur Dun)
  Hatch occurs May through June
  Duration of hatch 8 weeks
  Peak activity evening
  Best imitating fly—Pale Sulphur Dun, No. 14 & 16

*Ephemerella rotunda* (Pale Evening Dun)
  Hatch occurs in May
  Duration of hatch 4 weeks
  Peak activity midafternoon
  Best imitating fly—Pale Evening Dun, No. 12 & 14

*Leptophlebia cupida* (Early Blue Quill)
  Hatch occurs in April
  Duration of hatch 4 weeks
  Peak activity midday
  Best imitating fly—Early Blue Quill, No. 12 & 14

*Acroneuria nigrita* (Black Willow)
  Hatch occurs May through June
  Duration of hatch 8 weeks
  Peak activity midday
  Best imitating fly—Black Willow, No. 8 & 10

*Pteronarcys dorsata* (Giant Black Stonefly)
  Hatch occurs May through June
  Duration of hatch 8 weeks
  Peak activity twilight
  Best imitating fly—Giant Black Stonefly, No. 1 & 8

*Heptagenia hebe* (Little Evening Yellow)
    Hatch occurs June through August
    Duration of hatch 12 weeks
    Peak activity afternoon and evening
    Best imitating fly—Little Evening Yellow, No. 14 & 16

*Stenonema heterotarsale* (Pale Gray Fox Quill)
    Hatch occurs June through August
    Duration of hatch 12 weeks
    Peak activity afternoons and evening
    Best imitating fly—Pale Gray Fox Quill, No. 12 & 14

*Stenonema canadense* (Light Cahill)
    Hatch occurs June through August
    Duration of hatch 12 weeks
    Peak activity afternoon and evening
    Best imitating fly—Light Cahill, No. 14 & 16

*Stenonema rubrum* (Pale Cahill Quill)
    Hatch occurs June through August
    Duration of hatch 12 weeks
    Peak activity afternoon and evening
    Best imitating fly—Pale Cahill Quill, No. 14 & 16

*Hexagenia bilineata* (Brown Drake)
    Hatch occurs June and July
    Duration of hatch 8 weeks
    Peak activity twilight
    Best imitating fly—Brown Drake, No. 6 & 8

*Stenonema canadense*—female dun

*Siphlonmirus mirus* (Olive Drake)
    Hatch occurs June through September
    Duration of hatch 16 weeks
    Peak activity midday
    Best imitating fly—Olive Drake, No. 10 & 12

*Potamanthus rufus* (Golden Drake)
    Hatch occurs June through September
    Duration of hatch 16 weeks
    Peak activity twilight
    Best imitating fly—Golden Drake, No. 10 & 12

*Potamanthus distinctus* (Golden Drake)
    Hatch occurs June through August
    Duration of hatch 12 weeks
    Peak activity twilight
    Best imitating fly—Golden Drake, No. 12 & 14

*Isonychia bicolor* (March Brown)
    Hatch occurs in June
    Duration of hatch 4 weeks
    Peak activity evening
    Best imitating fly—March Brown, No. 10 & 12

*Isonychia albomanicata* (Mahogany Drake)
    Hatch occurs in June
    Duration of hatch 4 weeks
    Peak activity evening
    Best imitating fly—Mahogany Drake, No. 12 & 14

*Paraleptophlebia debilis* (Dark Blue Quill)
    Hatch occurs June through October
    Duration of hatch 20 weeks
    Peak activity midday
    Best imitating fly—Dark Blue Quill, No. 16 & 18

*Neocloeon almance* (Gray-Winged Yellow)
    Hatch occurs June through September
    Duration of hatch 16 weeks
    Peak activity midday
    Best imitating fly—Gray-Winged Yellow, No. 20 & 22

*Epeorus dispar* (Little Yellow Quill)
    Hatch occurs June and July
    Duration of hatch 8 weeks
    Peak activity twilight
    Best imitating fly—Little Yellow Quill, No. 16 & 18

*Epeorus rubidus* (Gray-Winged Quill)
    Hatch occurs June through August
    Duration of hatch 12 weeks
    Peak activity twilight
    Best imitating fly—Gray-Winged Quill, No. 16 & 18

*Ephemerella simplex* (Dark Slate-Winged Olive)
    Hatch occurs June through September
    Duration of hatch 16 weeks
    Peak activity midday
    Best imitating fly—Dark Slate-Winged Olive, No. 14 & 16

*Ephemerella serrata* (Dark Iron-Blue Quill)
    Hatch occurs June through August
    Duration of hatch 12 weeks
    Peak activity midday
    Best imitating fly—Dark Iron-Blue Quill, No. 16 & 18

*Ephemerella deficiens* (Dark Lead-Winged Olive)
    Hatch occurs June through August
    Duration of hatch 12 weeks
    Peak activity midday
    Best imitating fly—Dark Lead-Winged Olive, No. 16 & 18

*Ephemerella lata* (Light Blue-Winged Olive)
    Hatch occurs in June
    Duration of hatch 4 weeks
    Peak activity midday
    Best imitating fly—Light Blue-Winged Olive, No. 14 & 16

*Perla immarginata* (Orange Stonefly)
    Hatch occurs in June
    Duration of hatch 4 weeks
    Peak activity midday
    Best imitating fly—Orange Stonefly, No. 8 & 12

*Acroneuria lycoris* (Brown Stonefly)
    Hatch occurs June and July
    Duration of hatch 8 weeks
    Peak activity morning
    Best imitating fly—Brown Stonefly, No. 8 & 12

*Heptagenia aphrodite* (Evening Sulphur)
    Hatch occurs July through August
    Duration of hatch 8 weeks
    Peak activity twilight
    Best imitating fly—Evening Sulphur, No. 14 & 16

*Heptagenia thetis* (Pale Evening Dun)
    Hatch occurs July and August
    Duration of hatch 8 weeks
    Peak activity twilight
    Best imitating fly—Pale Evening Dun, No. 14 & 16

*Stenonema pollidum* (Little Pale Fox)
    Hatch occurs July and August
    Duration of hatch 8 weeks .
    Peak activity afternoon and evening
    Best imitating fly—Little Pale Fox, No. 16 & 18

*Stenonema integrum* (Pale Cahill Quill)
    Hatch occurs July and August
    Duration of hatch 8 weeks
    Peak activity afternoon and evening
    Best imitating fly—Pale Cahill Quill, No. 14 & 16

*Stenonema ithaca* (Light Gray Fox)
    Hatch occurs July and August
    Duration of hatch 8 weeks
    Peak activity afternoon and evening
    Best imitating fly—Light Gray Fox, No. 12 & 14

*Baetisca carolina* (Humpbacked Nymph)
    Hatch occurs in July
    Duration of hatch 4 weeks
    Peak activity afternoon
    Best imitating fly—Humpbacked Nymph, No. 12 & 18

*Bastica callosa* (Humpbacked Nymph)
    Hatch occurs in July
    Duration of hatch 4 weeks
    Peak activity afternoon
    Best imitating fly—Humpbacked Nymph, No. 12 & 18

*Baetis spinosus* (Slate-Wing Olive)
    Hatch occurs July and August
    Duration of hatch 8 weeks
    Peak activity mid-afternoon
    Best imitating fly—Slate-Wing Olive, No. 20 & 22

*Brachycercus nitidus* (White-Wing Red Quill)
    Hatch occurs July and August
    Duration of hatch 8 weeks
    Peak activity early morning
    Best imitating fly—White-Wing Red Quill, No. 16 & 18

*Caenis diminuta* (White-Winged Sulphur)
    Hatch occurs June through September
    Duration of hatch 16 weeks
    Peak activity twilight
    Best imitating fly—White-Winged Sulphur, No. 22 & 24

*Ephemerella cornuta* (Blue-Winged Olive)
    Hatch occurs in July
    Duration of hatch 4 weeks
    Peak activity midday
    Best imitating fly—Blue-Winged Olive, No. 12 & 14

*Ephemerella longicornis* (Medium Slate-Winged Olive)
    Hatch occurs in July
    Duration of hatch 4 weeks
    Peak activity midday
    Best imitating fly—Medium Slate-Winged Olive, No. 14 & 16

*Leuctra grandis* (Dark Stonefly)
    Hatch occurs July and August
    Duration of hatch 8 weeks
    Peak activity midday
    Best imitating fly—Dark Stonefly, No. 14 & 16

The best trout fishing occurs on the Upper Dan, Nantahala, and numerous other streams and small creeks that are hidden in the laurel thickets. Some are "spit across" size and a few are swift, boulder-studded rivers that demand the utmost in skillful wading and fly presentation. Lakes with trout include Nantahala, Cheoah, Santeelah, and Fontana reservoirs.

## SOUTH CAROLINA

This southeastern state has a certain amount of trout fishing, some of which is very good by anyone's standards. Rainbow and brown are the most common species, but some brook trout are taken from mountain streams.

The hatches that follow are based solely on those mountain creeks and rivers. Anyone concerning himself with insect emergences in the low-lying areas should subtract about seven days from the projected emergences.

*Baetis levitans* (Blue-Wing Olive)
 Hatch occurs April through November
 Duration of hatch about 32 weeks
 Peak activity afternoon
 Best imitating fly—Blue-Wing Olive, No. 22 & 24

*Baetis intercalaris* (Brown Quill)
 Hatch occurs April through November
 Duration of hatch 32 weeks
 Peak activity midafternoon
 Best imitating fly—Brown Quill, No. 20 & 22

*Baetis brunneicolor* (Rusty Dun)
 Hatch occurs April through November
 Duration of hatch 32 weeks
 Peak activity midafternoon
 Best imitating fly—Rusty Dun, No. 20 & 22

*Baetis vagans* (Little Iron Blue)
 Hatch occurs April through November
 Duration of hatch 32 weeks
 Peak activity midmorning
 Best imitating fly—Little Iron Blue, No. 18

*Leptophlebia nebulosa* (Brown Quill)
 Hatch occurs April and May
 Duration of hatch 8 weeks
 Peak activity midday
 Best imitating fly—Brown Quill, No. 12

*Ephemerella invaria* (Pale Evening Dun)
 Hatch occurs April and May
 Duration of hatch 8 weeks
 Peak activity midafternoon
 Best imitating fly—Pale Evening Dun, No. 12 & 14

*Ephemerella subvaria* (Red Quill/Hendrickson)
 Hatch occurs April through June
 Duration of hatch 12 weeks
 Peak activity midafternoon
 Best imitating fly—Red Quill or Hendrickson, No. 10 & 14

*Ephemera guttulata* (Green Drake)
 Hatch occurs in May
 Duration of hatch 4 weeks
 Peak activity evening
 Best imitating fly—Green Drake, No. 6 & 10

*Hexagenia carolina* (Sulphur Drake)
    Hatch occurs in May
    Duration of hatch 4 weeks
    Peak activity twilight
    Best imitating fly—Sulphur Drake, No. 10 & 12

*Hexagenia marlicanda* (Sulphur Drake)
    Hatch occurs May through June
    Duration of hatch 8 weeks
    Peak activity twilight
    Best imitating fly—Sulphur Drake, No. 10 & 12

*Ephemera simulans* (Brown Drake)
    Hatch occurs in May
    Duration of hatch 4 weeks
    Peak activity twilight
    Best imitating fly—Brown Drake, No. 10 & 12

*Ephemera triplex* (Pale Sulphur)
    Hatch occurs in May
    Duration of hatch 4 weeks
    Peak activity twilight
    Best imitating fly—Pale Sulphur, No. 12 & 14

*Siphlonurus quebecensis* (Brown Quill)
    Hatch occurs May through June
    Duration of hatch 8 weeks
    Peak activity midday
    Best imitating fly—Brown Quill, No. 12 & 14

*Callibaetis ferrugineus* (Speckle-Wing Olive)
    Hatch occurs May through October
    Duration of hatch 20 weeks
    Peak activity midday
    Best imitating fly—Speckle-Wing Olive, No. 16 & 18

*Pseudocloeon carolina* (Gray-Winged Brown)
    Hatch occurs May through August
    Duration of hatch 16 weeks
    Peak activity morning
    Best imitating fly—Gray-Winged Brown, No. 22 & 24

*Ephemerella lutulenta* (Yellow Quill)
    Hatch occurs May through June
    Duration of hatch 8 weeks
    Peak activity midday
    Best imitating fly—Yellow Quill, No. 12 & 14

*Pseudocloeon carolina*—male dun

*Ephemerella doris* (Blue-Winged Yellow Quill)
    Hatch occurs May and June
    Duration of hatch 8 weeks
    Peak activity midday
    Best imitating fly—Blue-Winged Yellow Quill, No. 14 & 16

*Ephemerella temporalis* (Yellow Quill)
    Hatch occurs May and June
    Duration of hatch 8 weeks
    Peak activity midday
    Best imitating fly—Yellow Quill, No. 12 & 14

*Ephemerella attenuata* (Blue-Winged Olive)
    Hatch occurs May and June
    Duration of hatch about 8 weeks
    Peak activity is sporadic
    Best imitating fly—Blue-Winged Olive, No. 14 & 16

*Ephemerella dorothea* (Pale Sulphur Dun)
    Hatch occurs May and June
    Duration of hatch 8 weeks
    Peak activity evening
    Best imitating fly—Pale Sulphur Dun, No. 14 & 16

*Ephemerella rotunda* (Pale Evening Dun)
    Hatch occurs in May
    Duration of hatch 4 weeks
    Peak activity midafternoon
    Best imitating fly—Pale Evening Dun, No. 12 & 14

*Leptophlebia cupida* (Early Blue Quill)
  Hatch occurs in April
  Duration of hatch 4 weeks
  Peak activity midday
  Best imitating fly—Early Blue Quill, No. 12 & 14

*Acroneuria nigrita* (Black Willow)
  Hatch occurs May and June
  Duration of hatch 8 weeks
  Peak activity midday
  Best imitating fly—Black Willow, No. 8 & 10

*Pteronarcys dorsata* (Giant Black Stonefly)
  Hatch occurs May and June
  Duration of hatch 8 weeks
  Peak activity twilight
  Best imitating fly—Giant Black Stonefly, No. 6 & 8

*Stenonema heterotarsale* (Pale Gray Fox Quill)
  Hatch occurs June through August
  Duration of hatch 12 weeks
  Peak activity afternoon and evening
  Best imitating fly—Pale Gray Fox Quill, No. 12 & 14

*Stenonema femoratum* (Light Cahill)
  Hatch occurs June through August
  Duration of hatch 12 weeks
  Peak activity afternoon and evening
  Best imitating fly—Light Cahill, No. 14 & 16

*Stenonema carolina* (Little Sulphur Cahill)
  Hatch occurs June and July
  Duration of hatch 8 weeks
  Peak activity afternoon and evening
  Best imitating fly—Little Sulphur Cahill, No. 14 & 16

*Stenonema canadense* (Light Cahill)
  Hatch occurs June through August
  Duration of hatch 12 weeks
  Peak activity afternoon and evening
  Best imitating fly—Light Cahill, No. 14 & 16

*Stenonema rubrum* (Pale Cahill Quill)
  Hatch occurs June through August
  Duration of hatch 12 weeks
  Peak activity afternoon and evening
  Best imitating fly—Pale Cahill Quill, No. 14 & 16

*Hexagenia bilineata* (Brown Drake)
    Hatch occurs June and July
    Duration of hatch 8 weeks
    Peak activity twilight
    Best imitating fly—Brown Drake, No. 6 & 8

*Siphlonmirus mirus* (Olive Drake)
    Hatch occurs June through September
    Duration of hatch 16 weeks
    Peak activity midday
    Best imitating fly—Olive Drake, No. 10 & 12

*Potamanthus rufus* (Golden Drake)
    Hatch occurs June through September
    Duration of hatch 16 weeks
    Peak activity twilight
    Best imitating fly—Golden Drake, No. 10 & 12

*Potamanthus distinctus* (Golden Drake)
    Hatch occurs June through August
    Duration of hatch 12 weeks
    Peak activity twilight
    Best imitating fly—Golden Drake, No. 12 & 14

*Isonychia bicolor* (March Brown)
    Hatch occurs in June
    Duration of hatch 4 weeks
    Peak activity evening
    Best imitating fly—March Brown, No. 10 & 12

*Paraleptophlebia debilis* (Dark Blue Quill)
    Hatch occurs June through October
    Duration of hatch 20 weeks
    Peak activity midday
    Best imitating fly—Dark Blue Quill, No. 16 & 18

*Neocloeon almance* (Gray-Winged Yellow)
    Hatch occurs June through September
    Duration of hatch 16 weeks
    Peak activity midday
    Best imitating fly—Gray-Winged Yellow, No. 20 & 22

*Epeorus dispar* (Little Yellow Quill)
    Hatch occurs June and July
    Duration of hatch 8 weeks
    Peak activity twilight
    Best imitating fly—Little Yellow Quill, No. 16 & 18

*Ephemerella simplex* (Dark Slate-Winged Olive)
   Hatch occurs June through September
   Duration of hatch 16 weeks
   Peak activity midday
   Best imitating fly—Dark Slate-Winged Olive, No. 14 & 16

*Ephemerella serrata* (Dark Iron-Blue Quill)
   Hatch occurs June through August
   Duration of hatch 12 weeks
   Peak activity midday
   Best imitating fly—Dark Iron-Blue Quill, No. 16 & 18

*Ephemerella deficiens* (Dark Lead-Winged Olive)
   Hatch occurs June through August
   Duration of hatch 12 weeks
   Peak activity midday
   Best imitating fly—Dark Lead-Winged Olive, No. 16 & 18

*Ephemerella lata* (Light Blue-Winged Olive)
   Hatch occurs in June
   Duration of hatch 4 weeks
   Peak activity midday
   Best imitating fly—Light Blue-Winged Olive, No. 14 & 16

*Perla immarginata* (Orange Stonefly)
   Hatch occurs in June
   Duration of hatch 4 weeks
   Peak activity midday
   Best imitating fly—Orange Stonefly, No. 8 & 12

*Acroneuria lycoris* (Brown Stonefly)
   Hatch occurs June and July
   Duration of hatch 8 weeks
   Peak activity morning
   Best imitating fly—Brown Stonefly, No. 8 & 12

*Stenonema pollidum* (Little Pale Fox)
   Hatch occurs July and August
   Duration of hatch 8 weeks
   Peak activity afternoon and evening
   Best imitating fly—Little Pale Fox, No. 16 & 18

*Stenonema integrum* (Pale Cahill Quill)
   Hatch occurs July and August
   Duration of hatch 8 weeks
   Peak activity afternoon and evening
   Best imitating fly—Pale Cahill Quill, No. 14 & 16

*Stenonema ithaca* (Light Gray Fox)
    Hatch occurs July and August
    Duration of hatch 8 weeks
    Peak activity afternoon and evenings
    Best imitating fly—Light Gray Fox, No. 12 & 14

*Baetisca carolina* (Humpbacked Nymph)
    Hatch occurs in July
    Duration of hatch 4 weeks
    Peak activity afternoon
    Best imitating fly—Humpbacked Nymph, No. 12 & 18

*Baetis spinosus* (Slate-Wing Olive)
    Hatch occurs July and August
    Duration of hatch 8 weeks
    Peak activity midafternoon
    Best imitating fly—Slate-Wing Olive, No. 20 & 22

*Brachycercus nitidus* (White-Wing Red Quill)
    Hatch occurs July and August
    Duration of hatch 8 weeks
    Peak activity early morning
    Best imitating fly—White-Wing Red Quill, No. 16 & 18

*Caenis diminuta* (White-Winged Sulphur)
    Hatch occurs June through September
    Duration of hatch 16 weeks
    Peak activity twilight
    Best imitating fly—White-Winged Sulphur, No. 22 & 24

*Ephemerella cornuta* (Blue-Winged Olive)
    Hatch occurs in July
    Duration of hatch 4 weeks
    Peak activity midday
    Best imitating fly—Blue-Winged Olive, No. 12 & 14

*Leuctra grandis* (Dark Stonefly)
    Hatch occurs July and August
    Duration of hatch 8 weeks
    Peak activity midday
    Best imitating fly—Dark Stonefly, No. 14 & 16

The best South Carolina trout waters are found in Oconee, Pickens, and Greenville counties—all in the northwest corner. The best of the streams include the famous Chattooga, Saluda, and Chauga rivers. Numerous smaller tributaries of these rivers contain trout in headwater areas.

## TENNESSEE

Tennessee has many varied fishing possibilities, from trout fishing in the large TVA lakes to mountain fishing for stream trout in the Cumberland and Smokey Mountains. Rainbow, brook, and brown trout are common in many areas and often coexist together in some streams. Rainbows are planted commonly in impoundment waters.

The weather is pretty standard throughout Tennessee, with the possible exception being in high mountainous areas. Spring or fall storms can dump a load of snow or cold rain in these regions and delay hatches for a week or more. Watch the weather for changes and/or cold weather if planning a trout-fishing trip to the mountains.

The tables listed below are based on both mountain stream hatches and emergences on some of the better trout lakes.

*Baetis levitans* (Blue-Wing Olive)
    Hatch occurs April through November
    Duration of hatch 32 weeks
    Peak activity afternoon
    Best imitating fly—Rusty Spinner or Little Blue Dun, No. 22 or 24

*Baetis intercalaris* (Brown Quill)
    Hatch occurs April through November
    Duration of hatch 32 weeks
    Peak activity midafternoon
    Best imitating fly—Brown Quill, No. 20 & 22

*Baetis brunneicolor* (Rusty Dun)
    Hatch occurs April through November
    Duration of hatch 32 weeks
    Peak activity midafternoon
    Best imitating fly—Rusty Dun, No. 20 & 22

*Baetis vagans* (Little Iron Blue)
    Hatch occurs April through November
    Duration of hatch 32 weeks
    Peak activity midmorning
    Best imitating fly—Rusty Spinner, No. 18

*Leptophlebia nebulosa* (Brown Quill)
    Hatch occurs April through May
    Duration of hatch 8 weeks
    Peak activity midday
    Best imitating fly—Brown Quill, No. 12

*Baetis vagans*—female spinner

*Ephemerella invaria* (Pale Evening Dun)
    Hatch occurs April and May
    Duration of hatch 8 weeks
    Peak activity midafternoon
    Best imitating fly—Pale Evening Spinner, No. 12 & 14

*Ephemerella subvaria* (Red Quill or Hendrickson)
    Hatch occurs April through June
    Duration of hatch 12 weeks, sporadically
    Peak activity midafternoon
    Best imitating fly—Hendrickson, No. 10 & 14

*Ephemera guttulata* (Green Drake)
    Hatch occurs in May
    Duration of hatch 4 weeks
    Peak activity evening
    Best imitating fly—Eastern Green Drake, No. 6 & 10

*Hexagenia carolina* (Sulphur Drake)
    Hatch occurs in May
    Duration of hatch 4 weeks
    Peak activity twilight
    Best imitating fly—Sulphur Drake, No. 10 & 12

*Hexagenia marlicanda* (Sulphur Drake)
    Hatch occurs May and June
    Duration of hatch 8 weeks
    Peak activity twilight
    Best imitating fly—Sulphur Drake, No. 10 & 12

*Ephemera simulans* (Brown Drake)
    Hatch occurs in May
    Duration of hatch 4 weeks
    Peak activity twilight
    Best imitating fly—Brown Drake, No. 10 & 12

*Ephemera blanda* (Sulphur Drake)
    Hatch occurs in May
    Duration of hatch 4 weeks
    Peak activity twilight
    Best imitating fly—Sulphur Drake, No. 14

*Ephemera triplex* (Pale Sulphur)
    Hatch occurs in May
    Duration of hatch 4 weeks
    Peak activity twilight
    Best imitating fly—Pale Sulphur Spinner, No. 12 & 14

*Siphlonurus quebecensis* (Brown Quill)
    Hatch occurs May and June
    Duration of hatch 8 weeks
    Peak activity midday
    Best imitating fly—Brown Quill, No. 12 & 14

*Callibaetis ferrugineus* (Speckle-Wing Olive)
    Hatch occurs May through October
    Duration of hatch 20 weeks
    Peak activity midday
    Best imitating fly—Speckle-Wing Olive, No. 16 & 18

*Leptophlebia johnsoni* (Dark Blue Quill)
    Hatch occurs in May
    Duration of hatch 4 weeks
    Peak activity midday
    Best imitating fly—Blue Quill, No. 14 & 16

*Paraleptophlebia swannanoa* (Iron Blue)
    Hatch occurs May and June
    Duration of hatch 8 weeks
    Peak activity midday
    Best imitating fly—Iron Blue Dun, No. 16 & 18

*Pseudocloeon carolina* (Gray-Winged Brown)
    Hatch occurs May through August
    Duration of hatch 16 weeks
    Peak activity morning
    Best imitating fly—Gray-Winged Brown, No. 22 & 24

*Ephemerella lutulenta* (Yellow Quill)
    Hatch occurs May and June
    Duration of hatch 8 weeks
    Peak activity midday
    Best imitating fly—Yellow Quill Spinner, No. 12 & 16

*Ephemerella doris* (Blue-Winged Yellow Quill)
    Hatch occurs May and June
    Duration of hatch 8 weeks
    Peak activity midday
    Best imitating fly—Yellow Quill Spinner, No. 14 & 16

*Ephemerella temporalis* (Yellow Quill)
    Hatch occurs May and June
    Duration of hatch 8 weeks
    Peak activity midday
    Best imitating fly—Yellow Quill Spinner, No. 12 & 14

*Ephemerella attenuata* (Blue-Winged Olive)
    Hatch occurs May and June
    Duration of hatch 8 weeks
    Peak activity is sporadic
    Best imitating fly—Dark Olive Spinner, No. 14 & 16

*Ephemerella dorothea* (Pale Sulphur Dun)
    Hatch occurs May and June
    Duration of hatch 8 weeks
    Peak activity evening
    Best imitating fly—Pale Evening Dun, No. 14 & 16

*Ephemerella rotunda* (Pale Evening Dun)
    Hatch occurs in May
    Duration of hatch 4 weeks
    Peak activity midafternoon
    Best imitating fly—Pale Evening Spinner, No. 12 & 14

*Acroneuria nigrita* (Black Willow)
    Hatch occurs May and June
    Duration of hatch 8 weeks
    Peak activity midday
    Best imitating fly—Willow, No. 8 & 10

*Pteronarcys dorsata* (Giant Black Stonefly)
    Hatch occurs May and June
    Duration of hatch 8 weeks
    Peak activity twilight
    Best imitating fly—Giant Black Stonefly, No. 6 & 8

*Heptagenia hebe* (Little Evening Yellow)
    Hatch occurs June through August
    Duration of hatch 12 weeks
    Peak activity twilight
    Best imitating fly—Little Evening Yellow, No. 14 & 16

*Stenonema heterotarsale* (Pale Gray Fox Quill)
    Hatch occurs June through August
    Duration of hatch 12 weeks
    Peak activity afternoon and evening
    Best imitating fly—Light Cahill, No. 12 & 14

*Stenonema carolina* (Little Sulphur Cahill)
    Hatch occurs June and July
    Duration of hatch 8 weeks
    Peak activity afternoon and evening
    Best imitating fly—Sulphur Cahill, No. 14 & 16

*Stenonema canadense* (Light Cahill)
    Hatch occurs June through August
    Duration of hatch 12 weeks
    Peak activity afternoon and evening ·
    Best imitating fly—Light Cahill, No. 14 & 16

*Stenonema rubrum* (Pale Cahill Quill)
    Hatch occurs June through August
    Duration of hatch 12 weeks
    Peak activity afternoon and evening
    Best imitating fly—Cream Cahill Spinner, No. 14 & 16

*Hexagenia bilineata* (Brown Drake)
    Hatch occurs June and July
    Duration of hatch 8 weeks
    Peak activity twilight
    Best imitating fly—Brown Drake, No. 6 & 8

*Siphlonmirus mirus* (Olive Drake)
    Hatch occurs June through September
    Duration of hatch 16 weeks
    Peak activity midday
    Best imitating fly—Brown Quill Spinner, No. 10 & 12

*Potamanthus rufus* (Golden Drake)
    Hatch occurs June through September
    Duration of hatch 16 weeks
    Peak activity twilight
    Best imitating fly—Golden Drake Spinner, No. 10 & 12

*Potamanthus distinctus* (Golden Drake)
    Hatch occurs June through August
    Duration of hatch 12 weeks
    Peak activity twilight
    Best imitating fly—Golden Drake Spinner, No. 12 & 14

*Isonychia bicolor* (March Brown)
    Hatch occurs in June
    Duration of hatch 4 weeks
    Peak activity evening
    Best imitating fly—Slate Drake, No. 10 & 12

*Paraleptophlebia debilis* (Dark Blue Quill)
    Hatch occurs June through October
    Duration of hatch 20 weeks
    Peak activity midday
    Best imitating fly—Dark Blue Quill or Jenny Spinner, No. 16 & 18

*Neocloeon almance* (Gray-Winged Yellow)
    Hatch occurs June through September
    Duration of hatch 16 weeks
    Peak activity midday
    Best imitating fly—Gray-Winged Yellow, No. 20 & 22

*Epeorus dispar* (Little Yellow Quill)
    Hatch occurs June and July
    Duration of hatch 8 weeks
    Peak activity twilight
    Best imitating fly—Yellow Quill, No. 16 & 18

*Epeorus rubidus* (Gray-Winged Quill)
    Hatch occurs June through August
    Duration of hatch 12 weeks
    Peak activity twilight
    Best imitating fly—Gray-Winged Quill, No. 16 & 18

*Ephemerella simplex* (Dark Slate-Winged Olive)
    Hatch occurs June through September
    Duration of hatch 16 weeks
    Peak activity midday
    Best imitating fly—Slate Wing Olive, No. 14 & 16

*Ephemerella serrata* (Dark Iron-Blue Quill)
    Hatch occurs June through August
    Duration of hatch 12 weeks
    Peak activity midday
    Best imitating fly—Dark Blue Quill, No. 16 & 18

*Ephemerella deficiens* (Dark Lead-Winged Olive)
    Hatch occurs June through August
    Duration of hatch 12 weeks
    Peak activity midday
    Best imitating fly—Dark Lead-Winged Olive, No. 16 & 18

*Ephemerella lata* (Light Blue-Winged Olive)
    Hatch occurs in June
    Duration of hatch 4 weeks
    Peak activity midday
    Best imitating fly—Light Blue-Winged Olive, No. 14 & 16

*Perla immarginata* (Orange Stonefly)
    Hatch occurs in June
    Duration of hatch 4 weeks
    Peak activity midday
    Best imitating fly—Orange Sedge, No. 8 & 12

*Acroneuria lycoris* (Brown Stonefly)
    Hatch occurs June and July
    Duration of hatch 8 weeks
    Peak activity morning
    Best imitating fly—Brown Stonefly, No. 8 & 12

*Stenonema pollidum* (Little Pale Fox)
    Hatch occurs July and August
    Duration of hatch 8 weeks
    Peak activity afternoon and evening
    Best imitating fly—Cream Cahill Spinner, No. 16 & 18

*Stenonema ithaca* (Light Gray Fox)
    Hatch occurs July and August
    Duration of hatch 8 weeks
    Peak activity afternoon and evening
    Best imitating fly—Ginger Quill Spinner or Light Cahill, No. 12 & 14

*Baetisca carolina* (Humpbacked Nymph)
    Hatch occurs in July
    Duration of hatch 4 weeks
    Peak activity afternoons
    Best imitating fly—Humpbacked Nymph, No. 12 & 14

*Baetis spinosus* (Slate-Wing Olive)
    Hatch occurs July and August
    Duration of hatch 8 weeks
    Peak activity sporadic
    Best imitating fly—Slate-Wing Olive, No. 20 & 22

*Brachycercus nitidus* (White-Wing Red Quill)
  Hatch occurs July and August
  Duration of hatch 8 weeks
  Peak activity early morning
  Best imitating fly—White-Wing Red Quill, No. 16 & 18

*Caenis diminuta* (White-Winged Sulphur)
  Hatch occurs June through September
  Duration of hatch 16 weeks
  Peak activity twilight
  Best imitating fly—White-Winged Sulphur, No. 22 & 24

*Ephemerella cornuta* (Blue-Winged Olive)
  Hatch occurs in July
  Duration of hatch 4 weeks
  Peak activity midday
  Best imitating fly—Blue-Wing Olive Dun, No. 12 & 14

*Leuctra grandis* (Dark Stonefly)
  Hatch occurs July and August
  Duration of hatch 8 weeks
  Peak activity midday
  Best imitating fly—Dark Stonefly, No. 14 & 16

Tailwater trout fishing occurs in spring and fall below many TVA lakes such as Dale Hollow, Center Hill, Daniel Boone, Watauga, Norris, and others. The best river fishing comes on small streams near Etowah in the Cherokee National Forest. It's located in southeast Tennessee along the North Carolina-Georgia-Tennessee border. Particularly productive are the Hiwassee River and its numerous tributaries.

Doe Creek, a tributary of Watauga Lake in northeastern Tennessee is another good river. The Little Tennessee (Little T) is a superb stream with plenty of large rainbows and browns.

Many other smaller streams or rivers in the Smoky Mountains offer exciting trout action. Some streams are seldom fished except by natives.

## VIRGINIA

This so-called "Southern" state has more trout fishing available than is commonly known. Rainbow, brown, and brook trout are found in the Piedmont, Blue Ridge Mountain and Valley region, and the Appalachian Plateau region.

The habitat in Virginia is conducive to good fly hatches and superb sport, in mountain-type streams, in tailwaters below large dams, and in the impoundments above dams.

Fishing in this state is different from that commonly found elsewhere. An angler, fishing early morning riseforms, can cast to the call of a bobwhite quail in a nearby field. Or he may wade the rocky streams of the Appalachian high country. Virginia offers something for every fly-fisherman.

*Baetis levitans* (Blue-Wing Olive)
    Hatch occurs April through November
    Duration of hatch 32 weeks
    Peak activity afternoon
    Best imitating fly—Blue-Wing Olive, No. 22 & 24

*Baetis intercalaris* (Brown Quill)
    Hatch occurs April through November
    Duration of hatch 32 weeks
    Peak activity midafternoon
    Best imitating fly—Brown Quill, No. 20 & 22

*Baetis brunneicolor* (Rusty Dun)
    Hatch occurs April through November
    Duration of hatch 32 weeks
    Peak activity midafternoon
    Best imitating fly—Rusty Dun, No. 20 & 22

*Baetis vagans* (Little Iron Blue)
    Hatch occurs April through November
    Duration of hatch 32 weeks
    Peak activity midmorning
    Best imitating fly—Rusty Spinner, No. 18

*Leptophlebia nebulosa* (Brown Quill)
    Hatch occurs April and May
    Duration of hatch 8 weeks
    Peak activity midday
    Best imitating fly—Brown Quill, No. 12

*Paraleptophelebia adoptiva* (Blue Quill)
    Hatch occurs April and May
    Duration of hatch 8 weeks
    Peak activity midday
    Best imitating fly—Blue Quill, No. 14 & 18

*Paraleptophlebia adoptiva*—female spinner

*Ephemerella invaria (Pale Evening Dun)*
    Hatch occurs April through May
    Duration of hatch 8 weeks
    Peak activity midafternoon
    Best imitating fly—Pale Evening Dun, No. 12 & 14

*Ephemerella subvaria (Red Quill or Hendrickson)*
    Hatch occurs April through June
    Duration of hatch 12 weeks
    Peak activity midafternoon
    Best imitating fly—Hendrickson, No. 10 & 14

*Ephemera guttulata (Green Drake)*
    Hatch occurs in May
    Duration of hatch 4 weeks
    Peak activity evening
    Best imitating fly—Eastern Green Drake, No. 6 & 10

*Hexagenia carolina (Sulphur Drake)*
    Hatch occurs in May
    Duration of hatch 4 weeks
    Peak activity twilight
    Best imitating fly—Sulphur Drake, No. 10 & 12

*Hexagenia marlicanda (Sulphur Drake)*
    Hatch occurs May and June
    Duration of hatch 8 weeks
    Peak activity twilight
    Best imitating fly—Sulphur Drake, No. 10 & 12

*Ephemera simulans* (Brown Drake)
    Hatch occurs in May
    Duration of hatch 4 weeks
    Peak activity twilight
    Best imitating fly—Brown Drake, No. 10 & 12

*Ephemera triplex* (Pale Sulphur)
    Hatch occurs in May
    Duration of hatch 4 weeks
    Peak activity twilight
    Best imitating fly—Pale Sulphur, No. 12 & 14

*Siploplecton signatum* (Olive Quill)
    Hatch occurs May and June
    Duration of hatch 8 weeks
    Peak activity midday
    Best imitating fly—Olive Quill, No. 12 & 14

*Siplonurus quebecensis* (Brown Quill)
    Hatch occurs May and June
    Duration of hatch 8 weeks
    Peak activity midday
    Best imitating fly—Brown Quill, No. 12 & 14

*Callibaetis ferrugineus* (Speckle-Wing Olive)
    Hatch occurs May through October
    Duration of hatch 20 weeks
    Peak activity sporadic
    Best imitating fly—Speckle-Wing Olive, No. 16 & 18

*Leptophlebia johnsoni* (Dark Blue Quill)
    Hatch occurs in May
    Duration of hatch 4 weeks
    Peak activity midday
    Best imitating fly—Blue Quill Spinner, No. 14 & 16

*Paraleptophlebia mollis* (Iron Blue Dun)
    Hatch occurs May and June
    Duration of hatch 8 weeks
    Peak activity midday
    Best imitating fly—Jenny Spinner, No. 16 & 18

*Paraleptophlebia assimilis* (Early Blue Quill)
    Hatch occurs May and June
    Duration of hatch 8 weeks
    Peak activity midday
    Best imitating fly—Early Blue Spinner, No. 14 & 16

*Pseudocloeon carolina* (Gray-Winged Brown)
    Hatch occurs May through August
    Duration of hatch 16 weeks
    Peak activity morning
    Best imitating fly—Gray-Winged Brown, No. 22 & 24

*Ephemerella lutulenta* (Yellow Quill)
    Hatch occurs May and June
    Duration of hatch 8 weeks
    Peak activity midday
    Best imitating fly—Yellow Quill, No. 12 & 16

*Ephemerella doris* (Blue-Winged Yellow Quill)
    Hatch occurs May and June
    Duration of hatch 8 weeks
    Peak activity midday
    Best imitating fly—Blue-Winged Yellow Quill, No. 14 & 16

*Ephemerella temporalis* (Yellow Quill)
    Hatch occurs May and June
    Duration of hatch 8 weeks
    Peak activity sporadic
    Best imitating fly—Yellow Quill, No. 12 & 14

*Ephemerella attenuata* (Blue-Winged Olive)
    Hatch occurs May and June
    Duration of hatch 8 weeks
    Peak activity sporadic
    Best imitating fly—Blue Quill Spinner, No. 14 & 16

*Ephemerella dorothea* (Pale Sulphur Dun)
    Hatch occurs May and June
    Duration of hatch 8 weeks
    Peak activity evening
    Best imitating fly—Pale Sulphur Dun, No. 14 & 16

*Ephemerella rotunda* (Pale Evening Dun)
    Hatch occurs in May
    Duration of hatch 4 weeks
    Peak activity midafternoon
    Best imitating fly—Pale Evening Dun, No. 12 & 14

*Leptophlebia cupida* (Early Blue Quill)
    Hatch occurs in April
    Duration of hatch 4 weeks
    Peak activity midday
    Best imitating fly—Black Quill Spinner, No. 12 & 14

*Acroneuria nigrita* (Black Willow)
    Hatch occurs in May through June
    Duration of hatch 8 weeks
    Peak activity midday
    Best imitating fly—Black Willow, No. 8 & 10

*Pteronarcys dorsata* (Giant Black Stonefly)
    Hatch occurs May and June
    Duration of hatch 8 weeks
    Peak activity twilight
    Best imitating fly—Giant Black Stonefly, No. 1–8

*Heptagenia hebe* (Little Evening Yellow)
    Hatch occurs June through August
    Duration of hatch 12 weeks
    Peak activity twilight
    Best imitating fly—Little Evening Yellow, No. 14 & 16

*Stenonema heterotarsale* (Pale Gray Fox Quill)
    Hatch occurs June through August
    Duration of hatch 12 weeks
    Peak activity afternoon and evening
    Best imitating fly—Pale Gray Fox Quill, No. 12 & 14

*Ephemerella allegheniensis* (Medium Olive Dun)
    Hatch occurs June and July
    Duration of hatch 8 weeks
    Peak activity midday
    Best imitating fly—Medium Olive Dun, No. 14 & 16

*Stenonema carolina* (Little Sulphur Cahill)
    Hatch occurs June and July
    Duration of hatch 8 weeks
    Peak activity afternoon and evening
    Best imitating fly—Little Sulphur Cahill, No. 14 & 16

*Stenonema canadense* (Light Cahill)
    Hatch occurs June through August
    Duration of hatch 12 weeks
    Peak activity afternoon and evening
    Best imitating fly—Light Cahill, No. 14 & 16

*Stenonema rubrum* (Pale Cahill Quill)
    Hatch occurs June through August
    Duration of hatch 12 weeks
    Peak activity afternoon and evening
    Best imitating fly—Pale Cahill Quill, No. 14 & 16

*Hexagenia bilineata* (Brown Drake)
    Hatch occurs June and July
    Duration of hatch 8 weeks
    Peak activity twilight
    Best imitating fly—Brown Drake, No. 6 & 8

*Siphlonurus mirus* (Olive Drake)
    Hatch occurs June through September
    Duration of hatch 16 weeks
    Peak activity midday
    Best imitating fly—Olive Drake, No. 10 & 12

*Potamanthus rufus* (Golden Drake)
    Hatch occurs June through September
    Duration of hatch 16 weeks
    Peak activity twilight
    Best imitating fly—Golden Drake, No. 10 & 12

*Potamanthus distinctus* (Golden Drake)
    Hatch occurs June through August
    Duration of hatch 12 weeks
    Peak activity twilight
    Best imitating fly—Golden Drake Spinner, No. 12 & 14

*Isonychia bicolor* (March Brown)
    Hatch occurs in June
    Duration of hatch 4 weeks
    Peak activity evening
    Best imitating fly—Grey Variant, No. 10 & 12

*Paraleptophlebia debilis* (Dark Blue Quill)
    Hatch occurs June through October
    Duration of hatch 20 weeks
    Peak activity midday
    Best imitating fly—Dark Blue Quill, No. 16 & 18

*Neocloeon almance* (Gray-Winged Yellow)
    Hatch occurs June through September
    Duration of hatch 12 weeks
    Peak activity midday
    Best imitating fly—Gray-Winged Yellow, No. 20 & 22

*Epeorus dispar* (Little Yellow Quill)
    Hatch occurs June and July
    Duration of hatch 8 weeks
    Peak activity twilight
    Best imitating fly—Little Yellow Quill, No. 16 & 18

*Epeorus rubidus* (Gray-Winged Quill)
   Hatch occurs June through August
   Duration of hatch 12 weeks
   Peak activity twilight
   Best imitating fly—Gray-Winged Quill, No. 16 & 18

*Ephemerella simplex* (Dark Slate-Winged Olive)
   Hatch occurs June through September
   Duration of hatch 16 weeks
   Peak activity midday
   Best imitating fly—Dark Slate-Winged Olive, No. 14 & 16

*Paraleptophlebia praedipita* (Little Summer Blue Quill)
   Hatch occurs June through September
   Duration of hatch 16 weeks
   Peak activity midday
   Best imitating fly—Little Summer Blue Quill, No. 16 & 18

*Ephemerella serrata* (Dark Iron-Blue Quill)
   Hatch occurs June through August
   Duration of hatch 12 weeks
   Peak activity midday
   Best imitating fly—Dark Iron-Blue Quill, No. 16 & 18

*Ephemerella deficiens* (Dark Lead-Winged Olive)
   Hatch occurs June through August
   Duration of hatch 12 weeks
   Peak activity midday
   Best imitating fly—Dark Lead-Winged Olive, No. 16 & 18

*Ephemerella lata* (Light Blue-Winged Olive)
   Hatch occurs in June
   Duration of hatch 4 weeks
   Peak activity midday
   Best imitating fly—Light Blue-Winged Olive, No. 14 & 16

*Perla immarginata* (Orange Stonefly)
   Hatch occurs in June
   Duration of hatch 4 weeks
   Peak activity midday
   Best imitating fly—Orange Stonefly, No. 8–12

*Acroneuria lycoris* (Brown Stonefly)
   Hatch occurs June and July
   Duration of hatch 8 weeks
   Peak activity morning
   Best imitating fly—Brown Stonefly, No. 8–12

*Ephemerella lata*—male dun

*Heptagenia thetis* (Pale Evening Dun)
    Hatch occurs July and August
    Duration of hatch 8 weeks
    Peak activity twilight
    Best imitating fly—Pale Evening Dun, No. 14 & 16

*Stenonema pollidum* (Little Pale Fox)
    Hatch occurs July and August
    Duration of hatch 8 weeks
    Peak activity afternoon and evening
    Best imitating fly—Little Pale Fox, No. 16 & 18

*Stenonema integrum* (Pale Cahill Quill)
    Hatch occurs July and August
    Duration of hatch 8 weeks
    Peak activity afternoon and evening
    Best imitating fly—Pale Cahill Quill, No. 14 & 16

*Stenonema ithaca* (Light Gray Fox)
    Hatch occurs July and August
    Duration of hatch 8 weeks
    Peak activity afternoon and evening
    Best imitating fly—Light Gray Fox, No. 12 & 14

*Baetis carolina* (Humpbacked Nymph)
Hatch occurs in July
Duration of hatch 4 weeks
Peak activity afternoon
Best imitating fly—Humpbacked Nymph, No. 12 & 18

*Baetis callosa* (Humpbacked Nymph)
Hatch occurs in July
Duration of hatch 4 weeks
Peak activity afternoon
Best imitating fly—Humpbacked Nymph, No. 12 & 18

*Baetis spinosus* (Slate-Winged Olive)
Hatch occurs July and August
Duration of hatch 8 weeks
Peak activity midafternoon
Best imitating fly—Slate-Winged Olive, No. 20 & 22

*Brachycercus nitidus* (White-Wing Red Quill)
Hatch occurs July and August
Duration of hatch 8 weeks
Peak activity early morning
Best imitating fly—White-Wing Red Quill, No. 16 & 18

*Caenis diminuta* (White-Winged Sulphur)
Hatch occurs June through September
Duration of hatch 16 weeks
Peak activity twilight
Best imitating fly—White-Winged Sulphur, No. 22 & 24

*Ephemerella cornuta* (Blue-Winged Olive)
Hatch occurs in July
Duration of hatch 4 weeks
Peak activity midday
Best imitating fly—Blue-Winged Olive, No. 12 & 14

*Ephemerella longicornis* (Medium Slate-Winged Olive)
Hatch occurs in July
Duration of hatch 4 weeks
Peak activity midday
Best imitating fly—Medium Slate-Winged Olive, No. 14 & 16

*Leuctra grandis* (Dark Stonefly)
Hatch occurs July through August
Duration of hatch 8 weeks
Peak activity midday
Best imitating fly—Dark Stonefly, No. 14 & 16

Virginia has some excellent hatches and good trout fishing on the Philpott tailwater, Dan River, Big Runk Broad Run, Jordan River, Rush River, Hughes River, Rapidan River, Robertson River, Rivanna River, Thornton River, St. Mary's River, Tye River, Pedlar River, North Fork Buffalo River, Irish Creek, Rocky Row Run, Bullpasture River, Smith Creek, Wilson Creek, Jackson River, Back Creek, North Fork Shenandoah River, Big Stony Creek, Little Stony Creek, Garth Run, Moormans River, Pound River, Levisa River, New River, Holston River, South Holston River, and Whitetop Laurel River.

## WEST VIRGINIA

Trout action in West Virginia is found solely in the mountainous eastern half. Here anglers can find brown, rainbow, and brook trout. Fly rod action can be good whenever anglers match emerging insects.

The tables that follow would apply to trout anywhere in the state. In some years mountain areas can be slower to warm to agreeable temperatures, and this may put emergences off for a short period. Once insects begin to hatch, good fishing usually follows.

*Baetis levitans* (Blue-Wing Olive)
    Hatch occurs April through November
    Duration of hatch 32 weeks, sporadically
    Peak activity afternoon
    Best imitating fly—Blue-Wing Olive, No. 22 & 24

*Baetis intercalaris* (Brown Quill)
    Hatch occurs April through November
    Duration of hatch 32 weeks, sporadically
    Peak activity midafternoon
    Best imitating fly—Brown Quill, No. 20 & 22

*Baetis brunneicolor* (Rusty Dun)
    Hatch occurs April through November
    Duration of hatch 32 weeks, sporadically
    Peak activity midafternoon
    Best imitating fly—Rusty Dun, No. 20 & 22

*Baetis vagans* (Little Iron Blue)
    Hatch occurs April through November
    Duration of hatch 32 weeks, sporadically
    Peak activity midmorning
    Best imitating fly—Rusty Spinner, No. 18

*Leptophlebia nebulosa* (Brown Quill)
Hatch occurs April and May
Duration of hatch 8 weeks
Peak activity midday
Best imitating fly—Brown Quill, No. 12

*Paraleptophelebia adoptiva* (Blue Quill)
Hatch occurs April and May
Duration of hatch 8 weeks
Peak activity midday
Best imitating fly—Dark Blue Quill, No. 14–18

*Ephemerella invaria* (Pale Evening Dun)
Hatch occurs April and May
Duration of hatch 8 weeks
Peak activity midafternoon
Best imitating fly—Pale Evening Spinner, No. 12 & 14

*Ephemerella subvaria* (Red Quill or Hendrickson)
Hatch occurs April through June
Duration of hatch 12 weeks
Peak activity midafternoon
Best imitating fly—Little Rusty Spinner, No. 10–14

*Ephemera guttulata* (Green Drake)
Hatch occurs in May
Duration of hatch 4 weeks
Peak activity evening
Best imitating fly—Male Coffin, No. 6–10

*Hexagenia atrocaudata* (Leadwing Drake)
Hatch occurs in May
Duration of hatch 4 weeks
Peak activity twilight
Best imitating fly—Dark Rusty Spinner, No. 6 & 8

*Hexagenia carolina* (Sulphur Drake)
Hatch occurs in May
Duration of hatch 4 weeks
Peak activity twilight
Best imitating fly—Sulphur Drake, No. 10 & 12

*Hexagenia recurvata* (Green Drake)
Hatch occurs May and June
Duration of hatch 8 weeks
Peak activity twilight
Best imitating fly—Brown Drake, No. 2 & 4

*Hexagenia recurvata*—female dun

*Hexagenia marlicanda* (Sulphur Drake)
    Hatch occurs May and June
    Duration of hatch 8 weeks
    Peak activity twilight
    Best imitating fly—Sulphur Drake, No. 10 & 12

*Ephemera simulans* (Brown Drake)
    Hatch occurs in May
    Duration of hatch 4 weeks
    Peak activity twilight
    Best imitating fly—Brown Drake, No. 10 & 12

*Ephemera blanda* (Sulphur Drake)
    Hatch occurs in May
    Duration of hatch 4 weeks
    Peak activity twilight
    Best imitating fly—Sulphur Drake, No. 14

*Ephemera triplex* (Pale Sulphur)
    Hatch occurs in May
    Duration of hatch 4 weeks
    Peak activity twilight
    Best imitating fly—Pale Sulphur, No. 12 & 14

*Siploplecton signatum* (Olive Quill)
    Hatch occurs May and June
    Duration of hatch 8 weeks
    Peak activity midday
    Best imitating fly—Olive Quill, No. 12 & 14

*Siphlonurus quebecensis* (Brown Quill)
　　Hatch occurs May and June
　　Duration of hatch 8 weeks·
　　Peak activity midday
　　Best imitating fly—Brown Quill, No. 12 & 14

*Callibaetis ferrugineus* (Speckle-Winged Olive)
　　Hatch occurs May through October
　　Duration of hatch 20 weeks, sporadically
　　Peak activity midday
　　Best imitating fly—Speckle-Winged Olive, No. 16 & 18

*Leptophlebia johnsoni* (Dark-Blue Quill)
　　Hatch occurs in May
　　Duration of hatch 4 weeks
　　Peak activity midday
　　Best imitating fly—Blue Quill Spinner, No. 14 & 16

*Paraleptophlebia mollis* (Iron Blue Dun)
　　Hatch occurs May and June
　　Duration of hatch 8 weeks
　　Peak activity midday
　　Best imitating fly—Jenny Spinner, No. 16 & 18

*Paraleptophlebia assimilis* (Early Blue Quill)
　　Hatch occurs May and June
　　Duration of hatch 8 weeks
　　Peak activity midday
　　Best imitating fly—Early Blue Quill, No. 14 & 16

*Pseudocloeon carolina* (Gray-Winged Brown)
　　Hatch occurs May through August
　　Duration of hatch 16 weeks, sporadically
　　Peak activity morning
　　Best imitating fly—Gray-Winged Brown, No. 22 & 24

*Ephemerella lutulenta* (Yellow Quill)
　　Hatch occurs May and June
　　Duration of hatch 8 weeks
　　Peak activity midday
　　Best imitating fly—Yellow Quill, No. 12 & 16

*Ephemerella doris* (Blue-Winged Yellow Quill)
　　Hatch occurs May and June
　　Duration of hatch 8 weeks
　　Peak activity midday
　　Best imitating fly—Blue-Winged Yellow Quill, No. 14 & 16

*Ephemerella temporalis* (Yellow Quill)
    Hatch occurs May and June
    Duration of hatch 8 weeks
    Peak activity midday
    Best imitating fly—Yellow Quill, No. 12 & 14

*Ephemerella attenuata* (Blue-Winged Olive)
    Hatch occurs May and June
    Duration of hatch 8 weeks
    Peak activity sporadic
    Best imitating fly—Blue Quill Spinner, No. 14 & 16

*Ephemerella dorothea* (Pale Sulphur Dun)
    Hatch occurs May and June
    Duration of hatch 8 weeks
    Peak activity evening
    Best imitating fly—Pale Evening Dun, No. 14 & 16

*Ephemerella rotunda* (Pale Evening Dun)
    Hatch occurs in May
    Duration of hatch 4 weeks
    Peak activity midafternoon
    Best imitating fly—Pale Evening Dun, No. 12 & 14

*Leptophlebia cupida* (Early Brown Spinner)
    Hatch occurs in April
    Duration of hatch 4 weeks
    Peak activity midday
    Best imitating fly—Early Brown Spinner, No. 12 & 14

*Acroneuria nigrita* (Black Willow)
    Hatch occurs May and June
    Duration of hatch 8 weeks
    Peak activity midday
    Best imitating fly—Black Willow, No. 8 & 10

*Pteronarcys dorsata* (Giant Black Stonefly)
    Hatch occurs May and June
    Duration of hatch 8 weeks
    Peak activity twilight
    Best imitating fly—Giant Black Stonefly, No. 1 & 8

*Heptagenia hebe* (Little Evening Yellow)
    Hatch occurs June through August
    Duration of hatch 12 weeks
    Peak activity twilight
    Best imitating fly—Pale Evening Dun, No. 14 & 16

*Stenonema heterotarsale* (Pale Gray Fox Quill)
   Hatch occurs June through August
   Duration of hatch 12 weeks
   Peak activity afternoon and evening
   Best imitating fly—Pale Gray Fox Quill, No. 12 & 14

*Ephemerella allegheniensis* (Medium Olive Dun)
   Hatch occurs June and July
   Duration of hatch 8 weeks
   Peak activity midday
   Best imitating fly—Medium Olive Dun, No. 14 & 16

*Stenonema carolina* (Little Sulphur Cahill)
   Hatch occurs June and July
   Duration of hatch 8 weeks
   Peak activity afternoon and evening
   Best imitating fly—Little Sulphur Cahill, No. 14 & 16

*Stenonema canadense* (Light Cahill)
   Hatch occurs June through August
   Duration of hatch 12 weeks
   Peak activity afternoon and evening
   Best imitating fly—Ginger Quill Spinner, No. 14 & 16

*Stenonema rubrum* (Pale Cahill Quill)
   Hatch occurs June through August
   Duration of hatch 12 weeks
   Peak activity afternoon and evening
   Best imitating fly—Pale Cahill Quill, No. 14 & 16

*Hexagenia bilineata* (Brown Drake)
   Hatch occurs June and July
   Duration of hatch 8 weeks
   Peak activity twilight
   Best imitating fly—Brown Drake, No. 6 & 8

*Siphlonurus mirus* (Olive Drake)
   Hatch occurs June through September
   Duration of hatch 16 weeks
   Peak activity midday
   Best imitating fly—Olive Drake, No. 10 & 12

*Potamanthus rufus* (Golden Drake)
   Hatch occurs June through September
   Duration of hatch 16 weeks
   Peak activity twilight
   Best imitating fly—Golden Drake, No. 10 & 12

*Potamanthus distinctus* (Golden Drake) .
    Hatch occurs June through August
    Duration of hatch 12 weeks
    Peak activity twilight
    Best imitating fly—Golden Spinner, No. 12 & 14

*Isonychia bicolor* (March Brown)
    Hatch occurs in June
    Duration of hatch 4 weeks
    Peak activity evening
    Best imitating fly—Gray Variant, No. 10 & 12

*Isonychia albomanicata* (Mahogany Drake)
    Hatch occurs in June
    Duration of hatch 4 weeks
    Peak activity evening
    Best imitating fly—Mahogany Drake, No. 12 & 14

*Paraleptophlebia debilis* (Dark Blue Quill)
    Hatch occurs June through October
    Duration of hatch 20 weeks
    Peak activity midday
    Best imitating fly—Dark Blue Quill, No. 16 & 18

*Neocloeon almance* (Gray-Winged Yellow)
    Hatch occurs June through September
    Duration of hatch 16 weeks
    Peak activity midday
    Best imitating fly—Gray-Winged Yellow, No. 20 & 22

*Epeorus dispar* (Little Yellow Quill)
    Hatch occurs June and July
    Duration of hatch 8 weeks
    Peak activity twilight
    Best imitating fly—Little Yellow Quill, No. 16 & 18

*Epeorus rubidus* (Gray-Winged Quill)
    Hatch occurs June through August
    Duration of hatch 12 weeks
    Peak activity twilight
    Best imitating fly—Gray-Winged Quill, No. 16 & 18

*Ephemerella simplex* (Dark Slate-Winged Olive)
    Hatch occurs June through September
    Duration of hatch 16 weeks
    Peak activity midday
    Best imitating fly—Dark Slate-Winged Olive, No. 14 & 16

*Ephemerella serrata* (Dark Iron-Blue Quill)
    Hatch occurs June through August
    Duration of hatch 12 weeks
    Peak activity midday
    Best imitating fly—Dark Iron-Blue Quill, No. 16 & 18

*Ephemerella deficiens* (Dark Lead-Winged Olive)
    Hatch occurs June through August
    Duration of hatch 12 weeks
    Peak activity midday
    Best imitating fly—Dark Lead-Winged Olive, No. 16 & 18

*Ephemerella lata* (Light Blue-Winged Olive)
    Hatch occurs in June
    Duration of hatch 4 weeks
    Peak activity midday
    Best imitating fly—Light Blue-Winged Olive, No. 14 & 16

*Perla immarginata* (Orange Stonefly)
    Hatch occurs in June
    Duration of hatch 4 weeks
    Peak activity midday
    Best imitating fly—Orange Stonefly, No. 8 & 12

*Acroneuria lycoris* (Brown Stonefly)
    Hatch occurs June and July
    Duration of hatch 8 weeks
    Peak activity morning
    Best imitating fly—Brown Stonefly, No. 8 & 12

*Stenonema pollidum* (Little Pale Fox)
    Hatch occurs July and August
    Duration of hatch 8 weeks
    Peak activity afternoon and evening
    Best imitating fly—Little Pale Fox, No. 16 & 18

*Stenonema integrum* (Pale Cahill Quill)
    Hatch occurs July and August
    Duration of hatch 8 weeks
    Peak activity afternoon and evening
    Best imitating fly—Pale Cahill Quill, No. 14 & 16

*Stenonema ithaca* (Light Gray Fox)
    Hatch occurs July and August
    Duration of hatch 8 weeks
    Peak activity afternoon and evening
    Best imitating fly—Light Cahill, No. 12 & 14

*Baetisca carolina* (Humpbacked Nymph)
    Hatch occurs in July
    Duration of hatch 4 weeks
    Peak activity sporadic
    Best imitating fly—Humpbacked Nymph, No. 12 & 18

*Bastica callosa* (Humpbacked Nymph)
    Hatch occurs in July
    Duration of hatch 4 weeks
    Peak activity afternoon
    Best imitating fly—Humpbacked Nymph, No. 12 & 18

*Baetis spinosus* (Slate-Winged Olive)
    Hatch occurs July and August
    Duration of hatch 8 weeks
    Peak activity midafternoon
    Best imitating fly—Slate-Winged Olive, No. 20 & 22

*Brachycercus nitidus* (White-Winged Red Quill)
    Hatch occurs July and August
    Duration of hatch 8 weeks
    Peak activity early morning
    Best imitating fly—White-Winged Red Quill, No. 16 & 18

*Caenis diminuta* (White-Winged Sulphur)
    Hatch occurs June through September
    Duration of hatch 16 weeks
    Peak activity midday
    Best imitating fly—White-Winged Sulphur, No. 22 & 24

*Ephemerella cornuta* (Blue-Winged Olive)
    Hatch occurs in July
    Duration of hatch 4 weeks
    Peak activity midday
    Best imitating fly—Dark Olive Spinner, No. 12 & 14

*Ephemerella longicornis* (Medium Slate-Winged Olive)
    Hatch occurs in July
    Duration of hatch 4 weeks
    Peak activity midday
    Best imitating fly—Medium Slate-Winged Olive, No. 14 & 16

*Leuctra grandis* (Dark Stone)
    Hatch occurs July and August
    Duration of hatch 8 weeks
    Peak activity midday
    Best imitating fly—Dark Stonefly, No. 14 & 16

Trout are found in Cranberry River, Williams River, Seneca Creek, Shaver's Fork River, Elk River tailwaters, and Anthony Creek. Some lakes such as Edwards Run Pond, Spruce Knob Lake, Seneca Impoundment, and Summit Lake hold trout. Turkey Creek can be a good bet, as is Blackwater River.

# 8

# Southern Hatches

Hatches of so-called "trout flies" are of lesser importance in the southern states simply because many of these states do not have trout. But, good catches of rock bass, largemouth bass, smallmouth bass (in some states), bluegill, sunfish, white bass, and other species can pick up the slack for fly-fishermen.

This grouping of southern states includes Alabama, Arkansas, Louisiana, Mississippi, Oklahoma, and Texas. Some of these states, such as Texas and Arkansas, have good-to-excellent trout action in certain areas, and the accompanying tables for each state can pinpoint the best times and imitating flies to use. As I have little firsthand knowledge of these hatches, I will not recommend imitating flies. I am also unfamiliar with popular names for these insects in this region, so have not noted those. However, by noting recommendations for the same insect species in other regions, you will probably be on the right track towards matching a particular hatch. You may also have to improvise a little.

## ALABAMA

According to one source, Alabama has 21,000 small ponds and lakes, 20 large reservoirs, some 250 creeks, and 50 rivers, all of which can provide good sport for fly-fishermen interested in matching emerging insects. Trout are virtually nonexistent in Alabama.

The important game fish species fly-rodders can tangle with include largemouth, smallmouth, spotted, and redeye bass; walleye and sauger; striped bass; rock and warmouth bass; and bluegill or redear sunfish.

*Ameletus lineatus*
Hatch occurs in March and April
Duration is 6 to 8 weeks
Peak activity occurs at dusk

*Siphlonurus decorus*
Hatch occurs from April to July
Duration is from late morning to late afternoon from late April on
Peak activity occurs after noon

*Siphlonurus luridipennis*
Hatch occurs from April to July
Duration is 8 weeks
Peak activity occurs in the afternoon

*Siphlonurus marginatus*
Hatch occurs from April to July
Duration is about 8 weeks
Peak activity occurs in the afternoon

*Siphlonurus mirus*
Hatch occurs from April through July
Duration is about 10 to 12 weeks
Peak activity occurs in afternoon

*Siphlonurus quebecensis*
Hatch occurs from April to July
Duration is 8 weeks
Peak activity occurs in late afternoon or early evening

*Isonychia annulata*
Hatch can occur all year
Duration is sporadic
Peak activity occurs at twilight

*Isonychia bicolor*
Hatch can occur all year during warm weather
Duration is sporadic
Peak activity normally occurs at dusk

*Isonychia georgiae*
Hatch can occur all year
Duration is sporadic
Swarms can occur at twilight

*Isonychia sadleri*—female dun


*Isonychia sadleri*
　　Hatch occurs all year in warm weather
　　Duration is sporadic
　　Peak activity occurs at twilight

*Baetis amplus*
　　Hatch occurs during summer months
　　Duration is 4 to 8 weeks
　　Peak activity occurs during daylight hours

*Baetis australis*
　　Hatch occurs during summer months
　　Duration is all summer if warm
　　Peak activity occurs during daylight hours

*Baetis pallidulus*
　　Hatch occurs during summer months
　　Duration is all summer if warm
　　Peak activity occurs in late morning to early afternoon

*Baetis spinosus*
　　Hatch occurs during summer months
　　Duration can take place all summer
　　Peak activity occurs during daylight hours

*Ephemerella attenuata*
　　Hatch occurs from May through September
　　Duration is 4 months
　　Peak activity occurs at dusk

*Ephemerella cornuta*
    Hatch occurs from May through September
    Duration can be 4 months, but usually shorter
    Peak activity occurs at dusk

*Ephemerella lata*
    Hatch occurs from May through September
    Duration of 4 months
    Peak activity occurs at dusk

*Ephemerella tuberculata*
    Hatch occurs from May through September
    Duration is 4 months
    Peak activity occurs at dusk

*Ephemerella walkeri*
    Hatch occurs from May through September
    Duration is 4 months
    Peak activity occurs at dusk

*Epeorus (Iron) dispar*
    Hatch occurs in late summer
    Duration is 4 weeks
    Peak activity occurs during low-light levels, at dusk

*Epeorus (Iron) pleuralis*
    Hatch begins in late summer
    Duration is 4 weeks
    Peak activity is sporadic, usually in midafternoon

*Ephemera guttulata*
    Hatch occurs from May through August
    Duration is 16 weeks
    Peak activity occurs during overcast periods, usually at midday

*Ephemera simulans*
    Hatch can occur from May through August
    Duration is sporadic, can be up to 16 weeks
    Peak activity occurs at sunset

Hatches can occur on Guntersville, Wheeler, Pickwick, Wilson reservoirs, and Bartlett's Ferry, Goat Rock, George, Martin, Weiss, Wheeler, Wilson Mitchell and other lakes. Fly hatches can take place on many streams, and the Tallapoosa, Coosa, Sipsey, Tombigbee, Cahaba, Tennessee, Mulberry, and Alabama rivers are the best bets.

## ARKANSAS

One of the greatest things going for Arkansas is the completion of numerous reservoirs. These impoundments, with their cold-water outlets, has added an exciting dimension to southern trout fishing.

Rainbow and brown trout are common in many cold-water streams below reservoirs. Smallmouth and largemouth bass, spotted bass, panfish, and striped bass are also favorites for local anglers. All respond well to existing hatches, and an emergence can deliver sporadic but good fly-fishing in these waters.

Some of the largest brown trout in the world are now being taken from the White River. Browns over thirty pounds have been taken, although not on a fly. Rainbows can weigh up to fifteen pounds, but the average is much smaller. Trout of two to ten pounds produce the best fly-fishing in these waters.

*Ameletus lineatus*
    Hatch occurs in April
    Duration is 6 to 8 weeks
    Peak activity occurs at dusk

*Siphlonurus decorus*
    Hatch occurs from April to July
    Duration is about 10 weeks
    Peak activity occurs in late afternoon

*Siphlonurus marginatus*
    Hatch occurs from April to July
    Duration is 10 to 12 weeks
    Peak activity occurs in the afternoon

*Siphlonurus quebecensis*
    Hatch occurs from April to July
    Duration is 10 to 12 weeks
    Peak activity occurs in early evening

*Isonychia annulata*
    Hatch can occur all year during warm weather
    Duration is sporadic
    Peak activity occurs at twilight

*Isonychia bicolor*
    Hatch can occur all year during warm weather
    Duration is sporadic
    Peak activity occurs at dusk

*Isonychia sadleri*
>   Hatch occurs all year in warm weather
>   Duration is sporadic
>   Peak activity occurs at twilight

*Baetis pallidulus*
>   Hatch occurs during summer months
>   Duration can continue all summer if warm
>   Peak activity occurs in late morning and early afternoon

*Baetis spinosus*
>   Hatch occurs from May through September
>   Duration is 4 months if warm
>   Peak activity occurs at any time during day

*Ephemerella cornuta*
>   Hatch occurs from May through September
>   Duration is 2 to 4 months
>   Peak activity occurs at dusk

*Ephemerella walkeri*
>   Hatch occurs from May through September
>   Duration is 2 to 4 months
>   Peak activity occurs at dusk

*Epeorus (Iron) dispar*
>   Hatch occurs in late summer
>   Duration is 4 weeks
>   Peak activity occurs at dusk

*Epeorus (Iron) pleuralis*
>   Hatch begins in late summer
>   Duration is 4 weeks
>   Peak activity is in midafternoon, can be sporadic

*Ephemera guttulata*
>   Hatch occurs from May through August
>   Duration is 16 weeks
>   Peak activity occurs at midday

*Ephemera simulans*
>   Hatch can occur from May through August
>   Duration is up to 16 weeks, sporadic in nature
>   Peak activity occurs at sunset

The best swarms of insects occur on faster streams and also deliver the best trout action. Look for hatches on Spring, White, Ouachita,

Saline, Black, and Little Missouri rivers. An emergence can take place on countless creeks and below or above Bull Shoals, Blakely, Narrows, Norfolk, Greers Ferry, Bull Shoals, Ozark, Ouachita lakes and reservoirs.

## LOUISIANA

This state has over four million acres of lakes, rivers, creeks, and bayous where fly-fishermen can find action with largemouth bass, warmouth bass, yellow bass, crappie, and several species of sunfish, including redear and bluegill.

Trout do not exist in Louisiana waters and few anglers consider studying the hatches to determine when the best angling opportunities exist for other species that can be taken with a fly rod. Insects hatch year round in these waters and a knowledge of emergence dates can lead to good fly-fishing.

*Ameletus lineatus*
　　Hatch occurs in March and April
　　Duration is 6 to 8 weeks
　　Peak activity occurs at dusk

*Siphlonurus decorus*
　　Hatch occurs from April to July
　　Duration is 12 to 16 weeks of sporadic activity
　　Peak activity occurs after noon

*Siphlonurus luridipennis*
　　Hatch occurs from April to July
　　Duration is 8 weeks, possibly longer in hot weather
　　Peak activity occurs in the afternoon

*Siphlonurus marginatus*
　　Hatch occurs from April to July
　　Duration is about 8 weeks
　　Peak activity occurs in the afternoon

*Siphlonurus mirus*
　　Hatch occurs from April through July
　　Duration is about 12 weeks
　　Peak afternoon activity

*Siphlonurus quebecensis*
　　Hatch occurs from April to July
　　Duration is 8 to 12 weeks
　　Peak activity occurs in late afternoon or early evening

*Isonychia annulata*
>    Hatch can occur all year
>    Duration is sporadic
>    Peak activity occurs at dusk

*Isonychia bicolor*
>    Hatch can occur all year during warm weather
>    Duration is sporadic
>    Peak activity occurs at dusk

*Isonychia georgiae*
>    Hatch can occur all year
>    Duration is sporadic
>    Swarms usually occur at twilight

*Isonychia sadleri*
>    Hatch occurs all year in warm weather
>    Duration is sporadic
>    Peak activity occurs at dusk

*Baetis amplus*
>    Hatch occurs during summer months
>    Duration is 4 to 8 weeks
>    Peak activity occurs during daylight hours

*Baetis australis*
>    Hatch occurs during summer months
>    Duration is all summer
>    Peak activity occurs during daylight hours

*Baetis pallidulus*
>    Hatch occurs during summer months
>    Duration is all summer
>    Peak activity takes place in late morning or early afternoon

*Baetis spinosus*
>    Hatch occurs during summer months
>    Duration is all summer, usually sporadic
>    Peak activity occurs during daylight hours

*Ephemerella attenuata*
>    Hatch occurs from May through September
>    Duration is 4 months, usually sporadic
>    Peak activity occurs at dusk

*Ephemerella cornuta*
   Hatch occurs May through September
   Duration is about 4 months but can be shorter and sporadic
   Peak activity occurs at dusk

*Ephemerella lata*
   Hatch occurs from May through September
   Duration is 4 months or longer
   Peak activity occurs at dusk

*Ephemerella tuberculata*
   Hatch occurs from May through September
   Duration is 4 or more months
   Peak activity occurs at dusk

*Ephemerella walkeri*
   Hatch occurs from May through September
   Duration is 4 or more months
   Peak activity occurs at dusk

*Epeorus (Iron) dispar*
   Hatch occurs in late summer
   Duration is 4 weeks
   Peak activity occurs at dusk or on overcast days

*Epeorus (Iron) pleuralis*
   Hatch begins in late summer
   Duration is 4 weeks
   Peak activity is sporadic, usually in midafternoon

*Ephemera guttulata*
   Hatch occurs from May through August
   Duration is 16 weeks, sometimes longer
   Peak activity at midday, often during overcast periods

Almost all Louisiana creeks, streams, lakes, and bayous will have hatches of one type or another. In some areas they are continuous. Try Pearl, Vermilion, Mermentau, and Ouachita rivers. Caddo, Spring Bayou, Cross, Sabine, Black, Bruin, and Verrett lakes can be good.

## MISSISSIPPI

Excellent largemouth bass, crappie, bluegill, redear sunfish, and other freshwater game fish species exists in Mississippi. The state has numerous lakes with public access, and it's in these areas that fly-rodders can find good sport during hatches.

*Ameletus lineatus*
>Hatch occurs in April
>Duration is 6 to 8 weeks
>Peak activity occurs at dusk

*Siphlonurus quebecensis*
>Hatch occurs from April to July
>Duration is 10 to 12 weeks
>Peak activity occurs in early evening

*Isonychia annulata*
>Hatch can occur all year
>Duration is sporadic
>Peak activity occurs at twilight

*Isonychia bicolor*
>Hatch can occur all year
>Duration is sporadic
>Peak activity occurs at dusk

*Isonychia sadleri*
>Hatch occurs all year
>Duration is sporadic
>Peak activity occurs at twilight

*Baetis pallidulus*
>Hatch occurs during summer months
>Duration is all summer
>Peak activity occurs in late morning or early afternoon

*Baetis spinosus*
>Hatch occurs from May through September
>Duration is 4 months
>Peak activity occurs during daylight hours

*Ephemerella cornuta*
>Hatch occurs from May through September
>Duration is 2 to 4 months
>Peak activity occurs at dusk

*Ephemerella walkeri*
>Hatch occurs from May through September
>Duration is 2 to 4 months, but sporadic
>Peak activity occurs at dusk

*Ephemera guttulata*
>   Hatch occurs from May through August
>   Duration is 16 weeks
>   Peak activity occurs at midday

*Ephemera simulans*
>   Hatch can occur from May through August
>   Duration is sporadic but can last up to 16 weeks
>   Peak activity occurs at sunset

Try looking for hatches along Strong, Chunky, Bowie, Pearl, Tombigbee, Buttahatchie, and other rivers or creeks. Pickwick Reservoir, Sardis Reservoir, Enid Reservoir, Moon Lake, Eagle Lake, Lake George, Mossy Lake, Big Black Lake, Sunflower Lake, and Grenada Reservoir may be good bets.

## OKLAHOMA

Oklahoma is considered by many to be arid and without good running water or trout streams. Such is really not the case; trout fishing may be somewhat different from other well known states, but this state does offer some good sport. Most of the rainbows are stocked into various reservoirs, but Oklahoma also offers largemouth bass, smallmouth bass, northern pike, walleye, catfish, white bass, and panfish.

*Ameletus lineatus*
>   Hatch occurs in April
>   Duration is 6 to 8 weeks
>   Peak activity occurs at dusk

*Siphlonurus quebecensis*
>   Hatch occurs from April to July
>   Duration is 10 to 12 weeks
>   Peak activity occurs in early evening

*Isonychia annualata*
>   Hatch can occur all year during warm weather
>   Duration is sporadic
>   Peak activity occurs at twilight

*Isonychia bicolor*
>   Hatch is sporadic, best during warm weather months
>   Duration is usually 2 months
>   Peak activity occurs at dusk

*Baetis pallidulus*
   Hatch occurs during summer months
   Duration can continue all summer if warm
   Peak activity occurs in late morning and early afternoon

*Baetis spinosus*
   Hatch occurs from May through September
   Duration is 4 months
   Peak activity occurs during daylight hours

*Ephemerella cornuta*
   Hatch occurs from May through September
   Duration is 2 to 4 months
   Peak activity occurs at dusk

*Ephemerella walkeri*
   Hatch occurs from May through September
   Duration is 2 to 4 months, but sporadic
   Peak activity occurs at dusk

*Ephemera guttulata*
   Hatch occurs from May through August
   Duration is 16 weeks
   Peak activity occurs at midday

*Ephemera simulans*
   Hatch can occur from May through August
   Duration is sporadic but can last up to 16 weeks
   Peak activity occurs at sunset

The following lakes and reservoirs should produce some good fly action: Lake Winster, Lake Humphreys, Lake Texoma, Eufaula Reservoir, Fort Cobb Reservoir, Fort Supply Reservoir, Foss Reservoir, Heyburn Reservoir, Hulah Lake, Tenkiller Lake, Canton Lake, Clayton Lake, and Lake Texoma.

## TEXAS

This state has hundreds, perhaps thousands, of reservoirs and smaller ranch tanks where a myriad of game fish are found. Largemouth bass are the most common, and are highly sought after. Some trout are found in scattered locations; often in ranch tanks fed by cool springs. Other species of fish include panfish, white bass, black crappie, white crappie, and catfish.

Hatches are sporadic in nature because of the intense heat in some areas, lack of rainfall, and nature of this land.

*Ephemera simulans*
   Hatch can occur from May to August, possibly as late as October
   Duration is sporadic
   Peak activity occurs at sunset

*Attenella margarita*
   Hatch begins in midsummer
   Duration is sporadic
   Peak activity is sporadic

*Thraulodes arizonicus*
   Hatch is sporadic
   Duration is sporadic
   Peak activity is at dusk

*Thraulodes brunneus*
   Hatch is sporadic
   Duration is sporadic
   Peak activity occurs at dusk

*Paraleptophlebia debilis*
   Hatch begins in September or October
   Duration is sporadic
   Peak activity occurs in early afternoon

*Paraleptophlebia memorialis*
   Hatch begins in the fall months
   Duration is sporadic
   Peak activity occurs in the afternoon

There is much work still to be done in identifying some of the southern hatches, particularly in the arid states such as Texas. The best fishing should come on larger impoundments such as Caddo Lake, Lake Texoma, Lake Travis, Toledo Bend Reservoir, Lake Sam Rayburn, Falcon Lake, and Lake Meredith.

# 9

# Midwest Hatches

Hatch periods in the Midwest can be the most productive time to fish for many anglers. Serious students of entomology have charted many emergences and many hatches can be pinpointed almost to the day.

This chapter gives hatch information for Illinois, Indiana, Iowa, Kansas, Michigan, Minnesota, Missouri, Nebraska, North Dakota, Ohio, South Dakota, and Wisconsin. States close to the Great Lakes have by far the most dependable emergences, but some of the other states are subject to good swarms of insects.

The fishing waters in these states run the gamut from sparkling clear streams to small tributaries of the Great Lakes, inland rivers, big lakes, small ponds, beaver ponds, and other conditions, and they produce classic hatches of mayflies, caddis flies, stoneflies, and other insects.

## ILLINOIS

This highly populated state offers little in the way of inland trout fishing. Some lakes and streams support a mediocre trout fishery, usually on a put-and-take basis. The best trout action occurs on Lake Michigan, which is not ideal for fly-fishing. Sporadic activity with planted browns and rainbows elsewhere is usually over as spring swings into summer. Some streams do have a good series of hatches and a heavy emergence can lure a wary trout up from bottom to feed.

*Ameletus ludens*
> Hatch begins in early April
> Duration is 4 to 8 weeks
> Peak activity occurs in early evening
> Best imitating fly—Black Quill, No. 18

*Siphlonurus typicus*
> Hatch begins in early April
> Duration is 6 weeks
> Peak activity occurs at dusk
> Best imitating fly—March Brown, No. 18

*Perla varians* (Stonefly)
> Hatch begins in mid-April
> Duration is 6 to 8 weeks
> Peak activity occurs at dusk
> Best imitating fly—Brown Stonefly, No. 18

*Perla capitata* (Brown Stonefly)
> Hatch begins in early-to-mid April
> Duration is 6 to 8 weeks
> Peak activity occurs from noon until dark
> Best imitating fly—Brown Stonefly, No. 16

*Siphlonurus marshalli* (Gray Mayfly)
> Hatch begins in late April
> Duration is 8 to 10 weeks
> Peak activity occurs at twilight
> Best imitating fly—Hare's Ear, No. 18

*Callibaetis fluctuans* (Pale Yellow Mayfly)
> Hatch begins in late April
> Duration is 10 to 14 weeks
> Peak activity occurs at dusk
> Best imitating fly—Golden Spinner, No. 16

*Callibaetis ferrugineus*
> Hatch begins in late April
> Duration is up to 20 weeks, usually much shorter
> Peak activity occurs from 7 P.M. to dark
> Best imitating fly—Coffin, No. 18

*Callibaetis skokianus* (Dark Red Mayfly)
> Hatch begins in early May
> Duration is 4 to 6 weeks
> Peak activity occurs from 6 P.M. until dusk
> Best imitating fly—Red Quill, No. 18

*Centroptilum walshi* (Pale Yellow Mayfly)
Hatch begins in late May or early June
Duration is 4 to 6 weeks
Peak activity occurs in the early evening
Best imitating fly—Pale Yellow Quill, No. 18

*Stenonema vicarium* (March Brown)
Hatch begins in late May or early June
Duration is 6 to 8 weeks
Peak activity occurs at any time during daylight hours
Best imitating fly—American March Brown or Great Red Spinner, No.
10 or 12

*Stenonema luteum* (Orange Mayfly)
Hatch begins in mid-May to early June
Duration is 12 weeks
Peak activity occurs in late afternoon
Best imitating fly—Rusty Spinner, No. 14

*Stenonema terminatum*
Hatch begins in mid-to-late May
Duration is about 2 months
Peak activity occurs from 7 P.M. to dusk
Best imitating fly—Jenny Spinner, No. 20

*Acroneuria ruralis* (Yellow Stonefly)
Hatch begins in early June
Duration is 6 weeks to all summer
Peak activity occurs at late afternoon
Best imitating fly—Yellow Stonefly, No. 18

*Acroneuria internata* (Dark Grey Stonefly)
Hatch begins in early June
Duration is all summer
Peak activity occurs at twilight
Best imitating fly—Grey Stonefly, No. 16

*Potomanthus verticis*
Hatch begins in mid-June
Duration is 4 weeks
Peak activity occurs from 6 P.M. until dark
Best imitating fly—Willow Quill, No. 18

*Tricorythodes stygiatus*
Hatch begins in mid-June
Duration is 8 weeks
Peak activity occurs at twilight
Best imitating fly—Grey Quill, No. 20

*Brachycercus prudens*
   Hatch begins in mid-June
   Duration is 8 to 10 weeks
   Peak activity occurs at dusk
   Best imitating fly—Brown Mayfly, No. 20

*Hexagenia limbata* (Caddis)
   Hatch begins in mid-June
   Duration is 2 to 3 weeks
   Peak activity occurs from sundown to midnight
   Best imitating fly—Michigan Caddis, No. 8 or 10

*Caenis jocosa*
   Hatch begins in late June
   Duration is 8 weeks
   Peak activity occurs from 5 P.M. until dusk
   Best imitating fly—Brown Drake, No. 18

*Caenis forcipata*
   Hatch begins in late June
   Duration is 6 to 8 weeks
   Peak activity occurs from 7 P.M. until dark
   Best imitating fly—Ginger Quill, No. 20

*Limnephiloidea fabria*
   Hatch begins in late June
   Duration is 4 weeks
   Peak activity occurs in early morning or late afternoon
   Best imitating fly—Brown Sedge, No. 10

Good hatches of some insects have been seen and fished on the Apple, Mississippi, Fox, Wabash, and Kankakee rivers. Anglers can find sporadic hatches on lakes such as Fox, Rend, Catherine, Channel, Marie, Bluff, Cedar, Crab Orchard, Devil's Kitchen, Horseshoe, Beaver Dam, Kinkaid, Sam Parr, Stump, Carlyle, Sangchris, and Springfield.

## INDIANA

This is another of the midwest states with little trout fishing except in Lake Michigan, where hatches mean little to salmonids that feed on healthy rations of smelt and alewives. A couple of streams deliver a small amount of fly-fishing for trout, and a couple lakes have these fish, but much of the fly-rodding action is for other species.

Largemouth and smallmouth bass are plentiful in many lakes and streams, as are bluegill, rock bass, white bass, yellow perch, crappies, bluegill, and sunfish. These species deliver the best action during a hatch.

*Epeorus pleuralis* (Blue Dun)
 Hatch begins in late April
 Duration is 4 weeks
 Peak activity occurs from noon to 2 P.M.
 Best imitating fly—Dark Gordon Quill or Gordon Quill, No. 12

*Paraleptophlebia adoptiva* (Iron Blue Dun)
 Hatch begins in late April
 Duration is 4 weeks
 Peak activity occurs from 4 P.M. until dark
 Best imitating fly—Dark Blue or Dark Red Quill, No. 18 or 20

*Iron fraudator* (Dark Gordon or Gordon Quill)
 Hatch begins in late April
 Duration is 4 weeks
 Peak activity occurs at midday
 Best imitating flies—Dark Gordon Quill or Gordon Quill, No. 14 & 12

*Ephemerella subvaria* (Hendrickson)
 Hatch begins in late April
 Duration is 6 weeks
 Peak activity occurs from noon until 2 P.M.
 Best imitating fly—Red Quill, No. 14

*Leptophlebia cupida* (Dark Hendrickson)
 Hatch begins in late April
 Duration is 4 weeks
 Peak activity occurs from 2 P.M. until dusk
 Best imitating fly—Early Brown Spinner or Black Quill Spinner, No. 14

*Stenonema vicarium* (Brown Drake or March Brown)
 Hatch begins in early May
 Duration is 4 weeks
 Peak activity occurs in the evening
 Best imitating fly—Great Red Spinner or American March Brown, No. 10 or 12

*Stenonema fuscum* (Ginger Quill)
 Hatch begins in mid-May
 Duration is 6 weeks
 Peak activity is sporadic
 Best imitating fly—Grey Fox, No. 12

*Paraleptophlebia adoptiva*—female dun

*Ephemera guttulata* (Green Drake)
    Hatch begins in late May
    Duration is 4 weeks
    Peak activity occurs in the evening
    Best imitating flies—Male or Female Green Drake, No. 8 & 10

*Isonychia bicolor* (Slate Drake, Slate-Winged Drake, or Leadwing Coachman)
    Hatch begins in late May
    Duration is up to 14 weeks of sporadic activity
    Peak activity occurs at twilight
    Best imitating flies—Grey Variant or White-Gloved Howdy, No. 10 & 12

*Hexagenia recurvata* (Drake)
    Hatch begins in early June
    Duration is 8 weeks
    Peak activity occurs in the evening
    Best imitating flies—Dark Green Drake or Brown Drake, No. 8 & 10

*Leptophlebia johnsoni* (Iron Blue Dun)
    Hatch begins in early June
    Duration is 4 weeks
    Peak activity occurs from 11 A.M. to 3 P.M.
    Best imitating fly—Blue Quill Spinner or Jenny Spinner, No. 14 or 16

*Stenonema canadense* (Light Cahill)
    Hatch begins in late June
    Duration is 4 weeks
    Peak activity occurs at twilight
    Best imitating fly—Light Cahill, No. 14

*Hexagenia limbata* (Michigan Caddis)
    Hatch begins in late June
    Duration is 4 weeks
    Peak activity occurs after dark
    Best imitating fly—Michigan Spinner, No. 6 & 8

*Potamanthus distinctus* (Golden Drake)
    Hatch begins in late June
    Duration is 4 weeks
    Peak activity occurs at twilight
    Best imitating fly—Paulinskill or Cream Variant, No. 12

*Ephemera varia* (Yellow Drake)
    Hatch begins in early June
    Duration is 4 weeks
    Peak activity occurs at twilight
    Best imitating flies—Cream Variant or Yellow Drake, No. 10 & 12

*Pteronarcys allonarcys*
    Hatch begins in early July
    Duration is 4 weeks
    Peak activity occurs in the evening
    Best imitating fly—Brown Stonefly, No. 18

Fly hatches occur on many lakes and streams. Good bets to consider would include the Little Calumet River and Trail Creek; the Wabash, Tippecanoe, Kankakee, Ohio, and St. Joseph rivers, and West Fork White River, and East Fork White River.


## IOWA

Iowa has very little to offer stream fishermen looking for fly rod action during hatches. The hatches are there, but are sparse in nature. Trout are scarce and most of the fishing is for largemouth and smallmouth bass, crappie, white bass, and panfish. However, these fish can produce some exciting fly rod sport when an emergence takes place.

*Nemoura delicatula*
    Hatch begins in early April
    Duration is 16 weeks of sporadic activity
    Peak activity occurs in the evening
    Best imitating fly—Brown Stonefly, No. 18

*Nemoura haysi*
    Hatch begins in early April
    Duration is up to 20 weeks
    Peak activity occurs from 6 P.M. to dark
    Best imitating fly—Salmon, No. 18

*Nemoura cinctipes*
    Hatch begins in early April
    Duration is up to 20 weeks of sporadic activity
    Peak activity occurs at dusk
    Best imitating fly—Black Stonefly, No. 16

*Sialis dorsata*
    Hatch begins in early April
    Duration is up to 20 weeks of sporadic activity
    Peak activity occurs at dusk
    Best imitating fly—Western Stonefly, No. 18

*Baetis alius*
    Hatch begins in early May
    Duration is 12 weeks
    Peak activity is sporadic
    Best imitating fly—March Brown, No. 16

*Cinygma dimicki* (Dark Spinner)
    Hatch begins in early May
    Duration is 12 weeks
    Peak activity occurs from 6 P.M. until dark
    Best imitating fly—Rusty Spinner, No. 18

*Pteronarcys nobilis*
    Hatch begins in mid-May
    Duration is 10 weeks
    Peak activity occurs in the evening
    Best imitating fly—Mallard Quill, No. 16

*Perla capitata*
    Hatch begins in mid-June
    Duration is 4 weeks
    Peak activity occurs in the early evening until twilight
    Best imitating fly—Stonefly, No. 16

*Epeorus nitidus* (Dark Red Quill)
    Hatch begins in mid-June
    Duration is 6 weeks
    Peak activity occurs about noon
    Best imitating fly—Red Quill, No. 18

*Epeorus longimanus* (Gordon Quill)
    Hatch begins in mid-June
    Duration is 6 weeks
    Peak activity occurs from noon to 2 P.M.
    Best imitating fly—Gordon Quill, No. 16

*Ephemerella inermis* (Olive Quill)
    Hatch begins in early July
    Duration is 8 weeks
    Peak activity occurs from 11 A.M. to 2 P.M.
    Best imitating fly—Pale Olive Quill, No. 16

*Heptagenia elegantula*
    Hatch begins in early July
    Duration is 8 weeks
    Peak activity occurs from 11 A.M. to 3 P.M.
    Best imitating fly—Dark Gordon Quill, No. 12 & 14

Some of the best hatches take place along the Mississippi River backwaters. Other rivers such as Iowa, Maquoketa, Raccoon, and Cedar produce some insect activity. Good bets to try are some of the larger lakes such as Spirit, Clear, Lost Island, Okoboji, Trumbel, and Storm.


## KANSAS

This state is much the same as Iowa. Largemouth, spotted, and occasionally smallmouth bass will show up in an angler's catch. The bulk of the fishing action revolves around white bass and panfish, and most of the fishing is done in man-made lakes scattered throughout the state.

*Nemoura delicatula*
    Hatch begins in early April
    Duration is 12 to 16 weeks
    Peak activity occurs at dusk
    Best imitating fly—Early Brown Stonefly, No. 18

*Nemoura haysi*
    Hatch begins in early April
    Duration is 20 weeks
    Peak activity occurs from 6 P.M. to dusk
    Best imitating fly—Western Stonefly, No. 16

*Nemoura oregonensis*
Hatch begins in early April
Duration is 20 weeks
Peak activity occurs at twilight
Best imitating fly—Black Stonefly, No. 16

*Nemoura cinctipes*
Hatch begins in early April
Duration is 20 weeks
Peak activity occurs in the evening
Best imitating fly—Mallard Quill, No. 18

*Sialis dorsata*
Hatch begins in early April
Duration is 20 weeks
Peak activity occurs in the evening
Best imitating fly—Stonefly, No. 18

*Baetis alius*
Hatch begins in early May
Duration is 8 weeks
Peak activity is sporadic
Best imitating fly—Brown March, No. 16

*Baetis caurinus*
Hatch begins in early May
Duration is 8 weeks
Peak activity is sporadic
Best imitating fly—Grey Mayfly, No. 16

*Cinygma dimicki* (Dark Spinner)
Hatch begins in early May
Duration is 12 weeks
Peak activity occurs from early afternoon to dusk
Best imitating fly—Rusty Spinner, No. 18

*Pteronarcys nobilis*
Hatch begins in mid-May
Duration is 10 weeks
Peak activity occurs in the evening
Note: An important hatch in this state.
Best imitating fly—Willow, No. 16

*Pteronarcys californica*
>   Hatch begins in early June
>   Duration is 12 to 16 weeks, somewhat sporadic
>   Peak activity occurs in the evening
>   Note: An important hatch for anglers to concentrate on.
>   Best imitating fly—Wulff Stonefly, No. 10 & 12

*Perla capitata*
>   Hatch begins in mid-June
>   Duration is about 12 weeks
>   Peak activity occurs in the evening
>   Best imitating fly—Mallard Quill, No. 16

*Perla kansensis*
>   Hatch begins in mid-June
>   Duration is 6 weeks
>   Peak activity occurs from 7 P.M. to dark
>   Best imitating fly—Brown Stonefly, No. 18

*Epeorus nitidus* (Dark Red Mayfly)
>   Hatch begins in mid-June
>   Duration is 6 weeks
>   Peak activity occurs around noon
>   Best imitating fly—Red Quill, No. 18

*Epeorus longimanus* (Gordon Quill)
>   Hatch begins in mid-June
>   Duration is 6 weeks
>   Peak activity occurs from noon to 2 P.M.
>   Best imitating fly—Gordon Quill, No. 16

*Ephemerella inermis* (Pale Olive Mayfly)
>   Hatch begins in early July
>   Duration is 8 weeks
>   Peak activity is from 10 A.M. to 2 P.M.
>   Note: An important hatch for fishermen.
>   Best imitating fly—Pale Olive Quill, No. 18

*Heptagenia elegantula* (Dark Gordon)
>   Hatch begins in early July
>   Duration is 8 weeks
>   Peak activity is from 11 A.M. to 2 P.M.
>   Best imitating fly—Dark Gordon, No. 18

Some of the best fishing holes in Kansas will support a measure of insect activity. Try Neosho, Marais, Fall, Verdigris, Elk, Caney, Walnut, Solomon, Saline, Spring, and Smokey Hill rivers. Good bets for lake fishing include Kirwin, Webster, Tuttle Creek, Council Grove, Cedar Bluff, Elk City, Melvern, Wilson, Cheney, and Perry reservoirs.

## MICHIGAN

There's not enough that can be said about Michigan's hatches. They are present almost year round, if one wishes to count some of the winter midge hatches. From spring through early fall an angler can find superb fly rod action. Trout available include rainbow, steelhead (lake-run fish), brown, brook, splake, lake, and an occasional tiger trout.

Some of the other Michigan game fish that feed avidly on hatching insects include bluegills, sunfish, largemouth bass, smallmouth bass, yellow perch (on occasion), whitefish, crappie, rock bass, warmouth bass, and others.

The tables that follow are based primarily on the Lower Peninsula. Hatches start about two weeks later in the Upper Peninsula. Cold weather, rain, or a late spring in either area can delay these by at least one week. Bear that in mind when planning a fishing trip to Michigan.

*Baetis vagans* (Blue-Wing Olive)
    Hatch begins in early April
    Duration is 4 months of sporadic activity
    Peak activity occurs on a sporadic basis
    Best imitating fly—Blue-Wing Olive, No. 16 & 18

*Ephemerella subvaria* (Hendrickson)
    Hatch begins in early April
    Duration is 2 months, best fishing at beginning of hatch
    Peak activity occurs about 2 P.M.
    *Note:* This is an important early hatch on most Michigan waters.
    Best imitating flies—Red Quill, Female Hendrickson, or Little Rusty
        Spinner, No. 12 & 14

*Leptophlebia cupida* (Black Quill)
    Hatch begins in early April
    Duration is 4 months of sporadic activity
    Peak activity occurs about 2 P.M.
    Best imitating fly—Black Quill or Whirling Dun, No. 12 or 14

*Paraleptophlebia adoptiva* (Slate-Wing Mahogany Dun)
    Hatch begins in early April
    Duration is 8 weeks
    Peak activity occurs at midday
    Best imitating flies—Dark Blue Quill or Dark Red Quill, No. 18 & 20

*Epeorus vitrea* (Pale Evening Dun)
 Hatch begins in early May
 Duration is 3 months
 Peak activity occurs in late afternoon and early evening
 *Note:* An important hatch for small Mayflies.
 Best imitating flies—Ginger Quill Spinner, Pale Watery Spinner, and
  Little Sulphur Dun, No. 16 & 18

*Ephemera simulans* (Brown Drake)
 Hatch begins in early May
 Duration is 2 months
 Peak activity occurs at twilight
 *Note:* A very important hatch for Michigan trout fishermen.
 Best imitating fly—Brown Drake, No. 12

*Ephemerella invaria* (Hendrickson)
 Hatch begins in early May
 Duration is 2 months
 Peak activity occurs at twilight
 Best imitating fly—Female Hendrickson, No. 12 & 14

*Ephemerella dorothea* (Sulphur Dun)
 Hatch begins in early May
 Duration is about 2 months
 Peak activity occurs at twilight
 *Note:* A very important hatch on trout streams.
 Best imitating flies—Pale Evening Spinner, Male Pale Evening Spinner,
  Pale Watery Dun, or Little Marryatt, No. 14 & 16

*Isonychia bicolor* (Large Mahogany Dun)
 Hatch begins in early May
 Duration is 4 months
 Peak activity occurs in late afternoon and evening
 Best imitating flies—Grey Variant or White-Gloved Howdy, No. 10 & 12

*Siphlonurus rapidus* (Grey Drake)
 Hatch begins in early May
 Duration is 1 month
 Peak activity occurs in late afternoon and early evening
 *Note:* These insects hatch from slow water.
 Best imitating flies—Cahill Quill or Red Quill Spinner, No. 12 & 14

*Siphlonurus quebecensis* (Grey Drake)
 Hatch begins in early to mid-May
 Duration is 1 month
 Peak activity occurs in late afternoon or early evening
 Best imitating flies— Brown Quill Spinner or Red Quill Spinner, No. 12
  & 14

*Stenonema fuscum* (Grey Fox)
>Hatch begins in early to mid-May
>Duration is 2 months
>Peak activity occurs at sporadic intervals, best at twilight
>*Note:* An important hatch.
>Best imitating flies—Ginger Quill Spinner or Grey Fox, No. 12 & 14

*Stenonema vicarium* (March Brown)
>Hatch begins in early May
>Duration is 1 month
>Peak activity occurs at twilight
>Best imitating fly—Grey Fox, No. 12 & 14

*Chimarra* species
>Hatch begins in early May
>Duration is 4 weeks
>Peak activity occurs in late morning or early afternoon
>Best imitating fly—Chimarra Caddis, No. 16 & 18

*Brachycentrus numerosus* (Grannom)
>Hatch begins in May
>Duration is 6 weeks
>Peak activity occurs in late morning and afternoon
>Best imitating flies—Grannom Pupa and Emergent Grannom, No. 10, 12
> & 14

*Ephemera varia* (Yellow Drake)
>Hatch begins in early June
>Duration is 1 month
>Peak activity occurs at twilight
>Best imitating fly—Yellow Drake or Paulinskill, No. 10 or 12

*Ephemerella needhami* (Red Quill)
>Hatch begins in early June
>Duration is 1 month
>Peak activity occurs during late afternoon or early evening
>Best imitating flies—Little Red Quill or Little Rusty Spinner, No. 16 & 18

*Hexagenia limbata* (Giant Michigan Mayfly or—improperly—Michigan
Caddis)
>Hatch begins in mid-June (usually third week)
>Duration is 3 to 4 weeks
>Peak activity occurs after dark until about midnight
>*Note:* One of Michigan's best known hatches and one that produces big
>trout on many streams. Look for this insect to hatch from silty areas
>and slow water.
>Best imitating flies—Dark Michigan Mayfly, Light Michigan Mayfly, or
>Michigan Spinner, No. 6 & 8

*Ephemerella needhami*—male dun

*Potamanthus distinctus* (Paulinskill)
  Hatch begins in early June
  Duration is 1 month
  Peak activity is at dusk and sporadically after dark
  *Note:* Look for hatches to take place from slow, quiet water.
  Best imitating flies—Golden Spinner or Paulinskill, No. 10 & 12

*Stenonema heterotarsale* (Light Cahill)
  Hatch begins in early June
  Duration is 2 months
  Peak activity occurs in late afternoon and early evening
  Best imitating fly—Light Cahill, No. 12 & 14

*Stenonema ithaca* (Light Cahill)
  Hatch begins in early June
  Duration is 1 month
  Peak activity occurs in late afternoon or early evening
  Best imitating fly—Ginger Quill Spinner, No. 12 & 14

*Brachycercus lacustris* (Tiny White-Winged Brown)
  Hatch begins in early July
  Duration is 3 weeks
  Peak activity occurs in early morning
  Best imitating fly—Tiny White-Winged Brown, No. 18 & 20

*Ephemerella lata* (Slate-Wing Olive)
  Hatch begins in early July
  Duration is 5 weeks
  Peak activity occurs in midafternoon
  Best imitating fly—Slate-Wing Olive, No. 12 & 14

*Tricorythodes stygiatus* (Tiny White-Winged Black)
    Hatch begins in mid-July
    Duration is 2 months
    Peak activity occurs at midday
    Best imitating fly—Tiny White-Winged Black, No. 20 & 22

*Tricorythodes minutus*
    Hatch begins the third week in July
    Duration is 8 weeks
    Peak activity occurs at 9:30 A.M. to 10:30 A.M.
    *Note:* This is an important hatch of midges. Many times an emergence
       assumes blanket proportions.
    Best imitating fly—Tiny White-Winged Black, No. 20 & 22

The list of Michigan streams with significant hatches would include the AuSable (and north and south branches), Manistee, Rifle, Pine, Little Manistee, Pere Marquette (and its branches), Sturgeon, Ontonagon, Platte, Betsie, upper Muskegon, Rogue, St. Joseph, Clam, Pigeon, Tahquamenon, and a host of others in both peninsulas. Good lakes with hatches include Green, Duck, Leelanau, Glen, Houghton, Higgins, Burt, Mullett, Gogebic, and many others.

## MINNESOTA

The land of sky-blue waters is one of varied rivers, creeks, lakes, ponds, and backwoods potholes. Trout figure highly in the plans of most Minnesota anglers, and steady, documented fly hatches provide the key to unlocking the secret of rainbows, browns, brookies, lakers, Kamloops rainbows, and Donaldson rainbows (a recent import).

The state boasts more than 10,000 lakes and some 15,000 miles of trout streams—small brushy creeks, large streams running into Lake Superior, and rivers that drain east and west into the Mississippi River.

It should be noted that hatches in northern Minnesota are approximately one to two weeks behind those in southern Minnesota, upon which the following tables are based.

*Toeniopteryx pacifica* (Salmon)
    Hatch begins in early April
    Duration is 16 weeks
    Peak activity is from noon until dark
    Best imitating fly—Western Salmon, No. 14 or 16

*Plecoptera strophopteryx* (Willow)
   Hatch begins in early April
   Duration is 12 weeks
   Peak activity occurs in the evening
   Best imitating fly—Willow Stonefly, No. 14

*Arcynopteryx megarcus* (Stonefly)
   Hatch begins in early May
   Duration is 16 weeks
   Peak activity is at twilight
   Best imitating fly—Mallard Quill, No. 16

*Isogenus chernokrilus*
   Hatch begins in early May
   Duration is 16 weeks
   Peak activity occurs at twilight
   Best imitating fly—Black Stonefiy, No. 16

*Stenonema vicarium* (March Brown)
   Hatch begins in early May
   Duration is 1 month
   Peak activity occurs at twilight
   Best imitating fly—Grey Fox, No. 12 & 14

*Alloperla suwallia*
   Hatch begins in early May
   Duration is 16 weeks
   Peak activity occurs from 6 P.M. until dark
   Best imitating fly—Green Stonefly, No. 16

*Brachycentrus numerosus* (Grannom)
   Hatch begins in May
   Duration is 6 weeks
   Peak activity occurs in late morning and early afternoon
   Best imitating fly—Emergent Grannom, No. 10, 12, & 14

*Ephemera varia* (Yellow Drake)
   Hatch begins in early June
   Duration is 1 month
   Peak activity occurs at twilight
   Best imitating fly—Yellow Drake, No. 10 or 12

*Cinygmula ramaleyi* (Red Quill)
   Hatch begins in early June
   Duration is 4 weeks
   Peak activity occurs in the late morning
   Best imitating fly—Red Quill Spinner, No. 16 & 18

*Epeorus longimanus* (Gordon Quill)
    Hatch begins in early June
    Duration is 8 weeks
    Peak activity occurs from 10 A.M. until 3 P.M.
    Best imitating fly—Gordon Quill, No. 16

*Hexagenia limbata* (Minnesota Caddis)
    Hatch begins in mid-to-late-June
    Duration is 3 weeks
    Peak activity occurs at sundown until midnight
    Best imitating fly—Michigan Spinner, No. 6 & 8

*Ephemerella grandis* (Big Red Quill)
    Hatch begins in early July
    Duration is 8 weeks
    Peak activity occurs from 9 A.M. until 1 P.M.
    Best imitating fly—Red Quill Spinner, No. 10

*Heptagenia elegantula* (Dark Gordon)
    Hatch begins in early July
    Duration is 8 weeks
    Peak activity occurs from 11 A.M. until 2 P.M.
    Best imitating fly—Dark Gordon Spinner, No. 18

*Paraleptophlebia packii* (Iron Quill)
    Hatch begins in early July
    Duration is 8 weeks
    Peak activity is in the late morning and sporadic after that
    Best imitating flies—Dark Blue Quill or Iron Blue Dun, No. 16 & 18

*Callibaetis pallidus* (Ginger Quill)
    Hatch begins in mid-July
    Duration is 6 weeks
    Peak activity is sporadic
    Best imitating fly—Ginger Quill, No. 16

*Callibaetis americanus* (Grey Mayfly)
    Hatch begins in late July
    Duration is 8 weeks
    Peak activity occurs from 1 P.M. until dark
    Best imitating fly—Black Quill, No. 16

The best bets for locating some of these hatches would be on the St. Croix, Baptism, Brule, Knife, Sucker, Root, Straight, St. Louis, Mississippi (upper reaches), and Whitewater rivers. Many streams in the southeast and southwest portions of the state have excellent hatches.

## MISSOURI

Trout fishing in the "show me" state is confined primarily to stocked rainbows. Some stream fishing occurs, but many trout are planted into the larger lakes and impoundments.

Other species available that offer promise to fly-fishermen include bluegill, largemouth bass, smallmouth bass, white bass, crappie, rock bass, and to a lesser degree, channel catfish.

The climate in Missouri is such that the following tables will apply to hatches anywhere in the state.

*Nemoura delicatula*
    Hatch begins in early April
    Duration is 14 weeks
    Peak activity occurs at dusk
    Best imitating fly—Early Brown Stonefly, No. 18

*Nemoura haysi*
    Hatch begins in early April
    Duration is 20 weeks
    Peak activity occurs from 6 P.M. until dark
    Best imitating fly—Black Stonefly, No. 16

*Nemoura oregonensis*
    Hatch begins in early April
    Duration is 20 weeks
    Peak activity occurs just before dark
    Best imitating fly—Willow, No. 18

*Sialis dorsata*
    Hatch begins in early April
    Duration is 20 weeks
    Peak activity occurs in the evening
    Best imitating fly—Mallard Quill, No. 18

*Baetis alius*
    Hatch begins in early May
    Duration is 8 to 12 weeks
    Peak activity is sporadic
    Best imitating fly—March Brown, No. 16

*Baetis caurinus*
    Hatch begins in early May
    Duration is 8 to 12 weeks
    Peak activity is sporadic
    Best imitating fly—Grey Mayfly, No. 18

*Heptagenia dimicki* (Dark Spinner)
 Hatch begins in early May
 Duration is 12 weeks
 Peak activity occurs from early afternoon until dark
 Best imitating fly—Rusty Spinner, No. 18

*Cinygmula ramaleyi* (Red Quill)
 Hatch begins in early May
 Duration is 8 to 12 weeks
 Peak activity occurs at midday
 Best imitating flies—Dark Red Quill and Red Quill Spinner, No. 16 & 18

*Epeorus nitidus* (Dark Red May)
 Hatch begins in mid-June
 Duration is 6 weeks
 Peak activity occurs at noon
 Best imitating fly—Red Quill, No. 18

*Epeorus longimanus* (Gordon Quill)
 Hatch begins in mid-June
 Duration is 6 weeks
 Peak activity occurs from 11 A.M. to 2 P.M.
 Best imitating fly—Gordon Quill, No. 16

*Perla capitata*
 Hatch begins in mid-June
 Duration is 16 weeks
 Peak activity occurs at dusk
 Best imitating fly—Black Stonefly, No. 18

*Perla kansensis* (Brown Stone)
 Hatch begins in mid-June
 Duration is 6 weeks
 Peak activity occurs from 7 P.M. until dark
 Best imitating fly—Brown Stonefly, No. 16

*Ephemerella inermis* (Pale Olive Mayfly)
 Hatch begins in early July
 Duration is 8 weeks
 Peak activity occurs from 10 A.M. until 3 P.M.
 Best imitating fly—Pale Olive Quill, No. 18

*Heptagenia elegantula* (Dark Gordon)
 Hatch begins in early July
 Duration is 8 weeks
 Peak activity occurs from 11 A.M. to 3 P.M.
 Best imitating fly—Dark Gordon Quill, No. 12 & 14

The hottest and safest bets for rainbow trout are in Bennet Spring, Montauk, Roaring, Capps, Niangua, Roubidoux, and Eleven Point rivers or creeks. Good trout fishing takes place at Lake Taneycomo and Bull Shoals Lake. Streams with other species include Osage, Platte, Nodaway, Lamine, South Grand, Gasconade, Fox, North, Missouri, Mississippi, Cuivar, Jacks Fork, Huzzah, Elk, Chariton, Wyaconda, and James rivers.

## NEBRASKA

Nebraska offers a flatland type of trout fishing, primarily in creeks and rivers. It's often thought that this prairie state has little water, but actually it boasts more than 11,000 miles of streams and some 3,000 lakes.

Nebraska also offers fly-fishermen a crack at largemouth and small-mouth bass, crappie, white bass, bluegill, and channel catfish.

The table that follows applies to rivers, streams, and lakes throughout the state.

*Baetis alius*
  Hatch begins in late April or early May
  Duration is 12 weeks
  Peak activity is sporadic
  Best imitating fly—March Brown, No. 16

*Nemoura delicatula*
  Hatch begins in April
  Duration is 12 weeks
  Peak activity occurs at twilight
  Best imitating fly—Brown Stonefly, No. 16

*Nemoura haysi*
  Hatch begins in April
  Duration is 20 weeks
  Peak activity occurs just before dark
  Best imitating fly—Mallard Quill, No. 18

*Nemoura oregonensis*
  Hatch begins in April
  Duration is 20 weeks
  Peak activity occurs from 6 P.M. to dusk
  Best imitating fly—Grey Stonefly, No. 18

*Nemoura cinctipes*
    Hatch begins in April
    Duration is 20 weeks
    Peak activity occurs in the evening
    Best imitating fly—Wulff Stonefly, No. 16

*Baetis caurinus*
    Hatch begins in early May
    Duration is 12 weeks
    Peak activity is sporadic
    Best imitating fly—Grey Mayfly, No. 18

*Heptagenia dimicki* (Dark Spinner)
    Hatch begins in early May
    Duration is 12 weeks
    Peak activity occurs from early afternoon until dusk
    Best imitating fly—Rusty Spinner, No. 18

*Cinygmula ramaleyi* (Red Quill)
    Hatch begins in early May
    Duration is 8 to 12 weeks
    Peak activity occurs from 8 A.M. until 1 P.M.
    Best imitating fly—Red Quill Spinner, No. 18

*Brachycentrus americanus*
    Hatch begins in May
    Duration is sporadic
    Peak activity takes place in the afternoon
    Best imitating flies—Goddard Caddis and Bucktail Caddis, No. 10 & 12

*Pteronarcys nobilis*
    Hatch begins in mid-May
    Duration is 10 weeks
    Peak activity occurs at twilight
    Best imitating fly—Yellow Stonefly, No. 16

*Pteronarcys californica*
    Hatch begins in early June
    Duration is 12 to 16 weeks
    Peak activity occurs from 6 P.M. until dark
    Best imitating fly—Black Stonefly, No. 14

*Perla capitata*
    Hatch begins in early June
    Duration is 12 to 16 weeks
    Peak activity occurs in the evening
    Best imitating fly—Brown Stonefly, No. 16

*Perla kansensis*
>Hatch begins in early June
>Duration is 6 to 8 weeks
>Peak activity occurs at twilight
>Best imitating fly—Mallard Quill, No. 16

*Epeorus nitidus* (Dark Red Mayfly)
>Hatch begins in mid-June
>Duration is 6 weeks
>Peak activity occurs from 11 A.M. to 1 P.M.
>Best imitating fly—Red Quill Spinner, No. 18

*Epeorus longimanus* (Gordon Quill)
>Hatch begins in mid-June
>Duration is 6 weeks
>Peak activity occurs at noon
>Best imitating fly—Gordon Quill Spinner, No. 16

*Clioperla ebria*
>Hatch begins in late June
>Duration is 4 weeks
>Peak activity occurs at dusk
>Best imitating fly—Wulff Stonefly, No. 16

*Ephemerella inermis* (Pale Olive Spinner)
>Hatch begins in early July
>Duration is 8 weeks
>Peak activity occurs from 10 A.M. to 1 P.M.
>Best imitating fly—Olive Quill Spinner, No. 16

*Heptagenia elegantula* (Dark Gordon)
>Hatch begins in early July
>Duration is 8 weeks
>Peak activity occurs from 11 A.M. to 2 P.M.
>Best imitating fly—Dark Gordon Spinner, No. 18

Look for insect activity to occur on South Loup, North Platte, White, Snake, Dismal, Niobara rivers and Otter, Deer, Long Pine, and Hot creeks. Other likely places include Lake McConaughy and Chadron Water Supply Reservoir.

## NORTH DAKOTA

This state has little to offer trout fishermen. It does have some good hatches. The principal game fish that feed on insects are bluegill, crappie, and white bass.

The table that follows applies to matching hatches anywhere in the state.

*Toeniopteryx pacifica* (Salmon Fly)
    Hatch begins in late March or early April
    Duration is 16 weeks
    Peak activity occurs from noon to dark
    *Note:* An important hatch in this state.
    Best imitating fly—Salmon Fly, No. 16

*Plecoptera strophopteryx* (Willow-Stonefly)
    Hatch begins in late March or early April
    Duration is 12 weeks
    Peak activity occurs at dusk
    Best imitating fly—Willow Fly, No. 14

*Arcynopteryx megarcys*
    Hatch begins in early May
    Duration is 16 weeks
    Peak activity occurs at dusk
    Best imitating fly—Brown Stonefly, No. 14

*Alloperla suwallia*
    Hatch begins in early May
    Duration is 16 weeks
    Peak activity occurs from 6 P.M. to dark
    Best imitating fly—Black Stonefly, No. 14

*Perla claassenia*
    Hatch begins in June
    Duration is 8 weeks
    Peak activity occurs at dusk
    Best imitating fly—Mallard Quill, No. 14

*Cinygmula ramaleyi* (Red Quill)
    Hatch begins in early June
    Duration is 7 weeks
    Peak activity occurs in late morning
    Best imitating fly—Red Quill Spinner, No. 16 & 18

*Epeorus longimanus* (Red Quill Spinner)
    Hatch begins in early June
    Duration is 8 weeks
    Peak activity occurs from 10 A.M. to 2 P.M.
    Best imitating flies—Female Red Quill Spinner and Red Quill Spinner,
      No. 12 & 14

*Ephemerella grandis* (Great Red Quill)
    Hatch begins in early July
    Duration is 8 weeks
    Peak activity occurs in late morning
    Best imitating flies—Dark Great Red Quill and Great Red Quill, No. 10

*Heptagenia elegantula* (Dark Gordon)
    Hatch begins in early July
    Duration is 8 weeks
    Peak activity occurs from noon to 3 P.M.
    Best imitating fly—Dark Gordon Quill, No. 12 & 14

*Paraleptophlebia packii* (Iron Quill)
    Hatch begins in early July
    Duration is 8 weeks
    Peak activity is sporadic all day
    Best imitating flies—Iron Blue Dun or Dark Blue Quill, No. 16 & 18

*Callibaetis pallidus* (Ginger Quill)
    Hatch begins in mid-July
    Duration is 6 weeks
    Peak activity occurs at sporadic intervals
    Best imitating flies—Ginger Quill Spinner or Pale Olive Quill, No. 14 &
        16

*Callibaetis americanus* (Gray Mayfly)
    Hatch begins in late July
    Duration is 8 weeks
    Peak activity occurs from 1 P.M. to dark
    Best imitating fly—Black Quill, No. 16

The hottest action on the above hatches occurs with panfish. I recommend the Little Missouri River, Douglas Creek, Lake Ashtabula, Heart Butte Reservoir, Jamestown Reservoir, Danzig Reservoir, Lake Darling, Garrison Reservoir, and Cedar Lake.


## OHIO

This Great Lakes state offers relatively little trout fishing. The Mad River, however, is one of the best streams in the state, both for rainbow and brown trout and for insect hatches.

Other species of interest to fly-fishermen are crappie, bluegill, white bass, sunfish, rock bass, warmouth bass, and occasionally yellow perch and channel catfish.

The table listed below applies to fly hatches anywhere in Ohio. A cold snap in the spring could delay hatches somewhat, but these are pretty close in all respects.

*Epeorus pleuralis* (Blue Dun)
    Hatch begins in late April
    Duration is 4 weeks
    Peak activity is from noon to 2 P.M.
    *Note:* The most important of the early hatches.
    Best imitating fly—Gordon Quill, No. 12

*Paraleptophlebia adoptiva* (Iron Blue Dun)
    Hatch begins in late April
    Duration is 4 weeks
    Peak activity occurs from 11 A.M. to dusk
    Best imitating flies—Dark Blue Quill and Dark Red Quill, No. 18 & 20

*Iron fraudator* (Dark Gordon)
    Hatch begins in late April
    Duration is 4 weeks
    Peak activity occurs at midday
    Best imitating flies—Dark Gordon Quill and Gordon Quill, No. 12 & 14

*Ephemerella subvaria* (Hendrickson)
    Hatch begins in late April
    Duration is 5 weeks
    Peak activity occurs from noon to 3 P.M.
    *Note:* An important early hatch on Ohio streams.
    Best imitating fly—Hendrickson, No. 14

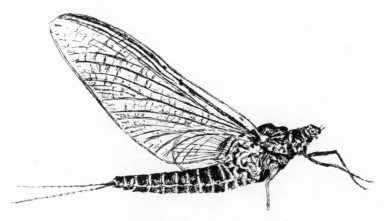

*Ephemerella subvaria*—female spinner

*Leptophlebia cupida* (Dark Hendrickson)
  Hatch begins in late April
  Duration is 4 weeks
  Peak activity occurs from 2 P.M. to dark
  Best imitating fly—Whirling Dun or Black Quill, No. 12 or 14


*Stenonema vicarium* (March Brown)
  Hatch begins in early May
  Duration is 4 weeks
  Peak activity occurs in the evening
  Best imitating fly—American March Brown, No. 10 or 12


*Stenonema fuscum* (Ginger Quill)
  Hatch begins in mid-May
  Duration is 4 weeks
  Peak activity is sporadic
  Best imitating fly—Grey Fox, No. 12


*Ephemera guttulata* (Green Drake)
  Hatch begins in late May
  Duration is 4 weeks
  Peak activity occurs in the evening
  *Note:* An important hatch of big Mayflies.
  Best imitating flies—Male Green Drake and Female Green Drake, No. 8 &
    10


*Isonychia bicolor* (Gray Variants)
  Hatch begins in late May
  Duration is 14 weeks
  Peak activity occurs from 5 P.M. to dark
  Best imitating fly—Grey Variant, No. 10 & 12


*Hexagenia recurvata* (Brown Drake)
  Hatch begins in early June
  Duration is 8 weeks
  Peak activity occurs just before and after dark
  *Note:* An important hatch on both lakes and streams.
  Best imitating fly—Brown Drake, No. 10


*Leptophlebia johnsoni* (Dark Iron Blue Dun)
  Hatch begins in early June
  Duration is 4 weeks
  Peak activity occurs from 11 A.M. to 2 P.M.
  Best imitating fly—Blue Quill Spinner, No. 16

*Stenonema canadense* (Light Cahill)
    Hatch begins in late June
    Duration is 4 weeks
    Peak activity occurs at twilight
    Best imitating fly—Light Cahill, No. 14

*Hexagenia limbata* (Michigan Caddis)
    Hatch begins in late June
    Duration is 4 weeks
    Peak activity occurs from twilight to midnight
    *Note:* An important early summer hatch. Good for big fish.
    Best imitating fly—Michigan Spinner, No. 6 & 8

*Potamanthus distinctus* (Creamy Dun)
    Hatch begins in late June
    Duration is 4 weeks
    Peak activity occurs at twilight
    Best imitating fly—Golden Spinner, No. 12

*Ephemera varia* (Yellow Drake)
    Hatch begins in early July
    Duration is 4 weeks
    Peak activity occurs in the evening
    Best imitating fly—Yellow Drake, No. 12

The Mad River is Ohio's best trout stream. Others that produce good-to-excellent fishing include Chagrin River, Conneaut Creek, Rocky River, Arcola Creek, and Turkey Creek. Trout are also found in Punderson, Turkey Creek, Wolf Run, Belmont, Dow, Monroe, and Fork Run lakes and in Jackson City and Barnesville reservoirs.

## SOUTH DAKOTA

The Black Hills area of South Dakota produces most of this state's trout. Numerous man-made lakes allow fly-fishermen to zero in on rainbow, brown, and brook trout. All these waters are stocked, trout populations that are established feed heavily on fly hatches.

Hatch information given below applies to the whole state but particularly to those lakes and streams in the Black Hills.

*Acroneuria pacifica* (Willow)
    Hatch begins in late March or early April
    Duration is 16 weeks
    Peak activity occurs from 1 P.M. to dusk
    Best imitating fly—Salmon, No. 16

*Nemoura linda*
 Hatch begins in early May
 Duration is 20 weeks
 Peak activity occurs from 6 P.M. to dark
 Best imitating fly—Mallard Quill, No. 16

*Neoperla clymeme* (Yellow Stonefly)
 Hatch begins in mid-June
 Duration is 8 to 10 weeks
 Peak activity occurs at dusk
 Best imitating fly—Yellow Stonefly, No. 18

*Cinygmula ramaleyi* (Red Quill)
 Hatch begins in early June
 Duration is 8 weeks
 Peak activity occurs from late morning to noon
 Best imitating fly—Red Quill Spinner, No. 16

*Epeorus longimanus* (Gordon Quill)
 Hatch begins in early June
 Duration is 8 weeks
 Peak activity occurs from 10 A.M. to 1 P.M.
 Best imitating fly—Gordon Quill, No. 18

*Ephemerella grandis* (Western Green Drake)
 Hatch begins in early July
 Duration is 8 weeks
 Peak activity occurs from 10 A.M. to 2 P.M.
 Best imitating fly—Red Quill Spinner or Green Drake, No. 8 or 10

*Paraleptophlebia packii* (Iron Quill)
 Hatch begins in early July
 Duration is 8 weeks
 Peak activity is sporadic
 Best imitating fly—Blue Quill Spinner, No. 16

*Heptagenia elegantula* (Dark Gordon)
 Hatch begins in early July
 Duration is 8 weeks
 Peak activity occurs from 11 A.M. to 2 P.M.
 Best imitating fly—Dark Gordon Quill, No. 16

*Pycnopsyche* species
 Hatch begins in August
 Duration is 8 weeks
 Peak activity occurs in early evening and at night
 Best imitating fly—Brown Sedge, No. 10 or 12

The best South Dakota fly-fishing occurs on Rapid Creek and Spearfish Creek. Trout have been planted in Sheridan, Sylvan, and Center lakes, and Deerfield Reservoir. Pactola Reservoir is another good bet for anglers.

## WISCONSIN

This midwestern state has some of the finest hatches and trout fishing known to man. Many of its thousands of miles of streams are seldom fished. Those near Madison in the southern portion have excellent hatches, and a man could fish out his lifetime without scratching the surface of possibilities.

Thousands of lakes are available, from massive Lakes Michigan and Superior, to small trout-only or "two-story" lakes containing both trout and warm-water species.

Hatch times can vary as much as seven to fourteen days between an emergence in the south and a similar one in the north. The schedules that follow are for the southern region. Take this into account and plan accordingly when fishing northern Wisconsin streams.

*Paraleptophlebia adoptiva* (Early Blue Quill)
    Hatch begins in early March on southern limestone streams
    Duration is 4 to 6 weeks
    Peak activity occurs from 10 A.M. to 3 P.M.
    *Note:* This is an excellent early season hatch.
    Best imitating flies—Dark Blue Quill or Dark Red Quill, No. 18 & 20

*Baetis vagans* (Blue-Wing Olive)
    Hatch begins in early April
    Duration is about 4 weeks
    Peak activity occurs from 10 A.M. to 6 P.M.
    *Note:* Feeding trout often prefer this hatch over other insects emerging at the same time.
    Best imitating flies—Little Dun or Rusty Spinner, No. 18

*Chimarra* species
    Hatch begins in April
    Duration is sporadic
    Peak activity occurs from late morning to early afternoon
    Best imitating fly—Chimarra Caddis, No. 18 & 20

*Epeorus pleuralis* (Quill Gordon)
  Hatch begins in mid-April
  Duration is 4 weeks
  Peak activity occurs from 1 to 4 P.M.
  Best imitating fly—Quill Gordon, No. 12 & 14

*Ephemerella subvaria* (Hendrickson)
  Hatch begins in late April
  Duration is 6 weeks
  Peak activity occurs between 2 and 4 P.M.
  *Note:* One of the most important spring hatches.
  Best imitating fly—Hendrickson, No. 12 & 14

*Leptophlebia cupida* (Black Quill)
  Hatch begins in late April
  Duration is sporadic, into August
  Peak activity occurs in mid-May around noon
  Best imitating fly—Black Quill Spinner, No. 12 & 14

*Baetis cingulatus* (Blue-Wing Olive)
  Hatch begins in mid-May
  Duration is sporadic, into August
  Peak activity occurs in the afternoon and evening
  Best imitating fly—Blue-Wing Olive, No. 20 & 22

*Baetis levitans* (Blue-Wing Olive)
  Hatch begins in mid-May
  Duration continues into August with sporadic hatches
  Peak activity occurs in the afternoon and evening
  Best imitating fly—Blue-Wing Olive, No. 22 & 24

*Ephemerella dorothea* (Sulphur Dun)
  Hatch begins in mid-May
  Duration is 10 weeks
  Peak activity occurs at midday and later as water warms
  Best imitating fly—Little Marryatt, No. 16 & 18

*Stenonema vicarium* (March Brown)
  Hatch begins in mid-May
  Duration is 4 weeks
  Peak activity occurs at 10 A.M.
  Best imitating fly—March Brown, No. 12

*Acroneuria ruralis* (Yellow Stonefly)
  Hatch begins in late May
  Duration is 3 months
  Peak activity occurs from 3 P.M. to dark
  Best imitating fly—Mallard Quill, No. 18

*Siphlonurus* species (Gray Drake)
    Hatch begins in late May
    Duration shows heaviest activity into July
    Peak activity occurs sporadically
    Best imitating fly—Brown Quill Spinner, No. 10 & 12

*Stenonema fuscum* (Grey Fox)
    Hatch begins in late May
    Duration is 6 weeks
    Peak activity occurs in late afternoon or early evening
    Best imitating fly—Grey Fox, No. 10

*Acroneuria internata* (Dark Grey Stonefly)
    Hatch begins in early June
    Duration is 2 months
    Peak activity occurs at twilight
    Best imitating fly—Mallard Quill, No. 16

*Stenonema ithaca* (Light Cahill)
    Hatch begins in mid-June
    Duration is 6 weeks
    Peak activity occurs at twilight
    *Note:* An important hatch.
    Best imitating fly—Ginger Quill Spinner, No. 12 & 14

*Ephemerella cornuta*
    Hatch begins in June
    Duration is 6 weeks
    Peak activity occurs sporadic
    Best imitating fly—Blue-Wing Olive, No. 12 & 14

*Epeorus vitrea* (Pale Evening Dun)
    Hatch begins in early June
    Duration is 1 month
    Peak activity is in the evening
    Best imitating fly—Pale Evening Dun, No. 10 or 12

*Isonychia bicolor* (Slate Drake)
    Hatch begins in mid-to late June
    Duration is 8 weeks
    Peak activity occurs just before dark (spinnerfall)
    Best imitating fly—Spent Slate Drake Spinner, No. 10 or 12

*Isonychia sadleri* (Great Mahogany Drake)
    Hatch begins in mid-June
    Duration is 4 weeks
    Peak activity occurs in the evening
    Best imitating fly—Dun Variant, No. 8

*Ephemera simulans*
>    Hatch occurs in June
>    Duration is 2 to 3 weeks
>    Peak activity occurs in the evening
>    Best imitating fly—Brown Drake, No. 10 or 12

*Hexagenia recurvata* (Dark Green Drake)
>    Hatch begins in June
>    Duration is 6 to 8 weeks
>    Peak activity occurs at dusk or after dark
>    *Note:* This is Wisconsin's largest Mayfly. Trout love it.
>    Best imitating fly—Dark Green Drake, No. 2 to 6

*Hexagenia limbata* (Michigan Caddis)
>    Hatch begins about third week in June in south
>    Duration is 8 weeks
>    Peak activity occurs at dusk and on until midnight
>    *Note:* A solid hatch of big flies, one that turns on trophy browns.
>    Best imitating fly—Michigan Spinner, No. 4 to 8

*Potomanthus distinctus* (Cream Dun)
>    Hatch begins end of June
>    Duration is 6 weeks
>    Peak activity occurs in late afternoon, at dusk, or later in warm weather
>    Best imitating fly—Cream Dun, No. 8

*Pseudocloeon anoka* (Tiny Dark Blue-Wing Olive)
>    Hatch begins in late June
>    Duration is 6 to 8 weeks. Look for second hatch in September.
>    Peak activity occurs in evening or on overcast days after 11 A.M.
>    Best imitating fly—Dark Blue-Wing Olive, No. 24

*Baetis levitans*
>    Hatch can occur all summer
>    Peak activity occurs in late afternoon or evening
>    Best imitating fly—Gray-Olive, No. 22 & 24

*Ephemera varia* (Yellow Drake)
>    Hatch begins in July
>    Duration is 6 weeks
>    Peak activity occurs from 6 P.M. until after dark
>    Best imitating fly—Yellow Drake, No. 10 & 12

*Ephemerella lata*
>    Hatch begins in July
>    Duration is 5 weeks
>    Peak activity occurs from 7 to 9 A.M.
>    Best imitating fly—Blue-Wing Olive, No. 18

*Tricorythodes* species
     Hatches begin in mid-July
     Duration is 2 months
     Peak activity occurs early in morning. Can blanket surface of river.
     *Note:* Great late-season hatch. Provides good, morning fishing.
     Best imitating fly—Tiny White-Wing Black, No. 24 to 28

*Baetis hiemalis*
     Hatch begins in September
     Duration is 6 weeks
     Peak activity occurs in the afternoon
     Best imitating fly—Slate-Wing Olive, No. 14

One of the biggest problems facing fly-fishermen in Wisconsin is determining where to fish. These spots are good for trout: Bad River, Neenah Creek, Butternut Creek, Trout Brook, Bark River, Brule River, Fish Creek, Reiboldt's Creek, Hibbards Creek, Sioux River, Siskowitt River, Little Brule River, Pokegama Creek, Nebagamon Creek, Heins Creek, Whitefish Bay Creek, Ahnapee River, Kewaunee River, Manitowoc River, Cranberry River, and hundreds of other streams.

# 10

## Western Hatches

Many western areas have fantastic hatches. I've seen clouds of Salmon Flies moving upstream on Colorado rivers that would boggle your mind. Trout are slashing, dimpling, rolling and nymphing as they feed. At times like this every angler should be able to catch fish, but, sad to say, some miss the boat and fail miserably.

Much of the secret to success is one's ability to offer fish a reasonable imitation of the natural dun or spinner. This is easier said than done and I've failed as often as other anglers. The key to unlocking the secret of these hatches is to gain an insight into the approximate times when each insect emerges. This too is difficult, because many western hatches are sporadic. A hatch that normally comes off in early July may be delayed for up to two weeks because of prevailing weather conditions or other factors.

Study the following charts, learn the habits and *normal* emergence dates for each insect, and then plan to be in the proper place at the expected date. Many trips planned around one emergence will fail simply because of the marked difference in hatching times from one river to another, or from one state to another.

### ALASKA

This northern-most state has some excellent fly hatches but weather plays a significant role in timing and productivity. Alaska has several regions, each with differing weather conditions, lake and stream conditions, and hatch times. Conditions can vary from a moderate climate in the Panhandle area to severe cold, snow, and low temperatures in mountainous areas.

Some of the best fishing occurs in the Panhandle where moderating currents offshore temper the existing weather conditions. The hatch information that follows is based on hatches in this area. Readers are advised to add one to two weeks to these emergence dates if fishing in mountainous or more northerly areas.

*Cinygmula ramaleyi* (Red Quill)
>   Hatch begins in early May
>   Duration of hatch is 12 weeks
>   Peak activity occurs from 8 A.M. to noon
>   *Note:* Hatches occur over a gravel bottom.
>   Best imitating fly—Red Quill, No. 18

*Isoperla signata* (Light Stonefly)
>   Hatch begins in early May
>   Duration of hatch is 16 weeks
>   Peak activity occurs in the evening
>   *Note:* Look for hatches over gravel bottom.
>   Best imitating fly—Early Brown Stonefly, No. 14

*Alloperla suwallia* (Stonefly)
>   Hatch begins in early May
>   Duration of hatch is 16 weeks
>   Peak activity occurs at dusk
>   *Note:* Gravel areas produce the best hatches.
>   Best imitating fly—Western Stonefly, No. 14

*Ephemerella walshi* (Brown Quill)
>   Hatch begins in early June
>   Duration of hatch is 20 weeks
>   Peak activity occurs in the evening
>   *Note:* Gravel areas produce the best hatch.
>   Best imitating fly—Brown Quill, No. 18

*Ephemerella tibiaus* (Mayfly)
>   Hatch occurs in early June
>   Duration of hatch is 20 weeks
>   Peak activity occurs in the evening
>   Best imitating fly—Ginger Quill, No. 18

*Baetis bicaudatus* (Rusty May or Rusty Spinner)
>   Hatch occurs in early June
>   Duration of hatch is 8 weeks
>   Peak activity occurs between 11 A.M. and 3 P.M.
>   Best imitating fly—Brown Quill, No. 16

*Callibaetis pallidus* (Ginger Quill)
    Hatch occurs in mid-June
    Duration of hatch is 6 weeks
    Peak activity is sporadic
    Best imitating fly—Ginger Quill, No. 16

*Siphlonurus validus* (Grey Mayfly—drake)
    Hatch occurs in mid-June
    Duration of hatch is 6 weeks
    Peak activity occurs in the evening
    Best imitating fly—Rusty Grey Spinner, No. 18

*Siphlonurus parameletus* (Mayfly)
    Hatch occurs in mid-June
    Duration of hatch is 4 weeks
    Peak activity occurs in the evening
    Best imitating fly—Grey Mayfly, No. 18

*Rhithrogena undulata* (Mayfly)
    Hatch occurs late in June
    Duration of hatch is 16 weeks
    Peak activity occurs in the evening
    Best imitating fly—Red Quill, No. 16

*Paraleptophlebia memorialis* (Mayfly)
    Hatch occurs early in July
    Duration of hatch is 10 weeks
    Peak activity occurs in the midafternoon
    Best imitating fly—Blue Quill, No. 18

*Ephemerella inermis* (Pale Olive Mayfly)
    Hatch occurs early in July
    Duration of hatch is 8 weeks
    Peak activity is from 10 A.M. to 2 P.M.
    Best imitating fly—Pale Olive Quill, No. 18

*Ephemerella verruca* (Olive Mayfly)
    Hatch occurs early in July
    Duration of hatch is 8 weeks
    Peak activity occurs from 10 A.M. to 3 P.M.
    Best imitating fly—Olive Quill, No. 18

*Ephemerella grandis* (Big Red Quill)
    Hatch occurs in early July
    Duration of hatch is 8 weeks
    Peak activity is sporadic
    Best imitating fly—Red Quill, No. 10

*Ephemerella doddsi* (Gray Spinner)
Hatch occurs in early July
Duration of hatch is 8 weeks
Peak activity is sporadic
Best imitating fly—Great Red Spinner or Quill Spinner, No. 16

Some insect activity has been found on the Naha, Karta, Situk, Eagle, Snake, Petersburg, Anchor, Deep, Karluk, Naknek, Sitkoh, and Ninilchik rivers and creeks. Periodic hatches can occur on Chickako, Star, Two, Wildhorse, Henderson, Muskiki, and Rat Lakes.

## ARIZONA

This semiarid southwestern state is often overlooked by fly-fishermen with their sights set on western streams. Few anglers consider fly hatches of major importance in Arizona, and trout are a distant thought.

The fact is that Arizona does have some trout fishing, and good sport at that. The best chances for hitting the emergences listed below occur in the northeast corner of the state. Good hatches are also found on some lakes in the White Mountains.

The tables of emergence information listed below apply to the whole state. A late spring can delay a hatch, but usually not more than one week.

*Chaoboridae eurorethra* (Phantom Midge)
Hatch occurs in early April
This hatch occurs daily
Best imitating fly—Black Gnat, No. 22

*Blephariceridae agathon* (Net-Wing Midge)
Hatch occurs in early April
Hatch occurs daily
Best imitating fly—Midge, No. 22

*Pteronarcys californica* (Dark Brown Stonefly)
Hatch occurs in late May
Duration of hatch is 14 weeks
Peak activity occurs at twilight
Best imitating fly—Early Brown Stonefly, No. 18

*Pteronarcella badia* (Black Stonefly)
      Hatch occurs in late May
      Duration of hatch is 8 weeks
      Peak activity occurs at 7 P.M. to dark
      Best imitating fly—Black Stonefly, No. 16

*Cinygmula ramaleyi* (Red Quill)
      Hatch occurs in late May
      Duration of hatch is 8 weeks
      Peak activity occurs at 9 A.M. to noon
      Best imitating fly—Red Quill Spinner, No. 18

*Perlodes signata* (Hagen Stone)
      Hatch occurs in early June
      Duration of hatch is 8 weeks
      Peak activity occurs at 6 P.M. to dusk
      Best imitating fly—Mallard Quill, No. 16

*Epeorus longimanus* (Gordon)
      Hatch occurs in mid-June
      Duration of hatch is 6 weeks
      Peak activity occurs at 11 A.M. to 1 P.M.
      Best imitating fly—Gordon Quill, No. 18

*Ephemerella infrequins* (Hendrickson)
      Hatch occurs in mid-June
      Duration of hatch is 6 weeks
      Peak activity occurs at 11 A.M. to 1 P.M.
      Best imitating fly—Rusty Spinner, No. 16

*Nemoura linda* (Stonefly)
      Hatch occurs in late June
      Duration of hatch is 16 weeks
      Peak activity occurs at dusk
      Best imitating fly—Grey Stonefly, No. 16

*Nemoura mogollonica* (Stonefly)
      Hatch occurs in late June
      Duration of hatch is 14 weeks
      Peak activity occurs at evening
      Best imitating fly—Willow, No. 18

*Nemoura glacier* (Stonefly)
      Hatch occurs in late June
      Duration of hatch is 14 weeks
      Peak activity occurs at evening
      Best imitating fly—Wulff Stonefly, No. 16

*Epeorus nitidus* (Dark Red Mayfly)
    Hatch occurs in early June
    Duration of hatch is 8 weeks
    Peak activity occurs at midday
    Best imitating fly—Red Quill, No. 20

*Ephemerella grandis* (Big Red)
    Hatch occurs in early July
    Duration of hatch is 8 weeks
    Peak activity occurs in late morning
    Best imitating fly—Red Spinner, No. 10

*Ephemerella inermis* (Pale Olive Mayfly)
    Hatch occurs in early July
    Duration of hatch is 8 weeks
    Peak activity occurs at 10 A.M. to 1 P.M.
    Best imitating fly—Pale Olive Quill, No. 18

*Heptagenia elegantula* (Dark Gordon)
    Hatch occurs in early July
    Duration is 8 weeks
    Peak activity occurs from noon to 3 P.M.
    Best imitating fly—Dark Gordon, No. 16

*Epeorus albertae* (Pink Lady)
    Hatch occurs in early July
    Duration of hatch is 8 weeks
    Peak activity occurs in the evening
    Best imitating fly—Pink Lady, No. 16

*Paraleptophlebia packii* (Iron Mayfly)
    Hatch occurs in early July
    Duration is 8 weeks
    Peak activity is sporadic
    Best imitating fly—Blue Quill, No. 18

*Stenophylax* (Caddis or Brown Sedge)
    Hatch occurs in early July
    Duration is 8 weeks
    Peak activity occurs in the evening
    Best imitating fly—Brown Sedge, No. 10

*Nemoura venusta* (Stonefly)
    Hatch occurs in early August
    Duration of hatch is 4 weeks
    Peak activity occurs at twilight
    Best imitating fly—Mallard Quill, No. 18

*Nemoura tumana* (Stonefly)
  Hatch occurs in early August
  Duration is 4 weeks
  Peak activity occurs at twilight
  Best imitating fly—Brown Stonefly, No. 16

Some good hatches have been noted on the White, Colorado, Little Colorado, and Verde rivers; Oak and Tonto creeks; and Nuna, Becker, Big Rainbow, and Lee Valley lakes; and in the reservoirs behind Glen Canyon Dam, the Grand Canyon Dam, and on Lake Powell and Lake Mohave.

## CALIFORNIA

This western state holds plenty of promise for fly-fishermen. Unfortunately, many anglers think of trout fishing in California only in terms of standing knee-deep in a rushing steelhead stream. Such is not always the case because a veritable wealth of hatches come off at pretty regular schedules. This enables the student of this book to zero in on some truly fantastic sport.

Rainbow, brown, brook, cutthroat, and lake trout are the predominant species, but some golden trout are found in high alpine lakes. Numerous streams, plus vast lakes, offer challenging possibilities.

*Hexagenia limbata* (Caddis)
  Hatch occurs in early mid-March
  Duration is 8 weeks, sporadically
  Peak activity occurs in the morning hours
  Best imitating fly—Michigan Caddis, No. 8 or 10

*Cinygmula ramaleyi* (Red Quill Spinner)
  Hatch occurs in mid-March
  Duration of hatch 8 weeks
  Peak activity occurs in the late morning
  Best imitating fly—Red Quill

*Peltoperudae yoraperla* (Stonefly)
  Hatch occurs February to April
  Peak activity occurs from dawn to 10 A.M.
  Best imitating fly—Brown Stonefly, No. 18

*Peltoperudae sierraperla*
  Hatch occurs from March through June
  Peak activity occurs from dawn to 9 A.M.
  Best imitating fly—Black Stonefly, No. 16

*Peltoperudae brevis*
>Hatch occurs mid-April
>Duration of hatch is 3 months
>Peak activity occurs at dawn
>Best imitating fly—Salmon Fly, No. 16 or 18

*Peltoperlidae quadrispinula*
>Hatch occurs mid-April
>Duration of hatch is 12 to 14 weeks
>Peak activity occurs from dawn to 10 A.M.
>Best imitating fly—Mallard Quill

*Nemoura visoka*
>Hatch occurs mid-April
>Duration of hatch 8 to 10 weeks
>Peak activity occurs in the early morning
>Best imitating fly—Mallard Quill

*Nemoura soyedina*
>Hatch occurs in April
>Duration of hatch is 12 weeks
>Peak activity occurs in the early morning
>Best imitating fly—Brown Stonefly

*Nemoura producta*
>Hatch occurs in April
>Duration of hatch is 12 weeks
>Peak activity occurs from dawn to 9 A.M.
>Best imitating fly—Black Stonefly

*Nemoura nevadensis*
>Hatch occurs in mid-April
>Duration of hatch 12 to 14 weeks
>Peak activity occurs from 7 A.M. to 10 A.M.
>Best imitating fly—Western Salmon Fly

*Nemoura frigida*
>Hatch occurs in mid-April
>Duration of hatch 10 weeks
>Peak activity occurs from dawn to 11 A.M.
>Best imitating fly—Willow Fly

*Nemoura cinctipes*
>Hatch occurs mid-April
>Duration of hatch 10 weeks
>Peak activity occurs from dawn to 10 A.M.
>Best imitating fly—Mallard Quill

*Sialis nevadensis* (Alder)
    Hatch occurs early April
    Duration of hatch 4 to 6 weeks
    Peak activity occurs from 11 A.M. to 2 P.M.
    Best imitating fly—Brown Alder Fly, No. 14

*Sialis rotunda* (Alder)
    Hatch occurs early April
    Duration of hatch 4 to 6 weeks
    Peak activity occurs from noon to 3 P.M.
    Best imitating fly—Dark Alder, No. 12

*Sialis occidens*
    Hatch occurs in mid-April
    Duration of hatch 4 weeks
    Peak activity occurs from 10 A.M. to 3 P.M.
    Best imitating fly—Brown Alder, No. 12

*Rhyacophila acropodes* (Brown Caddis)
    Hatch occurs end April
    Duration of hatch 4 weeks
    Peak activity occurs at dusk
    Best imitating fly—Dark Grannom, No. 16

*Rhyacophila agapetus*
    Hatch occurs end of April
    Duration of hatch 5 weeks
    Peak activity occurs at dusk
    Best imitating fly—Dark Sedge, No. 18

*Rhyacophila glossosoma*
    Hatch occurs end of April
    Duration of hatch 5 or 6 weeks
    Peak activity occurs at twilight
    Best imitating fly—Brown Caddis, No. 18

*Chimarra* species
    Hatch occurs end of April
    Duration of hatch 3 weeks
    Peak activity occurs at dusk
    Best imitating fly—Dark Brown Sedge

*Chimarra wormaldia*
    Hatch occurs end of April
    Duration of hatch 6 to 8 weeks
    Peak activity occurs from 5 P.M. to dark
    Best imitating fly—Black Sedge, No. 16

*Rhyacophila palaeagapetus*
    Hatch occurs in May
    Duration of hatch 4 weeks
    Peak activity occurs from 4 P.M. to dark
    Best imitating fly—Black Caddis, No. 16

*Rhyacophila protoptila*
    Hatch occurs in May
    Duration of hatch 4 weeks
    Peak activity occurs at dusk
    Best imitating fly—Brown Sedge, No. 20

*Odontoceridae mariua*
    Hatch occurs early in May
    Duration of hatch 6 to 8 weeks
    Peak activity occurs at dusk
    Best imitating fly—Dark Sedge

*Brachycentrus microsema* (Grannom)
    Hatch occurs in early May
    Duration of hatch 4 weeks
    Peak activity occurs at twilight
    Best imitating fly—Grannom, No. 10, 12, & 14

*Epeorus albertae*
    Hatch occurs early May
    Duration of hatch 4 weeks
    Peak activity occurs at twilight
    Best imitating fly—Pink Lady, No. 16 & 18

*Epeorus longimanus* (Gordon)
    Hatch occurs early May
    Duration of hatch 4 weeks
    Peak activity occurs at twilight
    Best imitating flies—Gordon Quill or Red Quill Spinner, No. 12 & 14

*Ephemerella hecuba*
    Hatch occurs early May
    Duration of hatch 4 weeks
    Peak activity occurs at twilight
    Best imitating fly—Dark Quill

*Ephemerella pelosa*
    Hatch occurs mid-May
    Duration of hatch 4 to 6 weeks
    Peak activity occurs from noon to 2 P.M.
    Best imitating fly—Dark Brown Quill, No. 12 & 14

*Brachycentrus oligopleltrum*
>   Hatch occurs in mid-May
>   Duration of hatch 3 to 5 weeks
>   Peak activity occurs at dusk
>   Best imitating fly—Dark Grannom, No. 10, 12, & 14

*Capniinae maculata*
>   Hatch occurs in May
>   Duration of hatch 8 weeks
>   Peak activity occurs from dawn to 11 A.M.
>   Best imitating fly—Tiny Dark Stonefly, No. 20

*Capnia spinulosa*
>   Hatch occurs early May
>   Duration of hatch 8 weeks
>   Peak activity occurs from 7 A.M. to 11 A.M.
>   Best imitating fly—Brown Stonefly, No. 18

*Capnia Barberi*
>   Hatch occurs in early May
>   Duration of hatch 8 weeks
>   Peak activity occurs at dawn to noon
>   Best imitating fly—Little Black Stonefly, No. 18

*Capnia columbiana*
>   Hatch occurs mid-May
>   Duration of hatch 6 weeks
>   Peak activity occurs dawn to 10 A.M.
>   Best imitating fly—Mallard Quill, No. 18

*Capnia grandis*
>   Hatch occurs mid-May
>   Duration of hatch 6 weeks
>   Peak activity occurs from 7 A.M. to 11 A.M.
>   Best imitating fly—Brown Stonefly, No. 18

*Sialis arvalis*
>   Hatch occurs early May
>   Duration of hatch 4 weeks
>   Peak activity occurs from 10 A.M. to 3 P.M.
>   Best imitating fly—Alder, No. 14

*Sialis californica*
>   Hatch occurs early mid-May
>   Duration of hatch 4 to 6 weeks
>   Peak activity occurs from 11 A.M. to 4 P.M.
>   Best imitating fly—Alder, No. 14-16

*Psychomyiidae psychomyia*
    Hatch occurs mid-May
    Duration of hatch 8 weeks
    Peak activity occurs at dusk
    Best imitating fly—Small Caddis, No. 20

*Psychomyiidae tinodes*
    Hatch occurs mid-May
    Duration of hatch 8 weeks
    Peak activity occurs at dusk
    Best imitating fly—Dark Caddis Quill, No. 18

*Hydropsyche* (Micro Caddis)
    Hatch occurs mid-May
    Duration of hatch 6 to 8 weeks
    Peak activity occurs from 6 P.M. to dark
    Best imitating fly—Brown Caddis, No. 20

*Choroterpes terratoma*
    Hatch occurs in late May
    Duration of hatch 4 weeks
    Peak activity occurs from 10 A.M. to 1 P.M.
    Best imitating fly—Olive Quill

*Peltoperlidae peltoperla*
    Hatch occurs end May
    Duration of hatch 4 weeks
    Peak activity occurs at early morning
    Best imitating fly—Dark Emerald Stonefly

*Peltoperlidae zipha*
    Hatch occurs end May
    Duration of hatch 6 to 8 weeks
    Peak activity occurs at dawn
    Best imitating fly—Brown Quill

*Peltoperlidae soliperla*
    Hatch occurs end May
    Duration of hatch 6 to 8 weeks
    Peak activity occurs at dawn
    Best imitating fly—Willow

*Nemoura ostrocerca*
    Hatch occurs end of May to early June
    Duration of hatch 4 to 6 weeks
    Peak activity occurs from 9 A.M. to 11 A.M.
    Best imitating fly—Mallard Quill

*Nemoura paranemoura*
   Hatch occurs end of May to early June
   Duration of hatch 4 to 6 weeks
   Peak activity occurs at dawn
   Best imitating fly—Salmon

*Nemoura tumana*
   Hatch occurs end of May to early June
   Duration of hatch 8 to 10 weeks
   Peak activity occurs from dawn to 10 A.M.
   Best imitating fly—Black Stonefly

*Tanyderidae protoplasa* (Crane)
   Hatch occurs early June
   Duration of hatch all summer
   Peak activity occurs from early morning to dark
   Best imitating fly—Badger Spider

*Tanyderidae protanyderus* (Crane)
   Hatch occurs early June
   Duration of hatch all summer
   Peak activity occurs from noon to dark
   Best imitating fly—Black Spider

*Tipula dorsimacula* (Crane)
   Hatch occurs early June
   Duration all summer
   Peak activity occurs from noon to dark
   Best imitating fly—Red Variant

*Namamyia* species
   Hatch occurs mid-June
   Duration of hatch 8 weeks
   Peak activity occurs at twilight
   Best imitating fly—Dark Sedge

*Odontoceridae nerophilus*
   Hatch occurs mid-June
   Duration of hatch 4 weeks
   Peak activity occurs from 6 P.M. to dark
   Best imitating fly—Dark Caddis, No. 12

*Odontoceridae parthina*
   Hatch occurs in mid-to-late June
   Duration of hatch 4 weeks
   Peak activity occurs from 6 P.M. to dark
   Best imitating fly—Dark Blue Sedge

*Lepidostoma athripsodes*
    Hatch occurs mid-to-late June
    Duration of hatch 8 weeks
    Peak activity occurs at dusk
    Best imitating fly—Dark Caddis

*Lepidostoma mystacides*
    Hatch occurs mid-to-late June
    Duration of hatch 8 weeks
    Peak activity occurs at dusk
    Best imitating fly—Small Brown Sedge

*Lepidostoma oecetis disjuncta*
    Hatch occurs late June
    Duration of hatch 4 weeks
    Peak activity occurs at twilight
    Best imitating fly—Willow Caddis

*Lepidostoma triaenodes*
    Hatch occurs late June
    Duration of hatch 4 weeks
    Peak activity occurs at twilight
    Best imitating fly—Dark Brown Caddis

*Brachycentrus americanus*
    Hatch occurs early June
    Duration of hatch 4 to 6 weeks
    Peak activity occurs at twilight
    Best imitating fly—Dark Brown Sedge, No. 18 or 20

*Nemoura columbiana*
    Hatch occurs late June
    Duration of hatch 4 weeks
    Peak activity occurs from 10 A.M. to noon
    Best imitating fly—Mallard Quill

*Nemoura haysi*
    Hatch occurs late June
    Duration of hatch 8 weeks
    Peak activity occurs at dawn to noon
    Best imitating fly—Green Stonefly, No. 16

*Nemoura amphinemoura*
    Hatch occurs late June
    Duration of hatch 8 weeks
    Peak activity occurs at dawn to 9 A.M.
    Best imitating fly—Salmon Fly

*Nemoura malenka*
    Hatch occurs early July
    Duration of hatch 12 weeks
    Peak activity occurs from 8 A.M. to 11 A.M.
    Best imitating fly—Willow Fly, No. 8 & 10

*Nemoura biloba*
    Hatch occurs early July
    Duration of hatch 12 weeks
    Peak activity occurs from 7 A.M. to noon
    Best imitating fly—Mallard Quill

*Nemoura depressa*
    Hatch occurs early July
    Duration of hatch 12 to 16 weeks
    Peak activity occurs from 7 A.M. to 11 A.M.
    Best imitating fly— Brown Stonefly

*Nemoura besametsa*
    Hatch occurs early July
    Hatch duration is all summer
    Peak activity occurs from dawn to 10 A.M.
    Best imitating fly—Salmon Fly, No. 8

*Nemoura delicatula*
    Hatch occurs mid-July
    Duration of hatch is all summer
    Peak activity occurs from dawn to noon
    Best imitating fly—Mallard Quill, No. 16

*Leuctrinae glabra* (Needle, Stonefly)
    Hatch occurs mid-July
    Duration of hatch 6 to 8 weeks
    Peak activity occurs from dawn to 10 A.M.
    Best imitating fly—Mallard Quill, No. 16

*Leuctrinae paraleuctra*
    Hatch occurs mid-July
    Duration of hatch 8 to 10 weeks
    Peak activity occurs from dawn to 10 A.M.
    Best imitating fly—Dark Gray Quill

*Leuctrinae claasseni*
    Hatch occurs mid-July
    Duration of hatch 8 to 10 weeks
    Peak activity occurs from dawn to 9 A.M.
    Best imitating fly—Dark Brown Stonefly, No. 16

*Leuctrinae moselia*
  Hatch occurs late July
  Duration of hatch 6 to 8 weeks
  Peak activity occurs from dawn to 9 A.M.
  Best imitating fly—Brown Stonefly, No. 18

*Leutrinae bradleyi*
  Hatch occurs late July
  Duration of hatch 6 to 8 weeks
  Peak activity occurs from 9 A.M. to noon
  Best imitating fly—Grey Quill, No. 18

*Leuctrinae sara*
  Hatch occurs late July
  Duration of hatch 8 to 10 weeks
  Peak activity occurs from 7 A.M. to 11 A.M.
  Best imitating fly—Brown Quill, No. 16

*Leuctrinae forcipata*
  Hatch occurs late July
  Duration of hatch 8 to 10 weeks
  Peak activity occurs from dawn to noon
  Best imitating fly—Dark Stonefly, No. 18

Good insect activity has been found on Willow, Red Rock, Horse, Owens, Butte, Mill, Middle Fork, Bear, Pine, Trinity, Ash, Butte, Yuba, Klamath, Salmon, Squaw, San Joaquin, Shasta, Joaquin, Sacramento, Rubicon, Merced, Truckee, Eel, Scott, Mattole, Smith, Mad, Russian, Garcia, and Kern rivers. Some good hatches can periodically be found on Shasta, Folsom, Pine, Isabella, Millerton, and Twitchell lakes.

## COLORADO

Colorado is a state with numerous trout fishing possibilities. Rivers and streams offer exciting hatches for the visiting or local angler to consider. Hatches, by and large, are pretty dependable, with the possible except of those occurring at high elevations.

The western two-thirds of Colorado is full of highly rated streams such as the Gunnison, Frying Pan, Taylor, and others equally famous for their fly hatches. The salmon fly hatch on the Gunnison has provided me with exceptional fishing over the years.

Hatches listed below are relatively stable and usually occur every year within seven days of the previous year's emergences. I would add a week to ten days to the dates listed below for hatches occurring at elevations over 6,000 feet.

*Nemoura delicatula* (Stonefly)
 Hatch occurs early April
 Duration of hatch 12 to 16 weeks
 Peak activity occurs at twilight
 Best imitating fly—Brown Stonefly, No. 16

*Nemoura haysi* (Stonefly)
 Hatch occurs early April
 Duration of hatch 16 to 20 weeks
 Peak activity occurs from 5 P.M. to dark
 Best imitating fly—Black Stone fly, No. 16

*Nemoura oregonensis* (Oregon Stonefly)
 Hatch occurs early April
 Duration of hatch 20 weeks
 Peak activity occurs at sunset
 Best imitating fly—Mallard Quill, No. 16

*Nemoura cinctipes* (Stonefly)
 Hatch occurs early April
 Duration 20 weeks
 Peak activity occurs at dusk
 Best imitating fly—Yellow Stonefly, No. 16

*Visoka cataractae* (Stonefly)
 Hatch occurs mid-April
 Duration of hatch 16 weeks
 Peak activity occurs from 6 P.M. to 9 P.M.
 Best imitating fly—Wulff Stonefly, No. 14

*Nemoura cecepta* (Light Brown Stonefly)
 Hatch occurs late April
 Duration of hatch 16 to 18 weeks
 Peak activity occurs at twilight
 Best imitating fly—Brown Stonefly, No. 16

*Nemoura californica* (California Stonefly, Brown)
 Hatch occurs early May
 Duration of hatch 20 to 24 weeks
 Peak activity occurs from 6 P.M. to dusk
 Best imitating fly—Brown Stonefly, No. 16

*Nemoura linda* (Stonefly)
    Hatch occurs in late May
    Duration of hatch 16 weeks
    Peak activity occurs from 7 P.M. to 10 P.M.
    Best imitating fly—Mallard Quill, No. 18

*Amphinemura-ris* (Dusky Brown Stonefly)
    Hatch occurs late May
    Duration of hatch 20 to 22 weeks
    Peak activity occurs at dusk
    Best imitating fly—Brown Stonefly, No. 16

*Sympetrum atripes* (Damselfly)
    Hatch occurs early May to June
    Duration is all summer
    Hatch occurs all day
    Best imitating fly—Blue Blackwing, No. 12

*Plathemis subornata* (Dragonfly)
    Hatch occurs early May to June
    Duration is all summer
    Hatch is sporadic, all day
    Best imitating fly, No. 10 Black Damselfly

*Somatochlora charadroea* (Flying Needle)
    Hatch occurs early May to June
    Duration is all summer
    Hatch is sporadic, all day
    Best imitating fly—Blue Blackwing, No. 12

*Raphidia bicolor* (Snake)
    Hatch occurs early May to June
    Duration is all summer
    Hatch is sporadic, all day
    Best imitating fly—Dragonfly, No. 10

*Hemerobiidae boriomyia* (Brown Lacewing)
    Hatch occurs early May to June
    Duration is all summer
    Peak activity occurs at dusk
    Best imitating fly—Brown Blackwing, No. 12

*Aedes squamiger* (Marsh Midge, Mosquito)
    Hatch occurs early May to June
    Duration of hatch all summer
    Hatch is sporadic, all day
    Best imitating fly—Badger Midge, No. 20

*Leptoconops torrens* (No-see-um)
    Hatch occurs early May to June
    Duration of hatch is all summer
    Hatch is sporadic, all day
    Best imitating fly—Claret Smut, No. 22

*Nemoura coloradensis* (Colorado Stonefly)
    Hatch occurs early June
    Duration of hatch is 8 to 12 weeks
    Peak activity occurs at dusk
    Best imitating fly—Mallard Quill, No. 16

*Malenka tina* (Stonefly)
    Hatch occurs early June
    Duration of hatch 8 to 12 weeks
    Peak activity occurs at twilight
    Best imitating fly—Wulff Stonefly, No. 18

*Limnephilus abbreviatus* (Caddis)
    Hatch occurs early June
    Duration of hatch 4 to 6 weeks
    Peak activity occurs in the evening
    Best imitating fly—Brown Caddis, No. 10

*Limnephilus coloradensis* (Colorado Caddis)
    Hatch occurs early June
    Duration is 8 weeks
    Peak activity occurs at dusk
    Best imitating fly—Grannom, No. 12

*Anabolina brevipennis* (Caddis)
    Hatch occurs early June
    Duration of hatch 4 to 8 weeks
    Peak activity occurs at dusk
    Best imitating fly—Caddis Quill, No. 12

*Neoperla clymene* (Yellow Stonefly)
    Hatch occurs mid-June
    Duration of hatch 8 to 10 weeks
    Peak activity occurs from 6 P.M. to dark
    Best imitating fly—Yellow Stonefly, No. 16

*Isogenus elongatus* (Black Stonefly)
    Hatch occurs late June
    Duration of hatch 8 to 10 weeks
    Peak activity occurs from 8 P.M. to dark
    Best imitating fly—Black Stonefly No. 16

*Hexagenia limbata* (Big Mayfly)
    Hatch occurs sporadically, all summer
    Duration is all summer
    Peak activity occurs from 7 P.M. to dark
    Best imitating fly—Hare's Ear, No. 14

*Ephemera infrequens* (Hendrickson)
    Hatch occurs in July
    Duration of hatch 3 weeks
    Peak activity occurs in late morning
    Best imitating fly—Hendrickson, No. 12 & 14

*Leptophlebiidae cupida* (Western Mayfly)
    Hatch occurs late July
    Duration of hatch 8 to 12 weeks
    Peak activity occurs from 10 A.M. to midday
    Best imitating fly—Yellow Mayfly, No. 16

*Leptophlebiidae gravastella* (Mayfly)
    Hatch occurs late July
    Duration of hatch 8 to 12 weeks
    Peak activity occurs from 10 A.M. to midday
    Best imitating fly—Paulinskill, No. 18

*Baetis tricaudatus* (Red Summer Mayfly)
    Hatch occurs late July
    Duration of hatch 4 weeks
    Peak activity occurs from 10 A.M. to 2 P.M.
    Best imitating fly—Pink Lady, No. 18

*Ametropus albarda* (Mayfly)
    Hatch occurs late July
    Duration of hatch 4 weeks
    Peak activity occurs at midday
    Best imitating fly—Watery Dun, No. 18

*Ephemerella inermis* (Pale Olive Quill)
    Hatch occurs July and early August
    Duration of hatch 6 weeks
    Peak activity occurs from 10 A.M. to 1 P.M.
    Best imitating fly—Pale Olive Quill, No. 12 & 14

*Hydropsyche gracilis* (Caddis)
    Hatch occurs mid-July
    Duration of hatch 6 to 8 weeks
    Peak activity occurs at twilight
    Best imitating fly—Adams, No. 12

*Sericostomitidae similis* (Caddis)
  Hatch occurs mid-July
  Duration of hatch 6 to 8 weeks
  Peak activity occurs at twilight
  Best imitating fly—Whitecraft, No. 10

*Rhyacophilia hyalinata* (Case)
  Hatch is sporadic all summer
  Peak activity occurs at dusk
  Best imitating fly—Blue Artman, No. 14

*Stenonema verticus* (Ginger Quill)
  Hatch occurs in August
  Duration of hatch 3 weeks
  Peak activity occurs in late afternoon and evening
  Best imitating fly—Ginger Quill Spinner, No. 14 & 16

*Callibaetis americanus* (Grey Quill)
  Hatch occurs in August
  Duration of hatch 2 to 3 weeks
  Peak activity occurs in afternoon
  Best imitating fly—Grey Quill, No. 16

*Callibaetis pallidus*
  Hatch occurs in August
  Duration of hatch is 2 weeks
  Hatch is sporadic during the day
  Best imitating fly—Pale Olive Quill, No. 14 & 16

*Heptagenia elegantula*
  Hatch occurs in August
  Duration of hatch 2 to 3 weeks
  Peak activity occurs from 11 A.M.
  Best imitating fly—Dark Gordon Quill, No. 12 & 16

*Epeorus albertae*
  Hatch occurs in August
  Duration of hatch 2 to 3 weeks
  Peak activity occurs at twilight
  Best imitating fly—Male Salmon Spinner, No. 16 & 18

*Ephemerella inermis*
  Hatch occurs in August
  Duration of hatch 2 weeks
  Peak activity occurs in the morning and at twilight
  Best imitating fly—Pale Olive Quill, No. 12 & 14

*Dicosmoecus (Orange Sedge)*
    Hatch occurs in September
    Duration of hatch about 4 weeks
    Peak activity occurs in the late evening
    Best imitating fly—Orange Sedge (wet), No. 6 & 8

I've experienced good hatches on the Roaring, Frying Pan, Gunnison, Taylor, Yampa, Colorado, White, and Arkansas rivers. Some excellent emergences take place on Jefferson, Eleven Mile, Dowdy, Seaman, and Tarryall lakes.

## IDAHO

This mountainous state has something to offer all fly-fishermen. Small streams are available that can offer the headiest challenge a dry-fly man could hope to find. Larger rivers deliver excellent hatches, and many trout lakes have emergences that bring big fish to the surface to feed.

Rainbow, brown, Kamloops, cutthroat, brook, and lake trout are plentiful. A handful of alpine lakes still harbor fair-to-good populations of golden trout, that colorful aristocrat of the craggy peaks. Dolly Varden trout are common in many lakes, and in streams as well.

The northern panhandle of Idaho can have a somewhat later hatch time for many insects. Adding seven days to the dates listed below should put the angler just about on schedule.

*Nemoura barri (Stonefly)*
    Hatch occurs early April
    Duration of hatch 4 weeks
    Peak activity occurs in the evening
    Best imitating fly—Brown Stonefly, No. 16

*Nemoura interrupta (Stonefly)*
    Hatch occurs early April
    Duration of hatch 16 weeks
    Peak activity occurs at twilight
    Best imitating fly—Grey Stonefly, No. 16

*Nemoura tina (Stonefly)*
    Hatch occurs in late May
    Duration of hatch 8 weeks
    Peak activity occurs at dusk
    Best imitating fly—Mallard Quill, No. 18

*Cinygmula ramaleyi* (Red Quill)
Hatch occurs early June
Duration of hatch 8 weeks
Peak activity occurs from 9 A.M. to noon
Best imitating fly—Dark Red Quill, No. 18

*Nemoura coloradensis* (Stonefly)
Hatch occurs early June
Duration of hatch 12 weeks
Peak activity occurs from 6 P.M. to dark
Best imitating fly—Wulff Stonefly, No. 16

*Epeorus nitidus* (Dark Red Mayfly)
Hatch occurs mid-June
Duration of hatch 6 weeks
Peak activity occurs at midday
Best imitating fly—Red Quill, No. 18

*Epeorus longimanus* (Gordon Quill)
Hatch occurs mid-June
Duration of hatch is 6 weeks
Peak activity occurs from noon to 2 P.M.
Best imitating fly—Gordon Quill, No. 16

*Ephemerella infrequens* (Hendrickson)
Hatch occurs mid-June
Duration of hatch 6 weeks
Peak activity occurs from noon to 2 P.M.
Best imitating fly—Rusty Spinner, No. 12

*Ephemerella grandis* (Great Red Mayfly)
Hatch occurs early July
Duration of hatch 8 weeks
Peak activity occurs in the late morning
Best imitating fly—Great Red Spinner, No. 10

*Ephemerella inermis* (Pale Olive Mayfly)
Hatch occurs early July
Duration of hatch 8 weeks
Peak activity occurs from 10 A.M. to 2 P.M.
Best imitating fly—Pale Olive Quill, No. 16

*Epeorus albertae* (Pink Lady)
Hatch occurs early July
Duration of hatch 8 weeks
Peak activity occurs at twilight
Best imitating fly—Pink Lady, No. 16

*Heptagenia elegantula* (Dark Gordon)
    Hatch occurs early July
    Duration of hatch 8 weeks
    Peak activity occurs from noon to 2 P.M.
    Best imitating fly—Dark Gordon, No. 14

*Paraleptophlebia packii* (Iron Quill)
    Hatch occurs early July
    Duration of hatch 8 weeks
    Hatch is sporadic
    Best imitating fly—Blue Quill, No. 18

*Nemoura apache* (Stonefly)
    Hatch occurs early July
    Duration of hatch 8 weeks
    Peak activity occurs at twilight
    Best imitating fly—Brown Stonefly, No. 16

*Perlesta placida* (Stonefly, Brown Stonefly)
    Hatch occurs early July
    Duration of hatch 8 weeks
    Peak activity occurs at twilight
    Best imitating fly—Brown Stonefly, No. 16

*Alloperla pacifica* (Stonefly)
    Hatch occurs early July
    Duration of hatch 8 weeks
    Peak activity occurs from 7 P.M. to dark
    Best imitating fly—Mallard Quill, No. 18

*Callibaetis pallidus* (Ginger Quill)
    Hatch occurs mid-July
    Duration of hatch 6 weeks
    Hatch is sporadic during the day
    Best imitating fly—Pale Olive, No. 16

*Callibaetis americanus* (Grey May)
    Hatch occurs late July
    Duration of hatch 8 weeks
    Peak activity occurs froom noon to dark
    Best imitating fly—Grey Quill, No. 16

*Baetis* species (Blue Quill)
    Hatch occurs late July
    Duration of hatch 4 weeks
    Peak activity occurs from 10 A.M. to 3 P.M.
    Best imitating fly—Blue Mayfly, No. 20

*Siphlonurus occidentalis* (Grey Quill)
    Hatch occurs early August
    Duration of hatch 4 weeks
    Peak activity occurs at twilight
    Best imitating fly—Grey Quill, No. 10

The listing of Idaho's trout streams with reliable hatches is like taking a breath of fresh air. The names connote delightful fly-fishing. Streams like the Henry's Fork, Gray's Lake Outlet, Snake, Salmon, Middle Fork of the Salmon, Clearwater, North Fork of the Clearwater, Little North Fork, Kootenai, Coeur d' Alene, Selway, and Buffalo rivers are famous. Henry's Lake is a favorite for many western anglers. Other good lakes include Priest, Pend Oreille, Coeur d' Alene, and Brownlee Reservoir.

## MONTANA

If I were to rank the states that I'd prefer fishing, Montana would rate No. 1. The streams, rivers, and lakes there offer a wide variety of character, with a sprinkling of spring creeks, large cobblestoned rivers with rushing currents, slow meadow-lined streams, and all set amid a backdrop of Rocky Mountain scenery. The fishing is superb.

Spring, and its hatches, often come late to Montana and few significant hatches are found before June. Hatches worthy of notice include the *Heptagenia elegantula, Ephemerella infrequens, Cinygma dimicki,* and *Rhithrogena futilis* spinner flights.

Regardless of location, the following tables should be as close to the emergence dates as possible. Western hatches are difficult to predict with accuracy, largely because of varying weather patterns.

Montana has a wealth of trout fishing, with the most common species including cutthroat, rainbow, brown, brook, Dolly Varden, and lakers. A remnant population of Montana grayling still exists in the Big Hole and Madison rivers, and in some high mountain lakes in Glacier National Park.

*Nemoura barri* (Stonefly)
    Hatch occurs early April
    Duration of hatch 4 weeks
    Peak activity occurs from 7 P.M. to dusk
    Best imitating fly—Mallard Quill, No. 16

*Nemoura delicatula* (Stonefly)
Hatch occurs early April
Duration of hatch is 20 weeks
Peak activity occurs at twilight
Best imitating fly—Grey Stonefly, No. 14

*Nemoura interrupta* (Stonefly)
Hatch occurs early April
Duration of hatch 16 weeks
Peak activity occurs in late evening
Best imitating fly—Willow, No. 16

*Nemoura tina* (Stonefly)
Hatch occurs late May
Duration of hatch 8 weeks
Peak activity occurs at dusk
Best imitating fly—Wulff Stonefly, No. 14

*Nemoura arctica* (Stonefly)
Hatch occurs late May
Duration of hatch 12 weeks
Peak activity occurs at twilight
Best imitating fly—Green Stonefly, No. 18

*Nemoura coloradensis* (Stonefly)
Hatch occurs early June
Duration of hatch is 12 weeks
Peak activity occurs from 7 P.M. to dark
Best imitating fly—Willow, No. 16

*Cinygmula ramaleyi* (Red Quill)
Hatch occurs early June
Duration of hatch 8 weeks
Peak activity occurs in the late morning
Best imitating fly—Dark Red Quill, No. 18

*Epeorus nitidus* (Dark Red Mayfly)
Hatch occurs mid-June
Duration of hatch 6 weeks
Peak activity occurs from 10 A.M. to 2 P.M.
Best imitating fly—Red Quill Spinner, No. 18

*Epeorus longimanus* (Gordon Quill)
Hatch occurs mid-June
Duration of hatch 6 weeks
Peak activity occurs from noon to 2 P.M.
Best imitating fly—Gordon Quill, No. 16

*Ephemerella infrequens*—male dun

*Ephemerella infrequens* (Hendrickson)
    Hatch occurs mid-June
    Duration of hatch 6 weeks
    Peak activity occurs from noon to 2 P.M.
    Best imitating fly—Rusty Spinner, No. 12

*Ephemerella grandis* (Western Green Drake)
    Hatch occurs early July
    Duration of hatch 8 weeks
    Peak activity occurs in the late morning
    Best imitating fly—Great Red Quill, No. 10

*Ephemerella inermis* (Pale Olive Mayfly)
    Hatch occurs early July
    Duration of hatch 8 weeks
    Peak activity occurs from 10 A.M. to 1 P.M.
    Best imitating fly—Pale Olive Quill, No. 16

*Epeorus albertae* (Pink Lady)
    Hatch occurs early July
    Duration of hatch 8 weeks
    Peak activity occurs at twilight
    Best imitating fly—Pink Lady, No. 16

*Heptagenia elegantula* (Pale Evening Spinner)
    Hatch occurs early July
    Duration of hatch 8 weeks
    Peak activity occurs from noon to 2 P.M.
    Best imitating fly—Dark Gordon Quill, No. 14

*Paraleptophlebia packii* (Iron Quill)
Hatch occurs early July
Duration of hatch 8 weeks
Hatch is sporadic during the day
Best imitating fly—Blue Quill, No. 18

*Cinygma dimicki*
Hatch occurs early July
Duration of hatch 4 weeks
Peak activity occurs in the evening
Best imitating fly—Light Cahill, No. 14

*Rhithrogena futilis*
Hatch occurs early July
Duration of hatch 4 weeks
Peak activity occurs in the evening
Best imitating fly—Quill Gordon, No. 12

*Nemoura apache* (Stonefly)
Hatch occurs early July
Duration of hatch 8 weeks
Peak activity occurs at dusk
Best imitating fly—Mallard Quill, No. 16

*Nemoura banksi* (Stonefly)
Hatch occurs early July
Duration of hatch 10 to 12 weeks
Peak activity occurs from 7 P.M. to dark
Best imitating fly—Black Stonefly, No. 18

*Trichoptera brachycentrus* (Grannon, Caddis)
Hatch occurs early July
Duration of hatch 8 weeks
Peak activity occurs from noon to dusk
Best imitating fly—Grannon, No. 14

*Trichoptera arctopsyche* (Dark Caddis Quill)
Hatch occurs early July
Duration of hatch 8 weeks
Peak activity occurs from noon to dusk
Best imitating fly—Dark Caddis, No. 16

*Nemoura mogollonica* (Stonefly)
Hatch occurs mid-July
Duration of hatch 10 to 12 weeks
Peak activity occurs in the evening
Best imitating fly—Mallard Quill, No. 16

*Trichoptera rhyacophila* (Brown Caddis)
    Hatch occurs mid-July
    Duration of hatch 6 to 8 weeks
    Peak activity occurs from 7 P.M. to dark
    Best imitating fly—Brown Caddis, No. 12

*Trichoptera platyphylax* (Dark Sedge)
    Hatch occurs mid-July
    Duration of hatch 6 to 8 weeks
    Peak activity occurs at twilight
    Best imitating fly—Brown Sedge, No. 8

*Callibaetis pallidus* (Ginger Quill)
    Hatch occurs mid-July
    Duration of hatch 6 weeks
    Hatch is sporadic
    Best imitating fly—Pale Olive Quill, No. 16

*Baetis* species (Blue Quill)
    Hatch occurs late July
    Duration of hatch 4 weeks
    Peak activity occurs from 10 A.M. to 4 P.M.
    Best imitating fly—Blue Quill, No. 20

*Callibaetis americanus* (Grey)
    Hatch occurs late July
    Duration of hatch 8 weeks
    Peak activity occurs from 1 P.M. to dark
    Best imitating fly—Grey Quill, No. 16

*Siphlonurus occidentalis* (Grey Drake)
    Hatch occurs early August
    Duration of hatch 4 weeks
    Peak activity occurs at dusk
    Best imitating fly—Grey May, No. 10

Reliable hatches occur on Spring Creek and Bitteroot, Clark Fork, Gallatin, South Fork Madison, Madison, Missouri, Yellowstone, Big Hole, Ruby, Beaverhead, Two Medicine, Flathead, McDonald, Jefferson, Stillwater, Blackfoot, South Fork Flathead rivers, and Rock Creek. Some hatches occur on Canyon Ferry, Flathead, Georgetown, Bear Paw, and St. Mary's lakes, and some reservoirs along the Missouri River.

## NEVADA

This so-called desert state is not totally lacking in trout fishing. Some fishing takes place in a few lakes and streams. Rainbow, brown, cutthroat, and lake trout are common game fish in these lakes and streams. Hatches are relatively few in comparison with other western states.

Fly-fishing is confined primarily to the few streams or rivers with sufficient flow to encourage insect activity. Hatch dates listed below apply to the entire state with the possible exception of high mountain areas where an emergence may be delayed as much as a week because of cold weather.

*Tanypteryx hageni* (Damselfly)
    Hatch occurs early spring
    Duration is all summer
    Hatch is sporadic all day
    Best imitating fly—Blue Blackwing, No. 12

*Diptera tanyderidae* (Gnat)
    Hatch occurs early spring
    Duration of hatch is all summer
    Hatch is sporadic during the day
    Best imitating fly—Black Gnat, No. 22

*Deuterophlebiidae coloradensis* (Midge)
    Hatch occurs early spring
    Duration of hatch is all summer
    Hatch is sporadic during the day
    Best imitating fly—Fisherman's Curse, No. 22

*Cinygmula ramaleyi* (Red Quill)
    Hatch occurs early June
    Duration of hatch 8 weeks
    Peak activity occurs from 8 A.M. to 11 A.M.
    Best imitating fly—Red Quill, No. 18

*Pteronarcys californica* (Dark Brown Stonefly)
    Hatch occurs early June
    Duration of hatch 12 weeks
    Peak activity occurs in the evening
    Best imitating flies—Stonefly and Early Brown Stonefly, No. 16

*Pteronarcella badia* (Black Stonefly)
    Hatch occurs early June
    Duration of hatch 8 weeks
    Peak activity occurs in the evening
    Best imitating fly—Black Stonefly, No. 16

*Epeorus nitidus* (Dark Red Mayfly)
    Hatch occurs mid-June
    Duration of hatch 6 weeks
    Peak activity occurs at midday
    Best imitating fly—Red Quill, No. 20

*Epeorus longimanus* (Gordon Quill)
    Hatch occurs mid-June
    Duration of hatch 6 weeks
    Peak activity occurs from 11 A.M. to 3 P.M.
    Best imitating fly—Gordon Quill, No. 16

*Ephemerella infrequens* (Hendrickson)
    Hatch occurs mid-June
    Duration of hatch 6 weeks
    Peak activity occurs from 11 A.M. to 3 P.M.
    Best imitating fly—Rusty Spinner, No. 14

*Perlodes signata* (Hagen Stonefly, Brown)
    Hatch occurs mid-June
    Duration of hatch 6 to 8 weeks
    Peak activity occurs from 7 P.M. to dark
    Best imitating fly—Mallard Quill, No. 16

*Ephemerella grandis* (Western Green Drake)
    Hatch occurs early July
    Duration of hatch 8 weeks
    Peak activity occurs in the late morning
    Best imitating fly—Red Spinner, No. 12

*Ephemerella inermis* (Pale Olive Mayfly)
    Hatch occurs early July
    Duration of hatch 8 weeks
    Peak activity occurs from 10 A.M. to 1 P.M.
    Best imitating fly—Pale Olive Quill, No. 18

*Heptagenia elegantula* (Dark Gordon)
    Hatch occurs early July
    Duration of hatch 8 weeks
    Peak activity occurs from noon to 3 P.M.
    Best imitating fly—Dark Gordon Quill, No. 16

*Epeorus albertae* (Pink Lady)
   Hatch occurs early July
   Duration of hatch 8 weeks
   Peak activity occurs at dusk
   Best imitating fly—Pink Lady, No. 16

*Paraleptopalebia packii* (Iron Mayfly)
   Hatch occurs early July
   Duration of hatch 8 weeks
   Hatch is sporadic
   Best imitating fly—Dark Blue Quill, No. 18

*Nemoura linda* (Stonefly)
   Hatch occurs early July
   Duration of hatch 12 weeks
   Peak activity occurs at dusk
   Best imitating fly—Grey Stonefly, No. 16

*Nemoura mogollonica* (Stonefly)
   Hatch occurs early July
   Duration of hatch 12 weeks
   Peak activity occurs from 7 P.M. to dark
   Best imitating fly—Brown Stonefly, No. 14

*Nemoura glacier* (Stonefly)
   Hatch occurs early July
   Duration is 4 weeks
   Peak activity occurs in the evening
   Best imitating fly—Willow, No. 14

*Nemoura venusta* (Stonefly)
   Hatch occurs early August
   Duration of hatch 4 weeks
   Peak activity occurs in the evening
   Best imitating fly—Salmon, No. 14

*Nemoura tumana* (Stonefly)
   Hatch occurs early August
   Duration of hatch 4 weeks
   Peak activity occurs in the evening
   Best imitating fly—Brown Stonefly, No. 16

The best trout fishing and hatches occur on the Truckee, East Walker, West Walker, and Humboldt rivers. Good fishing also takes place on Walker, Topaz, Pyramid, Tahoe lakes, and on Lake Mead.

## NEW MEXICO

This southwest state is considered by many anglers to be arid and without insect activity and trout fishing. This is far from true because New Mexico has an abundance of high mountain streams and lakes that support good fishing for rainbow, brown, and cutthroat.

Much of the better trout and insect activity occurs in the mountainous reaches along the New Mexico–Colorado border. It's here that anglers can find superb fly rod action with trout ranging up to ten pounds.

Because little insect activity takes place in the lower arid areas the tables that follow apply almost solely to trout-rich areas in the mountains.

*Ameletus aequivocus* (Mayfly)
    Hatch occurs early April
    Duration of hatch 12 to 16 weeks
    Peak activity occurs in the evening
    Best imitating fly—Brown Drake, No. 18

*Ameletus ludens* (Mayfly)
    Hatch occurs early April
    Duration of hatch 20 weeks
    Peak activity occurs from 7 P.M. to dark
    Best imitating fly—Grey Drake, No. 16

*Alloperla suwallia* (Stonefly)
    Hatch occurs early April
    Duration of hatch 16 weeks
    Peak activity occurs at dusk
    Best imitating fly—Mallard Quill, No. 16

*Chloroperlidae kathroperla* (Stonefly)
    Hatch occurs early April
    Duration of hatch 16 weeks
    Peak activity occurs at dusk
    Best imitating fly—Wulff Stonefly, No. 16

*Arcynopteryx megarcys* (Stonefly)
    Hatch occurs early April
    Duration of hatch 14 weeks
    Peak activity occurs at twilight
    Best imitating fly—Black Stonefly, No. 16

*Parameletus columbiae* (Mayfly)
Hatch occurs early May
Duration of hatch 8 weeks
Peak activity occurs from 9 A.M. to noon
Best imitating fly—Sulphur Dun, No. 18

*Ametropus albarda* (Mayfly)
Hatch occurs early May
Duration of hatch 12 weeks
Peak activity occurs from 10 A.M. to 2 P.M.
Best imitating fly—Grey Fox, No. 16

*Baetis anachris* (Mayfly)
Hatch occurs early May
Duration of hatch 12 weeks
Peak activity occurs from 10 A.M. to 2 P.M.
Best imitating fly—Gordon Quill, No. 16

*Baetis elachistus* (Mayfly)
Hatch occurs early May
Duration of hatch 12 weeks
Peak activity occurs from 10 A.M. to 2 P.M.
Best imitating fly—Cream Variant, No. 18

*Pteronarcella* (Stonefly)
Hatch occurs early June
Duration of hatch 8 weeks
Peak activity occurs from 7 P.M. to dusk
Best imitating fly—Little Black Stonefly, No. 14

*Peltoperla sierraperla* (Sierra Stonefly)
Hatch occurs early June
Duration of hatch 8 weeks
Peak activity occurs in the evening
Best imitating fly—Big Stonefly, No. 12

*Epeorus namatus* (Red Mayfly)
Hatch occurs mid-June
Duration of hatch 8 weeks
Peak activity occurs at midday
Best imitating fly—Red Quill, No. 18

*Perlidae dononeuria* (Stonefly)
Hatch occurs early July
Duration of hatch 8 weeks
Peak activity occurs from 6 P.M. to dark
Best imitating fly—Black Quill, No. 10-16

*Perlidae neoperla* (Stonefly)
    Hatch occurs early July
    Duration of hatch 8 weeks
    Peak activity occurs from 6 P.M. to dark
    Best imitating fly—Dark Stonefly, No. 10-14

*Stenophylax* (Caddis, Brown Sedge)
    Hatch occurs early July
    Duration of hatch 8 weeks
    Peak activity occurs at dusk
    Best imitating fly—Brown Sedge, No. 10

The best-known trout water in this state is the Rio Grande River. The Box Canyon area is justly famous for big browns and rainbows. Other streams with good hatches include Red, Latir, Costilla, Rio Pueblo, Santa Barbara, Vermejo, Ricardo, Mora, and Pecos rivers. Some good insect activity has been noted on Elephant Butte Lake, Caballo Lake, Hondo Lake, Spirit Lake, Latir Lake, Cabresto Lake, Eagle Nest Lake, Clayton Lake, and Fenton Lake.

## OREGON

This northwestern state has remarkable trout fishing and superb fly hatches. Oregon offers some 15,000 miles of trout streams and literally hundreds of lakes that contain trout and other species.

Trout species available include rainbow, steelhead (sea-going rainbow), cutthroat, sea-run (sea-going cutthroat), brown trout, and brook trout. Brookies seem to fare well in many mountain lakes as well as in some streams.

The hatch information listed below applies to the entire state. Little differences are to be noted with the exception that some streams traditionally have earlier or later emergences.

*Sympetrum atripes* (Damselfly)
    Hatch occurs early spring
    Duration of hatch all summer
    Hatch is sporadic all day
    Best imitating fly—Blue Blackwing, No. 12

*Plathemis subornata* (Dragonfly)
    Hatch occurs early spring
    Duration of hatch all summer
    Hatch is sporadic all day
    Best imitating fly—Grey Damselfly, No. 12

*Raphidia charadroea* (Flying Needle)
    Hatch occurs early spring
    Duration of hatch is all summer
    Hatch is sporadic during the day
    Best imitating fly—Damselfly, No. 14

*Raphidia bicolor* (Snakefly)
    Hatch occurs early spring
    Duration of hatch is all summer
    Hatch is sporadic during the day
    Best imitating fly—Black Lacewing, No. 12

*Adedes squamiger* (Marsh Midge)
    Hatch occurs early spring
    Duration of hatch is all summer
    Hatch is best hit at dusk
    Best imitating fly—Badger Midge, No. 22

*Hexagenia bilineata* (Mayfly)
    Hatch occurs early May
    Duration of hatch is 6 to 8 weeks
    Peak activity occurs at twilight and 10 A.M. to 2 P.M.
    Best imitating fly—Dark Mayfly, No. 18

*Hexagenia variabilis* (Mayfly)
    Hatch occurs early May
    Duration of hatch is 6 to 8 weeks
    Peak activity occurs at twilight to noon
    Best imitating fly—Quill Spinner, No. 20

*Leptophlebia vaciua* (Mayfly)
    Hatch occurs mid-May
    Duration of hatch 14 to 16 weeks
    Peak activity occurs 10 A.M. to 1 P.M.
    Best imitating fly—Brown Quill, No. 16

*Leptophlebia gregaus* (Mayfly)
    Hatch occurs mid-May
    Duration of hatch 6 to 8 weeks
    Peak activity occurs in the late morning
    Best imitating fly—Grey Quill, No. 18

*Callibaetis hageni* (Mayfly)
    Hatch occurs mid-to-late May
    Duration of hatch is 8 weeks
    Peak activity occurs from 9 A.M. to noon
    Best imitating fly—Pale Olive Quill, No. 18

*Callibaetis ferrugineus* (Mayfly)
    Hatch occurs mid-to-late May
    Duration of hatch 8 weeks
    Peak activity occurs at noon
    Best imitating fly—Ginger Quill, No. 20

*Brachycentrus* (Green Caddis)
    Hatch occurs late May or early June
    Duration of hatch 3 weeks
    Peak activity occurs in the late afternoon
    Best imitating fly—McKenzie Special, No. 6 or 8

*Siphlonurus occidentalis* (Grey Drake)
    Hatch occurs early June
    Duration of hatch 4 weeks
    Peak activity occurs from 10 A.M. to 1 P.M.
    Best imitating fly—Blue Quill, No. 18

*Epeorus nitidus* (Iron Mayfly)
    Hatch occurs early June
    Duration of hatch 8 weeks
    Peak activity occurs from noon to dark
    Best imitating fly—Dark Mayfly, No. 20

*Cinygma geminatum* (Little Mayfly)
    Hatch occurs early-to-mid June
    Duration of hatch is 6 to 8 weeks
    Peak activity occurs from 10 A.M. to noon
    Best imitating fly—Dark Quill, No. 18

*Paraperla frontalis* (Big Stonefly)
    Hatch occurs early June
    Duration of hatch 8 to 12 weeks
    Peak activity occurs at dusk
    Best imitating fly—Dark Stonefly, No. 16

*Pteronarcys californica* (Giant Stonefly)
    Hatch occurs early June to July
    Duration of hatch 12 weeks
    Peak activity occurs at dusk
    Best imitating flies—Stonefly Dry, No. 6 or Sofa Pillow, No. 4 & 6

*Nemoura delicatula* (Small Stonefly)
    Hatch occurs early June
    Duration of hatch 8 weeks
    Peak activity occurs at twilight
    Best imitating fly—Yellow Stonefly, No. 16

*Prostoia besametsa* (Stonefly)
Hatch occurs early June
Duration of hatch 8 weeks
Peak activity occurs at twilight
Best imitating fly—Black Stonefly, No. 18

*Visoka cataractae* (Stonefly)
Hatch occurs early June
Duration of hatch 8 weeks
Peak activity occurs from 1 P.M. to dark
Best imitating fly—Mallard Quill, No. 16

*Zapada cinctipes* (Stonefly)
Hatch occurs early June
Duration of hatch 8 weeks
Peak activity occurs from 1 P.M. to dark
Best imitating fly—Wulff Stonefly, No. 18

*Nemoura oregonensis* (Oregon Stonefly)
Hatch occurs early June
Duration of hatch 4 weeks
Peak activity occurs in the evening
Best imitating fly—Ginger Stonefly, No. 16

*Nemoura glacier* (Stonefly)
Hatch occurs mid-June
Duration of hatch 8 weeks
Peak activity occurs in the evening
Best imitating fly—Rusty Stonefly, No. 18

*Nemoura haysi* (Grey Stonefly)
Hatch occurs mid-June
Duration of hatch 8 weeks
Peak activity occurs in the evening
Best imitating fly—Grey Stonefly, No. 16

*Grammotaulius betteni* (Dark Caddis)
Hatch occurs mid-June
Duration of hatch 4 to 6 weeks
Peak activity occurs at dusk
Best imitating fly—Black Caddis, No. 10

*Nerophilus frontalis* (Grey Case)
Hatch occurs mid-June
Duration of hatch 8 weeks
Peak activity occurs in the evening
Best imitating fly—Brown Sedge, No. 12

*Mystacides alafimbriata* (Brown Caddis)
    Hatch occurs mid-June
    Duration of hatch 8 weeks
    Peak activity occurs in the evening
    Best imitating fly—Grannon, No. 12

*Dicosmeocus* (Orange Sedge or Caddis)
    Hatch occurs in October
    Duration of hatch 3 weeks
    Peak activity occurs in the afternoon
    *Note:* Important late-season hatch.
    Best imitating fly—Orange Sedge, No. 12

Hatches of some or all of the above insects have been noted in the Nestucca, Deschutes, Metolius, Williamson, White, Little Deschutes, Rogue, Molalla, Santiam, Clackamas, Umkqua, Chetco, Cooes, Nehalem, Siletz, Sixes, Smiths, Suislaw, Tualatin, Yamhill, Luckiamute, and other rivers.

Some lake fishing is possible during insect activity on Paulina, Diamond, East, Davis, South Twin, Elk, Morgan, Klamath, Big Lava, Crescent, Odell, Big Cultus, and Wallowa lakes.

## UTAH

This state is not known for producing awesome hatches, or for its trout fishing. But Utah does have some excellent emergences and produces some nice trout, even though it is overshadowed by the reputations of Montana, Wyoming, and Idaho.

*Tanypteryx hageni* (Damselfly)
    Hatch occurs early spring
    Duration of hatch is all summer
    Hatch is sporadic during the day
    Best imitating fly—Blue Blackwing, No. 12

*Cinygmula ramaleyi* (Red Quill)
    Hatch occurs early June
    Duration of hatch 8 weeks
    Peak activity occurs from 8 A.M. to 11 A.M.
    Best imitating fly—Red Quill Spinner, No. 18

*Pteronarcys californica* (Western Salmon)
    Hatch occurs early June
    Duration of hatch 12 weeks
    Peak activity occurs in the evening
    Best imitating fly—Salmon, No. 6

*Pteronarcella badia* (Black Stonefly)
    Hatch occurs early June
    Duration of hatch 8 weeks
    Peak activity occurs at twilight
    Best imitating fly—Black Stonefly, No. 14

*Epeorus nitidus* (Dark Red Mayfly)
    Hatch occurs mid-June
    Duration of hatch 6 weeks
    Peak activity occurs at midday
    Best imitating fly—Dark Red Quill, No. 12 & 14

*Epeorus longimanus* (Gordon Quill)
    Hatch occurs mid-June
    Duration of hatch 6 weeks
    Peak activity occurs from 11 A.M. to 2 P.M.
    Best imitating fly—Red Quill Spinner, No. 14

*Ephemerella infrequens* (Hendrickson)
    Hatch occurs mid-June
    Duration of hatch 6 weeks
    Peak activity occurs from 11 A.M. to 2 P.M.
    Best imitating fly—Rusty Spinner, No. 14

*Ephemerella grandis* (Western Green Drake)
    Hatch occurs early July
    Duration of hatch 8 weeks
    Peak activity occurs in the late morning
    Best imitating fly—Red Spinner, No. 14

*Ephemerella inermis* (Pale Olive Mayfly)
    Hatch occurs early July
    Duration of hatch 8 weeks
    Peak activity occurs from 10 A.M. to 2 P.M.
    Best imitating fly—Pale Olive Quill, No. 18

*Heptagenia elegantula* (Dark Gordon)
    Hatch occurs early July
    Duration of hatch 8 weeks
    Peak activity occurs from noon to 2 P.M.
    Best imitating fly—Dark Gordon, No. 16

*Epeorus albertae* (Pink Lady)
   Hatch occurs early July
   Duration of hatch 8 weeks
   Peak activity occurs at dusk
   Best imitating fly—Pink Lady, No. 16

*Paraleptophlebia packii* (Dark Brown Spinner)
   Hatch occurs early July
   Duration of hatch 8 weeks
   Hatch is sporadic during the day
   Best imitating fly—Dark Brown Spinner, No. 18

*Perlodes signata* (Hagen's Stonefly or Brown)
   Hatch occurs early June
   Duration of hatch 6 to 8 weeks
   Peak activity occurs from 7 P.M. to dark
   Best imitating fly—Brown Stonefly, No. 14

*Nemoura linda* (Stonefly)
   Hatch occurs early July
   Duration of hatch 12 weeks
   Peak activity occurs at dusk
   Best imitating fly—Grey Stonefly, No. 16

*Nemoura mogollonica* (Stonefly)
   Hatch occurs early July
   Duration of hatch 12 weeks
   Peak activity occurs from 7 P.M. to dark
   Best imitating fly—Mallard Quill, No. 16

*Nemoura glacier* (Stonefly)
   Hatch occurs early July
   Duration of hatch 4 weeks
   Peak activity occurs in the evening
   Best imitating fly—Wulff Stonefly, No. 18

*Nemoura venusta* (Stonefly)
   Hatch occurs early August
   Duration of hatch 4 weeks
   Peak activity occurs at dusk
   Best imitating fly—Yellow Stonefly, No. 16

*Nemoura tumana* (Stonefly)
   Hatch occurs early August
   Duration of hatch 4 weeks
   Peak activity occurs at dusk
   Best imitating fly—Green Stonefly, No. 16

*Stenonema verticus* (Ginger Quill Spinner)
    Hatch occurs in August
    Duration of hatch 3 weeks
    Peak activity occurs in the late afternoon and early evening
    Best imitating fly—Ginger Quill Spinner, No. 14 & 16

*Epeorus albertae*
    Hatch occurs early August
    Duration of hatch 2 to 3 weeks
    Peak activity occurs at twilight
    Best imitating fly—Pink Lady, No. 16 & 18

Good hatches have been seen on the Green, San Juan, Colorado, Bear, Logan, Blacksmith Fork, Weber, Provo, Duchesne, and Fremont rivers. Some good lake fishing takes place on Bear, Utah, Fish, and the Uinta Mountain lakes and Boulder Mountain lakes, and on such reservoirs as Flaming Gorge and Glen Canyon.

## WASHINGTON

This state offers something to every fly-fisherman. Wide-open choices include rushing streams, fullsize rivers that are host to steelhead and salmon runs, and high mountain lakes. More than 6,000 lakes are available, and many hold trout.

Washington has rainbow, steelhead, four subspecies of cutthroat, brown, brook, golden, Dolly Varden, and lake trout. Limited numbers of grayling are taken from some high country lakes. A sporty fish if taken on light fly tackle is the kokanee, a small fish that provides good sport and fine eating and that is very popular with many Washington anglers.

Very little variation is found in the following hatch charts. The only difference could be a week or 10 days between low-lying streams and lakes and those found in the mountains.

*Malenka californica* (Stonefly)
    Hatch occurs late March
    Duration of hatch is 32 weeks
    Peak activity occurs at twilight
    Best imitating fly—Brown Stonefly, No. 16

*Malenka flexura* (Stonefly)
    Hatch occurs late March
    Duration of hatch 30 weeks
    Peak activity occurs in the evening
    Best imitating fly—Black Stonefly, No. 18

*Deuterophlebiidae deuterophlebia* (Mountain Midge)
    Hatch occurs in the spring
    Duration of hatch is all summer
    Hatch is sporadic and best time is during day
    Best imitating fly—Badger Midge, No. 22

*Blephariceridae agathon* (Net-Wing Midge)
    Hatch occurs in the spring
    Duration is all summer
    Hatch is sporadic
    Best imitating fly—Black Midge, No. 20

*Chaoboridae eucorethra* (Phantom Midge)
    Hatch occurs in the spring
    Duration of hatch is all summer
    Hatch is sporadic
    Best imitating fly—Dun Midge, No. 22

*Ceratopogonidae heleidae* (No-see-um)
    Hatch occurs in the spring
    Duration of hatch is all summer
    Hatch is sporadic
    Best imitating fly—Black Gnat, No. 22

*Prostoia besametsa* (Stonefly)
    Hatch occurs early April
    Duration of hatch 20 weeks
    Peak activity occurs from 7 P.M. to dark
    Best imitating fly—Mallard Quill, No. 16

*Visoka cataractae* (Stonefly)
    Hatch occurs early April
    Duration of hatch is 16 weeks
    Peak activity occurs from 6 P.M. to dusk
    Best imitating fly—Wulff Stonefly, No. 16

*Zapada frigida* (Stonefly)
    Hatch occurs early April
    Duration of hatch 20 weeks
    Peak activity occurs at dusk
    Best imitating fly—Little Black Stonefly, No. 18

*Nemoura barri* (Stonefly)
   Hatch occurs early April
   Duration of hatch 4 weeks
   Peak activity occurs from 7 P.M. to dusk
   Best imitating fly—Brown Stonefly, No. 16

*Podmosta decepta* (Stonefly)
   Hatch occurs mid-April
   Duration of hatch 18 weeks
   Peak activity occurs in the evening
   Best imitating fly—Ginger Stonefly, No. 18

*Podmosta delicatula* (Stonefly)
   Hatch occurs mid-April
   Duration of hatch 18 weeks
   Peak activity occurs at twilight
   Best imitating fly—Mallard Quill, No. 18

*Nemoura interrupta* (Stonefly)
   Hatch occurs mid-April
   Duration of hatch 14 weeks
   Peak activity occurs from 7 P.M. to dark
   Best imitating fly—Green Stonefly, No. 16

*Cinygmula ramaleyi* (Red Quill)
   Hatch occurs end of May
   Duration of hatch 8 weeks
   Peak activity occurs from 9 A.M. to noon
   Best imitating fly—Red Quill, No. 18

*Epeorus nitidus* (Dark Red Mayfly)
   Hatch occurs early June
   Hatch duration 8 weeks
   Peak activity occurs at midday
   Best imitating fly—Dark Red Quill, No. 12 & 14

*Epeorus longimanus* (Gordon Quill)
   Hatch occurs early June
   Duration of hatch 6 weeks
   Peak activity occurs from 11 A.M. to 2 P.M.
   Best imitating fly—Red Quill Spinner, No. 14

*Callibaetis pallidus* (Ginger Quill)
   Hatch occurs mid-June
   Duration of hatch 4 weeks
   Peak activity occurs from 11 A.M. to 2 P.M.
   Best imitating fly—Ginger Quill, No. 18

*Ephemerella infrequens* (Hendrickson)
    Hatch occurs late June
    Duration of hatch 4 weeks
    Peak activity occurs from 11 A.M. to 2 P.M.
    Best imitating fly—Rusty Spinner, No. 14

*Ephemerella grandis* (Big Red)
    Hatch occurs early July
    Duration of hatch 8 weeks
    Peak activity occurs in the late morning
    Best imitating fly—Great Red Quill, No. 10

*Ephemerella inermis* (Pale Olive Mayfly)
    Hatch occurs early July
    Duration of hatch 4 weeks
    Peak activity occurs in the evening
    Best imitating fly—Pale Olive Quill, No. 14

*Epeorus albertae* (Pink Lady)
    Hatch occurs early July
    Duration of hatch 4 weeks
    Peak activity occurs in the evening
    Best imitating fly—Little Salmon Spinner, No. 16

*Zapada glacier* (Stonefly)
    Hatch occurs early July
    Duration of hatch 4 weeks
    Peak activity occurs at dusk
    Best imitating fly—Brown Stonefly, No. 18

*Amphinemura apache* (Stonefly)
    Hatch occurs early July
    Duration of hatch 8 weeks
    Peak activity occurs in the evening
    Best imitating fly—Willow, No. 18

*Callibaetis americanus* (Grey Quill)
    Hatch occurs mid-July
    Duration of hatch 8 weeks
    Hatch is sporadic
    Best imitating fly—Grey Quill, No. 16

*Heptagenia elegantula* (Dark Gordon)
    Hatch occurs mid-July
    Duration of hatch 4 weeks
    Peak activity occurs in the morning
    Best imitating fly—Dark Gordon Quill, No. 14

*Paraleptophlebia packii* (Iron Mayfly)
    Hatch occurs mid-July
    Duration of hatch 6 weeks
    Hatch is sporadic
    Best imitating fly—Blue Quill, No. 16

*Stenonema verticus* (Paulinskill)
    Hatch occurs late July
    Duration of hatch 4 weeks
    Hatch is sporadic
    Best imitating fly—Paulinskill, No. 16

*Siphlonurus occidentalis* (Grey Quill)
    Hatch occurs early August
    Duration of hatch 6 weeks
    Hatch is sproadic
    Best imitating fly—Grey Quill, No. 18

Good hatches of some of the insects shown above have been seen on the Cowlitz, Green, Hoh, Duckabush, Kalama, Queets, Humptulips, Skagit, Quinault, Skykomish, Stillaguamish, Washougal, Columbia, Nasell, Toutle, East Fork of the Lewis, North Fork of the Lewis, Elochoman rivers, and Icicle Creek. Lake fishing exists on Green, Merrill, Merwin, Spirit, Crescent, Silver, Spencer, Banks, Jamestown, Clear, Curlew, Pierre, Deed, Grandy, Browns, and Sutherland lakes.

## WYOMING

If any western state holds a decided edge in reputation as producing good hatches and good fly-fishing, it has to be Wyoming. This state offers anglers some of the finest western fishing available today.

More than 5,000 lakes are nestled in the peaks of the western mountains and many hold trout. Countless miles of spring creeks, clear rushing trout streams, and major river systems are available, all with trout and trout-supporting hatches.

Several species provide fly-fishermen with action. Top on the list is the trout species—rainbow, brown, cutthroat, brook, laker, and golden. If this smorgasbord of trout doesn't turn on even the most jaded angler, consider the grayling and Rocky Mountain whitefish. Both are excellent feeders on emerging insects.

Some, not all, of Wyoming's top trout waters are found within the confines of Yellowstone National Park and Grand Teton National Park. As very specific rules apply to fishing these waters, you should inquire with the National Park Service before concluding plans to fish in them.

*Nemoura barri* (Stonefly)
    Hatch occurs early April
    Duration of hatch 4 weeks
    Peak activity occurs from 7 P.M. to dusk
    Best imitating fly—Green Stonefly, No. 16

*Nemoura decepta* (Stonefly)
    Hatch occurs mid-April
    Duration of hatch 20 weeks
    Peak activity occurs from 7 P.M. to dark
    Best imitating fly—Brown Stonefly, No. 16

*Nemoura delicatula* (Stonefly)
    Hatch occurs mid-April
    Duration of hatch 20 weeks
    Peak activity occurs at dusk
    Best imitating fly—Grey Stonefly, No. 18

*Nemoura nevadensis interrupta* (Stonefly)
    Hatch occurs mid-April
    Duration of hatch 12 to 16 weeks
    Peak activity occurs in the evening
    Best imitating fly—Yellow Stonefly, No. 18

*Nemoura tina* (Stonefly)
    Hatch occurs in late May
    Duration of hatch 4 weeks
    Peak activity occurs from 5 P.M. to dark
    Best imitating fly—Mallard Quill, No. 14

*Nemoura arctica* (Stonefly)
    Hatch occurs in late May
    Duration of hatch 16 weeks
    Peak activity occurs in the evening
    Best imitating fly—Wulff Stonefly, No. 16

*Nemoura coloradensis* (Stonefly)
    Hatch occurs early in June
    Duration of hatch 12 weeks
    Peak activity occurs at twilight
    Best imitating fly—Brown Stonefly, No. 16

*Cinygmula ramaleyi* (Red Quill)
   Hatch occurs in early June
   Duration of hatch 8 weeks
   Peak activity occurs in late morning
   Best imitating fly—Little Red Quill, No. 18

*Epeorus nitidus* (Dark Red Quill)
   Hatch occurs mid-June
   Duration of hatch 6 weeks
   Peak activity occurs from 11 A.M. to 1 P.M.
   Best imitating fly—Red Quill Spinner, No. 18

*Epeorus longimanus* (Gordon Quill)
   Hatch occurs in mid-June
   Duration of hatch 6 weeks
   Peak activity occurs from 11 A.M. to 2 P.M.
   Best imitating fly—Dark Gordon Quill, No. 14

*Ephemerella infrequens* (Hendrickson)
   Hatch occurs mid-June
   Duration of hatch 6 weeks
   Peak activity occurs from 11 A.M. to 2 P.M.
   Best imitating fly—Rusty Spinner, No. 12

*Ephemerella doddsi* (Western Green Drake)
   Hatch occurs mid-June
   Duration of hatch 3 to 4 weeks
   Peak activity occurs in late morning and early afternoon
   Best imitating fly—Green Drake, No. 10

*Nemoura linda* (Stonefly)
   Hatch occurs late June
   Duration of hatch 8 to 10 weeks
   Peak activity occurs at twilight
   Best imitating fly—Wulff Stonefly, No. 16

*Nemoura mogollonica* (Stonefly)
   Hatch occurs in early July
   Duration of hatch 8 weeks
   Peak activity occurs in the evening
   Best imitating fly—Mallard Quill, No. 18

*Branchycentrus fuliginosus* (Grannom)
   Hatch occurs early July
   Duration of hatch 8 weeks
   Peak activity occurs from noon to dark
   Best imitating fly—Male Grannom, No. 14

*Ephemerella grandis* (Western Green Drake)
    Hatch occurs early July
    Duration of hatch 8 weeks
    Peak activity occurs in late morning and at twilight
    Best imitating fly—Great Red Quill, No. 10

*Ephemerella inermis* (Pale Olive Mayfly)
    Hatch occurs early July
    Duration of hatch 8 weeks
    Peak activity occurs from 10 A.M. to 2 P.M.
    Best imitating fly—Pale Olive Quill, No. 14

*Epeorus albertae* (Pink Lady)
    Hatch occurs early July
    Duration of hatch 8 weeks
    Peak activity occurs at twilight
    Best imitating fly—Pink Lady, No. 16

*Heptagenia elegantula* (Dark Gordon)
    Hatch occurs early July
    Duration of hatch 8 weeks
    Peak activity occurs from 10 A.M. to noon
    Best imitating fly—Dark Gordon Quill, No. 14

*Paraleptophlebia packii* (Iron Blue Quill)
    Hatch occurs early July
    Duration of hatch 8 weeks
    Hatch is sporadic
    Best imitating fly—Blue Quill, No. 18

*Arctopsyche* species (Dark Caddis)
    Hatch occurs early July
    Duration of hatch is 8 weeks
    Peak activity occurs at dusk
    Best imitating fly—Dark Caddis Quill, No. 16

*Rhyacophila* species (Brown Caddis)
    Hatch occurs mid-July
    Duration of hatch 6 to 8 weeks
    Peak activity occurs from 7 P.M. to dark
    Best imitating fly—Brown Caddis, No. 12

*Platyphylax* species (Dark Sedge)
    Hatch occurs mid-July
    Duration of hatch 6 to 8 weeks
    Peak activity occurs at twilight
    Best imitating fly—Dark Brown Sedge, No. 8

*Callibaetis pallidus* (Ginger Quill)
    Hatch occurs mid-to-late July
    Duration of hatch 6 to 8 weeks
    Hatch is sporadic
    Best imitating fly—Pale Olive Quill, No. 16

*Callibaetis americanus* (Grey Mayfly)
    Hatch occurs mid-to-late July
    Duration of hatch 8 to 12 weeks
    Hatch is sporadic
    Best imitating fly—Grey Quill, No. 16

*Nemoura apache* (Stonefly)
    Hatch occurs early July
    Duration of hatch 8 weeks
    Peak activity occurs at dusk
    Best imitating fly—Black Stonefly, No. 16

*Nemoura banksi* (Stonefly)
    Hatch occurs early July
    Duration of hatch 8 to 12 weeks
    Peak activity occurs from 7 P.M. to 9 P.M.
    Best imitating fly—Brown Stonefly, No. 16

*Baetis* species (Blue Quill)
    Hatch occurs late July
    Duration of hatch 8 weeks
    Peak activity occurs from 10 A.M. to 4 P.M.
    Best imitating fly—Blue Wing Olive, No. 22

*Siphlonurus occidentalis* (Grey Drake)
    Hatch occurs early August
    Duration of hatch 4 weeks
    Peak activity occurs at dusk
    Best imitating fly—Grey Mayfly, No. 10

Excellent hatches occur on the Yellowstone, Big Hole, Madison, Gardiner, Gros Ventre, Firehole, North Fork Shoshone, Gibbon, Clark's Fork, Green, Snake, Lewis, Gallatin rivers, and hundreds of small creeks. Good fishing occurs on Yellowstone, Shoshone, Jenny, North Piney, Atlantic, Lonesome, Hidden, Jackson, Bridger, Tomahawk, Cook, and Grave lakes, and Lake DeSmet and Cloud Peak Reservoir.

## HAWAII

This state has insignificant insect activity and few, if any, hatches of interest to anglers.

Some good trout fishing does occur on several island streams. The best chance of success occurs on Kauaikinana, Kawaikoi, Waiakoali, Mohihi, Koaie, and Waialae streams, all on the island of Kauai.

# 11

## Canadian Hatches

Canada is seldom thought of as having significant fly hatches. The typical angler generally associates hatches and spinnerfalls with more southerly streams. In reality, major emergences take place in the Canadian provinces and territories.

While a hatch generally takes place on a more-or-less regular schedule along state-side lakes and streams, in Canada, severe weather, changing climatic conditions, and other factors are often at work to delay emergences. Hatch dates can vary as much as a month with late spring break-ups. Canadian hatches are less apt to occur on the dates which follow than any of the others in this book. I've seen expected hatches of western Hendricksons (*Ephemerella infrequens*) in Alberta begin in late July in the northern region of the province. This hatch *normally* occurs in late June.

The key to pinpointing hatches in Canada is to break each province or territory into northern and southern zones. Emergences can vary as much as four weeks from one zone to the other. Such factors only increase the odds, and the challenge, of hitting good fishing during peak insect activity.

Latitude plays an important role in determining the approximate emergence date for Canadian insects. Cold weather, late ice conditions, or snow has been known to delay or eliminate certain hatches for several years in a row. This is more common in the northern zones, but it can occur in the south as well.

The following information was gathered by Jack Martin of the Canadian Federal Department of Agriculture in Ottawa. He is the resident expert on Canadian insects and he notes that a certain amount of overlapping. occurs with each species. He thinks anglers with a general knowledge of when the hatches *should* occur can plan a fishing trip with some certainty of hitting one or more emergences.

## ALBERTA

This western province offers anglers a moderate blend of snow-capped mountains, foothills, and reasonably dry farmland areas. It has more than 3,000 miles of fast trout streams along the foothills of the Rockies, as well as numerous trout lakes in the mountains. The predominant trout species include rainbow, brown, cutthroat, Dolly Varden, some lake trout, and grayling, with Rocky Mountain whitefish as a bonus.

Two basic types of stream conditions prevail—the clearwater rivers, and glacier-fed, slightly discolored mountain streams. The former are commonly found in the foothills and at lower elevations.

The dividing line between north and south regions is considered to be an east-west line running through Calgary. Students of this book should be prepared to add two to three weeks to the following table if a fishing trip is planned for the northern zone.

*Cinygmula ramaleyi* (Dark Red or Red Quill)
Hatch begins in early June
Duration of hatch is 6 to 8 weeks
Peak activity occurs at midday
Note: Look for hatches to occur over gravel.
Best imitating fly—Red Quill Spinner, No. 18

*Epeorus nitidus* (Big Red)
Hatch occurs in early June
Duration of hatch is 6 to 8 weeks
Peak activity occurs at midday
Note: This is a very important insect for anglers to know. Hatches occur
over a gravel bottom.
Best imitating fly—Hendrickson, No. 14

*Epeorus longimanus* (Little Spinner)
Hatch occurs in mid-June
Duration is 4 weeks
Peak activity occurs in the late morning and early evening
Note: This is an important hatch in Alberta. Gravel areas produce the
best hatches.
Best imitating fly—Quill Gordon, No. 14

*Ephemerella infrequens* (Western Hendrickson)
    Hatch occurs in late June
    Duration is 3 to 4 weeks
    Peak activity occurs from 11 A.M. to 1 P.M.
    *Note:* Look for hatches near gravel areas. A good hatch for trout
        fishermen. It produces fast fishing.
    Best imitating fly—Little Rusty Spinner, No. 14

*Ephemerella grandis* (Giant Red)
    Hatch occurs in early July
    Duration is 6 to 7 weeks
    Peak activity occurs from 10 A.M. to 1 P.M.
    *Note:* This is an extremely productive hatch for anglers to hit. Look for
        hatches in high altitude waters to occur over gravel.
    Best imitating fly—Great Red Quill, No. 10

*Ephemerella inermis* (Olive Quill)
    Hatch occurs in late July
    Duration is 4 to 5 weeks of sporadic activity
    Hatches are sporadic and can occur almost any time
    *Note:* The Olive Quill can offer superb or very slow fishing.
    Best imitating fly—Pale Olive Quill, No. 12

*Epeorus albertae* (Salmon)
    Hatch occurs in late July
    Duration is 4 to 5 weeks
    Peak activity occurs at dusk
    *Note:* This can produce some of the biggest fish. Trout feed heavily on
        salmon flies whenever and wherever they occur.
    Best imitating fly—Pink Lady, No. 16

*Paraleptophlebia packii* (Gray or Dark Blue Dun)
    Hatch begins in late July
    Duration is 4 to 5 weeks
    Emergences can occur anytime during daylight hours
    *Note:* This can be important to anglers if heavy spinnerfalls occur.
        Hatches occur over streams with good gravel bottom.
    Best imitating fly—Iron Blue Dun, No. 18

*Filipalpia peltoperlidae* (Stonefly)
    Hatch occurs in mid-to-late June
    Duration is 4 to 6 weeks
    Peak activity occurs after 11 A.M.
    Best imitating fly—Black Stonefly, No. 14

*Leuctrinae perlomyia* (Western Stonefly)
    Mid-July marks the beginning of this hatch
    Duration is 3 to 4 weeks
    Peak activity occurs from midday to dusk
    Best imitating fly—Stonefly, No. 14

*Trichoptera arctoecia* (Cinnamon Brown)
    Hatch occurs in late June and through July
    Duration is 4 to 5 weeks
    Peak activity can occur from 11 A.M. until dark
    Note: This is an important hatch in much of Alberta.
    Best imitating fly—Cinnamon Sedge, No. 12

*Trichoptera psilotreta* (Dark Blue Sedge)
    Hatch begins in late June through early July
    Duration is 4 to 5 weeks
    Activity is sporadic
    Note: This hatch is of importance to many trout fishermen.
    Best imitating fly—Dark Blue Sedge, No. 12

*Tanyderidae protoplasa* (Crane)
    Common from late June through summer
    Sporadic through all hours of the day
    Note: This insect does not figure too significantly among many anglers.
    Best imitating fly—Black Spider, No. 14

Alberta has a wealth of good areas where insect activity has led to superb fly-fishing. Highly rated are Big Mountain Lake, Kakwa River, Sheep River, Smokey River, Athabasca River, Wapiti River, Cutbank River, Highwood River, Sulphur River, Snake Indian River, Lubicon River, Muskwa River, Pinto River, and Clearwater, South Fork, and Muskwa lakes.

## BRITISH COLUMBIA

This western-most province offers many varieties of lake and stream conditions. It is bordered by the Pacific Ocean and is rimmed with many bays and inlets and towered over by the knifelike edges of the Rocky Mountains.

This province can be divided into three zones: northern, southern, and Vancouver Island. Insect activity in the northern zone may be as much as a month later than hatches found in the southern and Vancouver Island zones. The latter area is often wet, and hatches can occur considerably earlier on some lakes and streams, although this, as with all hatches, is totally dependent upon weather conditions and water temperatures.

Numerous lakes and streams are found in British Columbia and the large majority offer one or more species of trout. Common to this province are rainbow, steelhead (migratory rainbow), cutthroat and sea-run cutthroat, brown trout, Dolly Varden, brook trout, lake trout, and Arctic grayling.

The north-south dividing line can generally be described as running east and west through the town of Prince George. The southern zone would include all of Vancouver Island while the Queen Charlotte Islands would be in the northern zone. Fishermen find that hatches can occur from two to four weeks later in the northern zone. The dates that follow are based on the southern hatches.

*Heptagenidae cinygma* (Red Quill Spinner)
    Hatch begins in early June
    Duration is 4 weeks
    Peak activity occurs in late morning
    *Note:* This emergence is very important to anglers. Hatches occur in
        gravel areas.
    Best imitating fly—Red Quill, No. 16

*Heptagenidae anepeorus* (Dark Mayfly)
    Hatch begins in early June
    Duration is about 4 weeks
    Peak activity occurs from 11 A.M. to 2 P.M.
    Best imitating fly—Dark Red Quill Spinner, No. 12

*Callibaetis americanus* (Gray Mayfly)
    Hatch begins in late June
    Duration is 8 weeks
    Peak activity occurs from midday to dusk
    Best imitating fly—Gray Quill, No. 16

*Ephemerella inermis* (Olive Mayfly)
    Hatch begins in late June
    Duration is 8 weeks
    Peak activity occurs in early morning and late evening
    Best imitating fly—Pale Olive Quill, No. 14

*Epeorus albertae* (Salmon Mayfly)
    Hatch begins in late June
    Duration is 8 weeks
    Peak activity occurs at twilight
    *Note:* This is a very important insect for trout fishermen.
    Best imitating fly—Pink Lady, No. 16

*Heptagenia elegantula* (Gordon Mayfly)
 Hatches begin in late June
 Duration is 8 weeks
 Peak activity occurs in the morning
 *Note:* A very important hatch, but can be sporadic in nature.
 Best imitating fly—Dark Quill Gordon, No. 12 or 14

*Rhyacophilidae glossosomo* (Mountain Caddis)
 Hatch occurs from mid-to-late June
 Duration is 4 weeks
 Peak activity occurs at dusk
 *Note:* This insect is of major importance to trout fishermen. Heaviest
  emergences are found in clear, fast water over gravel.
 Best imitating fly—Black Caddis, No. 12

*Rhyacophilidae anagapetus* (Black Caddis)
 Hatch occurs in mid-to-late June
 Duration is 4 weeks
 Peak activity occurs at dusk
 Best imitating fly—Black Caddis, No. 18

*Filipalpia peltoperlidae* (Fast Water Stonefly)
 Hatches occur in mid-to-late June
 Duration is 4 weeks
 Peak activity occurs in early morning in gravel areas
 *Note:* An important insect for British Columbia anglers.
 Best imitating fly—Black Stonefly, No. 14

*Nemouridae nemoura* (Willow)
 Hatches occur in mid-to-late June
 Duration is approximately 4 weeks
 Peak activity occurs in early morning
 *Note:* This offers anglers a chance at some hefty feeding fish during the
  peak of the hatches.
 Best imitating fly—Willow, No. 16

*Nemouridae cornuta* (Stone Willow)
 Hatches occur in mid-to-late June
 Duration is 6 weeks
 Peak activity occurs in early morning
 *Note:* A very popular hatch that produces some big fish. Look for best
  hatches over gravel areas.
 Best imitating fly—Black Stonefly, No. 14

*Nemouridae ostrocera* (Mountain Stonefly)
   Hatches occur in mid-to-late June
   Duration is 6 weeks
   Peak activity occurs in early morning
   Note: Another good hatch for fly-fishermen to hit.
   Best imitating fly—Black Stonefly, No. 14 or 16

*Deuterophlebiidae coloradensis* (Rocky Mountain Midge)
   Hatches occur in mid-to-late June
   Duration is all summer
   Activity is sporadic, can occur anytime during day
   Best imitating fly—Black Gnat, No. 22

*Philopotamidae chimarra* (Brown Caddis)
   Hatches begin in late June
   Duration is approximately 4 weeks
   Peak activity occurs at dusk
   Best imitating fly—Dark Sedge Caddis, No. 14 or 16

*Paraleptophlebia packii* (Blue Quill)
   Hatches begin in late July
   Duration is 4 weeks
   Activity is sporadic
   Best imitating fly—Iron Blue Dun, No. 16

*Callibaetis pallidus* (Ginger Quill)
   Hatches begin in late July
   Duration is 4 weeks
   Activity is sporadic and can occur anytime
   Note: Quiet rocky water is a good place to look for hatches.
   Best imitating fly—Pale Ginger Quill, No. 16

*Stenonema verticus* (Creamy Mayfly)
   Hatches begin in late July
   Duration varies from stream to stream
   Peak activity occurs from 4 P.M. until dark
   Note: Gravel areas show heaviest activity.
   Best imitating fly—Ginger Quill Spinner, No. 16

Fly-fishermen can expect to find acceptable to excellent hatches on the Redwillow, Narraway, Frazer, Wolverine, Beaver, Caribou, Skeena, Babine, Dease, Stikine, Gold, Stamp, Ash, Kitimat, Wapiti, and Chilcotin rivers.

## MANITOBA

This prairie province is noted as an agricultural area in the south, but sparkling streams, large lakes, and spruce-rimmed ponds are more common in the northern zone. There are no mountainous areas and the elevation is less than 3,000 feet.

The southern zone is well covered by highways but the northern region is still a fly-in proposition. A fairly distinct line can be drawn separating the two zones by drawing an east-west line through The Pas. Hatches can and will be from two to four weeks later in the north, and may run up to six weeks later in waters fronting on the Northwest Territories.

Common species of game fish encountered by fly-fishermen are brook, rainbow, brown, lake trout, lake whitefish, and to a lesser degree, Arctic grayling, Arctic char, and smallmouth bass. Trout are common in both lakes and rivers, as are grayling and whitefish.

*Plecoptera pteronarcys* (Salmon)
    Hatches occur in early June
    Duration is 4 to 6 weeks
    Peak activity occurs at dusk and after dark
    *Note:* This is a very important hatch. Heaviest concentrations occur over
        gravel bars and progress upstream.
    Best imitating fly—Salmon Fly or Western Salmon Fly, No. 6 or 8

*Plecoptera alloperla* (Yellow Stonefly)
    Hatches occur in early June
    Duration is 4 to 6 weeks
    Peak activity occurs at dusk
    *Note:* This is another important Stonefly emergence.
    Best imitating fly—Little Green Stonefly, No. 14

*Plecoptera isoperla* (Yellow Sally)
    Hatches occur in early-to-late June
    Duration is 4 weeks
    Dusk shows the most activity
    *Note:* Another important hatch.
    Best imitating fly—Yellow Stonefly, No. 12 or 14

*Trichoptera psilotreta* (Blue Sedge)
    Hatch occurs in early June
    Duration can be all summer
    This hatch is sporadic and difficult to pinpoint
    *Note:* Look for gravel stretches for best action.
    Best imitating fly—Dark Sedge, No. 14

*Petaluridae tanypteryx* (Flying Needle)
    Early June is the best time
    Sporadic occurrence
    *Note:* Common areas are gravel, mud, and silt.
    Best imitating fly—Blackspider, No. 14

*Prosimulium hirtipes* (Black)
    Early June is when these insects are most common
    Duration is throughout warm summer weather
    Hatches are sporadic
    Best imitating fly—Black Gnat, No. 22

*Cinygmula ramaleyi* (Red Quill)
    Hatches occur in mid-June
    Duration is 6 to 8 weeks
    Heaviest activity is during midday
    *Note:* Gravel areas are best.
    Best imitating fly—Red Quill, No. 18

*Ephemerella infrequens* (Hendrickson)
    Hatches occur in late June
    Duration is 4 weeks
    Peak activity occurs from 11 A.M. to 2 P.M.
    *Note:* This is another very important hatch for fly-fishermen.
    Best imitating fly—Little Rusty Spinner or Female Hendrickson, No. 1

*Ephemerella grandis* (Red)
    Hatches occur in early July
    Duration is 6 to 8 weeks province-wide, but averages about 14 days
    Peak activity occurs in early morning or at dusk
    *Note:* This may be the most important hatch in Manitoba. Edges of large
        riffles are good spots to check.
    Best imitating fly—Dark Great Red Quill or Great Red Quill, No. 10

*Ephemerella inermis* (Olive Quill)
    Hatches occur in mid-July. Can extend into August with regularity.
    Duration is 6 to 8 weeks
    Peak activity occurs from 10 A.M. to 1 P.M. and at dusk
    *Note:* This insect can produce exciting fishing on some streams,
        although it is not found on all streams. Emergences usually take place
        in slow water.
    Best imitating fly—Pale Olive Quill, No. 12

*Epeorus albertae* (Salmon Fly)
    Hatches occur in mid-July
    Duration is 4 weeks
    Peak activity occurs at dusk

*Note:* This hatch can be heavy, with large trout feeding on adult duns and nymphs underwater. Look for hatches in fast water riffles or white water.
Best imitating flies—Male Salmon Spinner and Little Salmon Spinner, No. 18 & 16 respectively.

*Heptagenia elegantula* (Gordon Quill)
Hatches occur in mid-July to early August
Duration is 6 to 8 weeks, with 2 to 3 weeks average on most rivers
Peak activity usually occurs from 11 A.M. to 1 P.M.
*Note:* Another important hatch for fly-fishermen.
Best imitating fly—Dark Gordon Quill, No. 12 or 14

*Callibaetis pallidus* (Ginger Quill)
Hatches occur in late July through late August depending on latitude
Duration of hatch is 4 to 5 weeks
This hatch is characteristically sporadic
*Note:* Quiet meadow streams, beaver ponds, or slow moving currents are ideal places to look for this western Mayfly.
Best imitating flies—Pale Olive Quill and Ginger Quill Spinner, No. 14 & 16

*Stenonema verticus* (Creamy Mayfly)
Hatches occur in late July and through August
Duration of hatch is about 3 weeks
Late afternoon and early evening are peak periods
*Note:* A pale creamy-colored Mayfly that often has massive blanket hatches on some streams.
Best imitating fly—Ginger Quill Spinner, No. 14 & 16

*Callibaetis americanus* (Gray Mayfly)
Hatches occur in late July and through August
Duration of hatch is 4 to 5 weeks
Hatches usually take place in the afternoon
Best imitating fly—Grey Quill, No. 16

*Siphlonurus occidentalis* (Big Grey Mayfly)
Hatches occur in August, occasionally September in southerly areas
Duration is 4 to 6 weeks
Peak activity is during the day and may be sporadic
*Note:* Good hatches can occur in beaver ponds or slow moving streams. The nymphs are large and highly sought after by trout. Adult spinners are a favorite trout food as well.
Best imitating flies—Dark Grey Drake and Light Grey Drake, No. 10 & 8 respectively

Good-to-excellent hatches of some or all of these insects can be found on Caribou, Seal, Wolverine, Nueltin, Reindeer, South Knife, Machichi, Egg, Cochrane, and Kaskattama rivers and Gods, Clearwater, Bain, Reed, Molson, Athapapuskow, Cormorant, High Rock, Neultin, and Thompson lakes.

## NEW BRUNSWICK

This eastern province is rich in fishing opportunities, especially for brook trout, Atlantic and landlocked salmon, and smallmouth bass. Fly hatches can figure significantly in increased pleasure and productiveness during fish trips to this area.

New Brunswick has countless beaver ponds, small lakes, small streams, and large rivers with an abundance of marine life.

Unlike many of the western provinces and territories, this province is small enough that a hatch occurring today on one stream will probably be in evidence on any other stream. The weather is the same throughout the province which helps greatly when planning any fly-fishing trip.

The province has nearly four hundred fifty miles of public water, another seven hundred miles of leased club water on trout and salmon rivers, and more backwoods ponds than a porcupine has quills. This adds up to making this largest of the Maritime provinces a natural for the hatch-seeking fly-fisherman.

*Epeorus pleuralis* (Blue Dun)
    Hatch begins the end of April
    Duration is 3 to 4 weeks
    Peak activity normally occurs from 1 to 2 P.M.
    *Note:* These insects demand fast clear water with no .pollution. This is
        usually the first major hatch and is eagerly awaited by many
        fly-fishermen.
    Best imitating flies—Dark Gordon Quill, Gordon Quill, and Red Quill
        Spinners, No. 12 & 14

*Paraleptophlebia adoptiva* (Little Blue Mayfly)
    Hatch begins the end of April
    Duration is about 3 weeks
    Peak activity occurs at midday
    *Note:* These small mayflies are like gourmet food to hungry spring trout.
        The fish often feed exclusively on hatching duns.
    Best imitating flies—Blue Quill Spinner and Female Blue Quill Spinner,
        No. 20 & 18 respectively.

*Leptophlebia cupida* (Black Quill)
   Hatch begins the end of April or first week in May
   Duration is 3 to 4 weeks
   Peak activity occurs about 2 P.M. and continues through the afternoon on
      a sporadic basis
   *Note:* Look for these hatches to take place in areas with little current.
   Best imitating flies—Black Quill Spinner and Early Brown Spinner, No.
      14

*Ephemerella attenuata* (Blue-Wing Olive Dun)
   Hatch begins the end of April or first week in May
   Duration is 4 weeks
   Peak activity occurs at 1 or 2 P.M.
   *Note:* These insects prefer clear, fast river water with gravel. This hatch
      is of importance to fly-fishermen.
   Best imitating fly—Blue-Wing Olive Dun, No. 14

*Ephemerella subvaria* (Hendrickson)
   Hatch begins in late April or early May
   Duration is about 4 weeks
   Peak activity occurs about 2 P.M.
   *Note:* A very important hatch to hit at peak periods in slow water, silty
      areas. Fish are active during peak periods of activity.
   Best imitating flies—Red Quill, Hendrickson, Little Rusty Spinner,
      Female Hendrickson, No. 12 & 14

*Iron humeralis* (Pale Evening Dun)
   Hatch begins in early May
   Duration is 6 to 8 weeks
   Peak activity occurs at dusk
   *Note:* Another very important hatch for anglers to learn.
   Best imitating fly—Pale Watery Dun, No. 18

*Brachycentrus fuliginosus* (Grannon)
   Hatch begins in mid-May
   Duration is 4 weeks
   Peak activity occurs at dusk
   Best imitating fly—Cinnamon Sedge, No. 14

*Trichoptera dolophilodes* (Black Caddis)
   Hatch begins in mid-May
   Duration is nearly 8 weeks, although peak activity may be limited to 2
      weeks on certain streams
   Peak activity occurs at dusk
   Best imitating fly—Black Caddis, No. 10

*Protoplasa fitchii* (Crane)
    Hatch occurs in mid-May to early June
    Duration is about 10 weeks
    Peak activity occurs in the morning
    Best imitating fly—Black Ivis, No. 10

*Psychomyiidae nomada* (Dark Caddis)
    Hatch begins in late May
    Duration is 6 to 8 weeks
    Peak activity occurs during late evening hours
    Best imitating fly—Adams, No. 12

*Stenonema fuscum* (Ginger Quill)
    Hatch occurs in mid-May to early June
    Duration is 4 to 6 weeks
    Peak activity occurs at dusk
    Note: These insects prefer fast water over gravel. Learn this hatch
        because it is one of the best.
    Best imitating fly—Ginger Quill Spinner, No. 12 & 14

*Paraleptophlebia mollis* (Jenny Spinner)
    Hatch occurs in late May and through June
    Duration is 3 to 5 weeks
    Peak activity takes place between 11 A.M. and 1 P.M.
    Note: An important hatch, but a difficult one to fish. Insects are very
        small and light tippets are needed.
    Best imitating flies—Jenny Spinner and Blue Quill Spinner, No. 20 & 18
        respectively

*Ephemera guttulata* (Shad or Green Mayfly)
    Hatch occurs in late May
    Duration is 3 weeks
    Peak activity occurs in the evening
    Note: These large Mayflies can and will hatch in from slow or fast water,
        among silt or large boulders. Trout particularly welcome the Green
        Drake (another local name) hatch, as do local anglers. Big fish go on
        the prowl when these insects come off.
    Best imitating flies—Male Green Drake, Female Green Drake, Coffin,
        White Wulff, all in No. 8 or 10

*Isonychia bicolor* (Leadwing Coachman)
    Hatches occur primarily in June but can extend into August
    Duration is normally about 10 weeks
    Peak activity occurs during the late afternoon and into the evening
    Note: An important hatch of large slate-colored Mayflies that stimulates
        big fish into active feeding. These insects hatch from fast water after
        crawling onto rocks in shallow water.
    Best imitating flies—Grey Variant and White-Gloved Howdy, No. 12 & 14

*Stenonema vicarium* (March Brown)
  Hatch occurs in early June
  Duration is 4 weeks
  Peak activity occurs from noon until dusk
  Best imitating fly—March Brown, No. 10 & 12

*Leptophlebia johnsoni* (Blue Spinner)
  Hatch occurs in early June
  Duration is about 3 weeks
  Peak activity occurs in the evening
  Best imitating flies—Jenny Spinner and Blue Quill Spinner, No. 16 & 14
    respectively, or Iron Blue Dun, No. 16

*Plecoptera capnia* (Little Black Stonefly)
  Hatch occurs in mid-June
  Duration is 6 to 10 weeks
  Peak activity occurs at dusk
  *Note:* This is an important Stonefly in New Brunswick.
  Best imitating fly—Brown Stonefly, No. 14

*Stenonema canadense* (Ginger Cahill)
  Hatch occurs in late June or early July
  Duration is about 3 weeks
  Peak activity occurs at dusk with sporadic hatching during the day
  *Note:* Fast water is the key to locating these insects. Spinners are present
    for two days and drift with the current. This makes them vulnerable to
    fish. A very popular hatch.
  Best imitating flies—Ginger Quill Spinner, Little Salmon Spinner, and
    Light Cahill, No. 12 & 14

*Ephemera varia* (Yellow Drake)
  Hatch occurs in July
  Duration is about 4 weeks
  Peak activity occurs at dusk
  *Note:* Mating occurs over riffles. The Yellow Drakes mate and then float
    downstream with the current to oviposit. They are vulnerable to trout
    and this makes them valuable to fly-fishermen.
  Best imitating flies—Cream Variant and Yellow Drake, No. 10 & 12

Good fly-fishing to match these emergences can be had on the Little
Miramichi, Tobique, Upsalquitch, Tracadie, Serpentine, Cains, Northwest Miramichi, Nipisiquit, Salmon, Restigouche, Miramichi,
Kedgwick, and Dungarvon rivers. Lakes with some good hatches include Nipisiquit, Long, and other lakes or beaver ponds.

## NEWFOUNDLAND (LABRADOR)

Labrador is considered to be that portion of Newfoundland that is found along the mainland. Newfoundland lies at the mouth of the St. Lawrence River and is surrounded on the south, east, and north by the Atlantic Ocean, and on the west by the Gulf of St. Lawrence.

The primary species of interest to anglers are Atlantic salmon, brook trout, and sea-run brown trout. Some landlocked salmon are taken in interior lakes, ponds, and streams.

Fly hatches seldom begin before mid-May and are often completed by mid-July. Cold weather deters many hatches.

Seasons can be delayed as much as two weeks between more southerly Newfoundland and the harsh climate of Labrador. Anglers should bear this in mind when planning a fishing trip to this province. Add ten days to two weeks to the hatch times shown for Newfoundland when contemplating a trip to the Labrador mainland.

*Ephemerella subvaria (Hendrickson)*
  Hatch occurs in early to mid-May
  Duration is about 4 weeks
  Peak activity occurs at midday
  *Note:* An important early hatch in both areas.
  Best imitating fly—Hendrickson or Red Quill, No. 14

*Epeorus pleuralis* (Red Spinner)
  Hatch occurs in early to mid-May
  Duration is 4 to 8 weeks
  Peak activity occurs from 1 to 3 P.M.
  *Note:* Another important early hatch.
  Best imitating fly—Gordon Quill, No. 12

*Epeorus vitrea* (Sulphur Dun)
  Hatch begin in mid-May
  Duration is 4 to 6 weeks with sporadic hatches all summer
  Peak activity occurs at twilight
  *Note:* This is often a good hatch with much activity.
  Best imitating flies—Little Marryatt, No. 16 (fished wet during a hatch)
    or Pale Watery Dun, Dark Gordon Quill, or Little Sulphur Dun, No. 16
    & 18

*Stenonema vicarium* (March Brown)
  Hatch begins in mid-May
  Duration is 4 weeks
  Peak activity occurs from noon to 6 P.M.

Note: A big fly that hatches during daylight hours. Produces heavy
feeding activity, often with big fish. Look for action near pocket water,
riffles, or runs, although a hatch can occur almost anywhere.
Best imitating flies—March Brown, American March Brown, or Great
Red Spinner, No. 10 & 12

Iron Fraudator (Iron Dun)
Emergence begins in mid-May
Duration is 4 weeks
Peak activity occurs in midday and sometimes in early evening
Note: Trout often rise well to spinner flights.
Best imitating flies—Gordon Quill and Dark Gordon Quill, No. 12 & 14

Paraleptophlebia mollis (Jenny or Jenny Spinner)
Emergence starts in late May
Duration is approximately 4 weeks
Peak activity occurs about 11 A.M.
Note: These small dark Mayflys can develop into an amazingly heavy
hatch and lure big fish to the surface.
Best imitating flies—Jenny Spinner or Blue Quill Spinner, No. 18

Ephemera guttulata (Green Mayfly or Green Drake)
Hatch begins in late May
Duration is 4 to 5 weeks
Peak activity occurs from late afternoon to dusk
Note: Look for hatches in silty or boulder-filled streams. The Green
Drake hatch can be heavy on one stream and nonexistent on another
stream 10 miles away. These big insects bring heavy fish up to the
surface to feed on duns and spinners.
Best imitating flies—Male Green Drake, Female Green Drake, Male
Coffin, Female Coffin, or Grey Fox Variant, No. 8 & 10

Isonychia bicolor (Coachman)
Hatch begins in late May
Some emergences take place all summer. Best in June.
Peak activity occurs in late afternoon
Note: Look for hatches near fast water.
Best imitating flies—Grey Variant or Leadwing Coachman (wet), No. 10
or 12

Hexagenia recurvata (Dark Drake)
Hatch begins in early June
Duration is approximately 8 weeks, much less in northern areas
Peak activity occurs in the evening
Note: This large insect is known as a Brown Drake on some lakes and
streams and it provides fish with a good meal. Trout, in particular, are

fond of feeding on nymphs, duns, and spinners. Look for hatches to occur in silty areas or slow backwater stretches of a stream.
Best imitating flies—Dark Greek Drake and Brown Drake, No. 8 or 10

*Ephemerella needhami* (Rusty Spinner)
Hatch begins in early June
Duration is 4 weeks
Peak activity is from 11 A.M. to 2 P.M.
Best imitating fly—Rusty Spinner, No. 18 & 20

*Plecoptera acroneuria* (Willow)
Hatch begins in early June
Duration is 4 to 6 weeks
Peak activity occurs from 11 A.M. to 3 P.M.
Best imitating fly—Willow, No. 12

*Brachycentrus fuliginosus* (Grannon)
Hatch begins in early June
Duration is about 4 weeks
Activity is sporadic with good hatches on some streams
Best imitating fly—Male Grannon, No. 12 & 14

*Ephemerella attenuata* (Olive Dun)
Hatch begins in mid-June
Duration is 2 to 3 weeks
Peak activity occurs in early morning, but I have seen hatches in late afternoon and just before dark
Best imitating fly—Blue Quill Spinner, No. 16

*Stenonema canadense* (Light Cahill)
Hatch occurs in late June
Duration is 3 weeks
Peak activity takes place throughout the day, heaviest at dusk
Note: A good hatch wherever it occurs. Look for hatches in fast water stretches.
Best imitating flies—Light Cahill or Ginger Quill Spinner, No. 12 & 14

*Hexagenia limbata* (Caddis or Caddis Mayfly)
Hatch begins in late June
Duration is about 3 weeks
Peak activity occurs from dusk until 11 P.M.
Note: This hatch can deliver some of the biggest fish of the season for anglers willing to fish at night. Look for insects in quiet water stretches with silt beds along the riverbanks.
Best imitating flies—Light Mayfly, Light Michigan Mayfly, Dark Michigan Mayfly, or Michigan Spinner, No. 6 or 8

Rhithrogena impersonata (Olive Quill)
    Hatch begin the end of June
    Duration is 4 weeks
    Peak activity is sporadic
    Note: Look for hatches to occur in swift trout streams.
    Best imitating fly—Dark Gordon Quill, No. 10 & 12

Plecoptera rhyacophila (Brown Caddis or Brown Cad)
    Activity begins in late June
    Duration is 3 to 4 weeks
    Peak activity is from 2 P.M. until dark
    Best imitating fly—Brown Caddis, No. 14

Plecoptera stenophylax (Brown Sedge)
    Hatch begin in late June
    Duration is approximately 2 months
    Peak activity occurs in the evening
    Note: This is a very important hatch for anglers to concentrate on.
    Best imitating fly—Dark Sedge, No. 8

Anglers planning a trip to Labrador and Newfoundland should be aware that weather conditions are changeable in the North, and hatches can be sporadic, or nonexistent, depending upon climatic patterns at the time. Good hatches have been noted on the White Bear, Humber, Pinware, White, Gray, Victoria, and Exploits rivers; Dunns and Fishells brooks; and in many backwoods ponds.


## NORTHWEST TERRITORIES

The Northwest Territories is awesome in size, comprising approximately thirty-eight percent of Canada's landmass. This subArctic area is rich in insect life, but only during brief periods of summer weather. The season is short, usually from late June through mid-August, and then winter sets in again for nine months.

The population is about 50,000 people, mostly natives of Indian or Eskimo descent. Many streams are seldom fished with a fly, but outstanding opportunities are available for traveling fly-fishermen. The lake trout is the big attraction, but anglers can also tangle with Arctic char and grayling, and many of these fish have never seen a fly. The fishing can be phenomenal.

Air travel is the only way to find good fishing in this remote land. Lakes and streams are rugged and difficult to get to without the aid of a floatplane. Land travel is limited primarily to one small area in the Yellowknife area.

Many major islands are found in the northern regions, some extending to within five hundred miles of the North Pole. Fishing possibilities exist on Victoria, Banks, Melville, Bathurst, Cornwallis, Prince of Wales, Somerset, Devon, Prince Charles, and Baffin islands.

*Rhyacophilidae glossosoma* (High Water Caddis)
    Hatch begins with ice-out, usually late June
    Duration is 3 weeks
    Peak activity occurs from 4 P.M. until twilight
    Note: Look for hatches to occur over gravel in fast water.
    Best imitating fly—Dark Caddis, No. 20

*Rhyacophilidae protoptila* (Black Caddis)
    Hatch begins at ice-out
    Duration is 3 weeks
    Peak activity occurs in late afternoon
    Best imitating fly—Black Caddis, No. 18

*Phryganeidae glyphopsyche* (Arctic Caddis)
    Hatch begins with ice-out or early June
    Duration is 3 to 4 weeks
    Peak activity occurs at dusk
    Note: This is an important northern hatch.
    Best imitating fly—Dark Sedge, No. 16

*Nemourinae frigida* (Whirling Stonefly)
    Hatch occurs at ice-out or early July
    Duration is 3 to 4 weeks
    Peak activity occurs in the morning
    Best imitating fly—Stonefly, No. 14

*Nemourinae ostrocerca* (Stonefly)
    Hatch occurs at ice-out or early July
    Duration is 3 to 4 weeks
    Peak activity occurs in the morning
    Best imitating fly—Black Stonefly, No. 14

*Deuterophlebiidae coloradensis* (Mountain Midge)
    Hatch occurs at ice-out or early July
    Duration is all summer
    Peak activity occurs whenever the wind is moderate
    Best imitating fly—Dark Midge, No. 20

*Simuliidae gymnopais* (Black)
    Hatch occurs at ice-out or early July
    Duration is all summer
    Peak activity occurs during low wind periods
    Best imitating fly—Black Gnat, No. 22

*Ephemeroptera siphlonuridae* (Grey Drake)
    Hatches occur shortly after ice-out
    Duration is 3 weeks
    Peak activity occurs from midday to twilight
    Best imitating fly—Grey Drake, No. 12

*Heptagenidae stenonema* (Dark Cahill)
    Hatches occur from ice-out until early July
    Duration is 3 to 4 weeks
    Activity is sporadic
    Best imitating fly—Dark Cahill, No. 14

*Nemourinae oregonensis* (Mountain Stonefly)
    Hatch occurs in late June or early July
    Duration is 3 weeks
    Peak activity occurs in the morning
    Best imitating fly—Dark Sedge, No. 16

*Nemoura shipsa* (Arctic Stonefly)
    Hatch occurs in late June or early July
    Duration is 3 to 4 weeks
    Peak activity occurs from 4 P.M. until twilight
    Best imitating fly—Dark Stonefly, No. 16

*Leuctrinae glabra* (Coldwater Stonefly)
    Hatch occurs in late June or early July
    Duration is 3 to 4 weeks
    Peak activity takes place in late afternoon or early evening
    Best imitating fly—Black Sedge, No. 14

*Leptophlebiidae paraleptophlebia* (Blue-wing Dun)
    Hatch begins in early July
    Duration is 3 weeks
    This hatch is very sporadic
    Best imitating fly—Turkey Cahill, No. 12

As the reader can see, hatches in the Northwest Territories have a tendency to occur at much the same time. It's not uncommon to see three or four decidedly different hatches in progress at once. Fish can be very selective and may feed actively on one emerging dun to the exclusion of all others. This produces very challenging yet satisfying sport.

An area the size of the Northwest Territories has an abundance of lakes and streams with fly hatches. The difficult thing is to pinpoint areas where anglers are assured of hitting one or more hatches. Good emergences have been noted on the Mackenzie, Rengleng, Hay,

Nahanni, Liard, Slave, Little Buffalo, Yellowknife, Thelon, and Camsell rivers; and on Mills, Campbell, Great Bear, Great Slave, Kakisa, Marian, Dismal, Dubawnt, and Lac St. Theres lakes.

## NOVA SCOTIA

This Maritime province offers fly-fishermen a wealth of opportunities. Year-round cool weather, moderate rainfall, and stable temperatures combine to bring off adequate hatches.

Nova Scotia has more than 2,500 freshwater lakes and ponds and some 550 rivers and streams. More than 300 of these rivers are managed for trout and Atlantic salmon. Brook, sea-run brook, brown, sea-run brown, rainbow, landlocked salmon, and Atlantic salmon are the principal species available to fly-fishermen.

*Epeorus pleuralis* (Blue Dun)
    Hatch begins in late April
    Duration is 3 to 4 weeks
    Peak activity normally occurs after 1 P.M. but can occur in morning
    *Note:* The first hatch of importance to anglers. Look for hatches in fast
        water areas.
    Best imitating flies—Dark Gordon Quill, Hare's Ear, and Gordon Quill,
        No. 12 & 14

*Iron fraudator* (Dark Gordon Quill)
    Hatch begins in late April
    Duration is about 4 weeks
    Peak activity occurs in midday
    Best imitating flies—Gordon Quill, Red Quill Spinner, and Dark Gordon
        Quill, No. 12 & 14

*Paraleptophlebia adoptiva* (Little Blue Dun)
    Hatch begins in late April
    Duration is 3 weeks
    Peak activity occurs in midday
    *Note:* Medium current areas have the best hatches, but these insects can
        hatch out anywhere.
    Best imitating flies—Blue Quill, Dark Blue Quill, and Dark Red Quill,
        No. 18 & 20

*Leptophlebia cupida* (Twirling Dun or Dark Hendrickson)
    Hatch begins in early May
    Duration is 3 to 4 weeks
    Peak activity occurs about 2 P.M.
    *Note:* Look for hatches of this fairly large Mayfly over fast water.

Best imitating flies—Dark Quill, Black Quill Spinner, Black Quill, and
   Whirling Dun, No. 12 & 14

*Stenonema vicarium* (March Brown or Brown Drake)
   Hatch begins in early May
   Duration is about 4 weeks but can extend well into June
   Peak activity occurs from noon to twilight
   *Note:* Look for emergences in fairly fast water.
   Best imitating flies—March Brown, American March Brown, and Great
      Red Spinner, No. 10 & 12

*Iron humeralis* (Pale Evening Dun)
   Hatch begins in early May
   Duration is 6 to 8 weeks
   Peak activity occurs at dusk
   Best imitating fly—Pale Dun, No. 16

*Ephemerella subvaria* (Hendrickson)
   Hatch begins in early May
   Duration is about 4 weeks
   Peak activity occurs around 2 P.M.
   *Note:* A widespread insect with good hatches.
   Best imitating flies—Red Quill, Hendrickson, Female Hendrickson, and
      Little Rusty Spinner, No. 12 & 14

*Stenonema fuscum* (Ginger Quill)
   Hatch begins in mid-May
   Duration is 4 to 6 weeks
   Peak activity can be sporadic
   *Note:* Another important hatch and one that can produce fast sport. Look
      for insects to hatch from fast water.
   Best imitating flies—Grey Fox and Ginger Quill Spinner, No. 12 & 14

*Diptera chironomidae* (No-see-um)
   Hatches begin in mid-May
   Duration is all summer during warm weather
   Peak activity occurs on warm days with little wind
   Best imitating fly—Black Midge, No. 20 & 22

*Megaloptera sialidae* (Alder)
   Insect activity begins in mid-May
   Duration is all summer
   Best imitating fly—Alder, No. 14

*Paraleptophlebia mollis* (Jenny Spinner)
   Hatch begins in late May
   Duration is 3 to 4 weeks

Peak activity occurs between 11 A.M. and 1 P.M.
*Note:* An important hatch to hit. Look for emergences in slow water over small gravel and pebbles.
Best imitating flies—Jenny Spinner, Blue Quill Spinner, and Dark Blue Quill, No. 18 & 20

*Ephemera guttulata* (Shad Mayfly, Green Mayfly, or Green Drake)
Hatch begins in late May
Duration is 3 weeks
Peak activity occurs after dark
*Note:* This hatch can produce big fish and fast action. Look for emergences around silt-covered boulders.
Best imitating flies—Green Drake, Female Green Drake, Female Coffin, and Male Coffin, No. 8 & 10

*Isonychia bicolor* (Slate Drake or Leadwing Coachman)
Hatches occur in late May
Duration is 10 weeks
Peak activity begins at dusk
*Note:* Look for emergences from shallow water.
Best imitating flies—Grey Variant and White-Gloved Howdy, No. 10 & 12

*Brachycentrus fuliginosus* (Grannon)
Hatch begins in early to mid-June
Duration is about 8 weeks
Peak activity is sporadic and difficult to pinpoint
Best imitating fly—Male Grannon, No. 14

*Chimarra dolophilodes* (Little Black Caddis)
Hatch begins in early to mid-June
Duration is approximately 8 weeks
Emergence is sporadic
Best imitating fly—Black Caddis, No. 16, 18, or 20

*Stenonema ithaca* (Light Cahill)
Hatch begins in mid-June
Duration is about 4 weeks
Peak activity occurs from midday to evening
Best imitating fly—Ginger Quill Spinner, No. 14

*Potamanthus distinctus* (Evening Dun)
Hatch begins in late June
Duration is 4 weeks
Peak activity occurs at twilight
*Note:* Look for emergences over quiet water or in eddies.
Best imitating flies—Golden Spinner or Cream Variant, No. 10 & 12

*Ephemera varia* (Yellow Mayfly or Yellow Drake)
    Hatch begins in late June
    Duration is 6 weeks
    Peak activity occurs at twilight
    Best imitating fly—Yellow Drake, No. 12

Good hatches have been known to occur on the Jordan, Clyde, Sable, Wallace, Gold, Indian, St. Francis, French, Rosemary, Aspy, Medway, and Little Caribou rivers. Look for hatches to show on Smith, Grant, Banook, Dobson, Lake William, Pisca, Corkum, Tinker, Simpsons, and Jeddore lakes.

## ONTARIO

This is Canada's second largest province, with more than 65,000 square miles of water area. At first glance from the air some areas seem to contain more water than land. Ontario is a mixture of spruce-lined bog lakes, large natural lakes left by retreating glaciers, and a maze of streams flowing into lakes Superior, Huron, Ontario, Erie, and north toward James and Hudson bays.

Brook trout retain their preeminent position among Ontario's salmonids, but this province also has healthy populations of splake (brook–lake trout cross), rainbow, brown, and lake trout. Lake whitefish are common in many lakes and can provide a wealth of fly-fishing for anglers fortunate enough to be on the water when dimpling riseforms crease the lake.

This vast province stretches more than 1,000 miles from the metropolitan areas near Toronto to the barren windswept reaches to the north and west of James Bay. This frontier country is home to outsize brookies, big pike, heavy walleyes, and the subarctic angler may be treated to a rare sighting of a wolf, caribou, or even more rarely, a polar bear. Ontario divides into a northern and southern zone for fly-fishermen. Dividing the two would be an east-west line drawn from Timmins to Kenora. The southern zone would encompass the Great Lakes region and north to that line. As much as three weeks difference in hatch times should be noted between the two zones. Many northern hatches overlap, giving anglers a crack at several emergences during one trip.

The dates of Ontario emergences which follow should serve only as a guide. A week of warm weather can trigger massive hatches, while a cool spell can delay them. As a rule, I normally add two weeks to the following dates if the weather is cool and three additional weeks if a cool spring is noted in the northern zone.

*Epeorus pleuralis* (Grey Quill)
    Hatch begins in late April
    Duration is 4 weeks
    Peak activity occurs from noon to 2 P.M.
    *Note:* The first important hatch to occur in both zones.
    Best imitating flies—Blue Dun, Gordon Quill, and Dark Gordon Quill,
       No. 12 & 14

*Iron Fraudator* (Red Quill Spinner)
    Hatch begins in late April
    Duration is 3 to 4 weeks
    Peak activity occurs from 11 A.M. to twilight
    *Note:* Another valuable early hatch for fly-fishermen.
    Best imitating fly—Blue Quill Spinner, No. 18

*Ephemerella subvaria* (Whirling Dun)
    Hatch begins in mid-to-late May
    Duration is 3 to 4 weeks
    Peak of the action occurs from 1 to 3 P.M.
    *Note:* The Hendrickson hatch is No. 1 among Ontario anglers.
    Best imitating flies—Red Quill and Hendrickson, No. 14

*Ephemerella rotunda* (Spinning Dun)
    Hatch begins in late May
    Duration is 3 to 4 weeks
    Peak activity occurs between 1 and 3 P.M.
    *Note:* Another important hatch in Ontario waters.
    Best imitating fly—Hendrickson, No. 12 & 14

*Ephemerella dorothea* (Pale Evening Dun)
    Hatch begins in late May
    Duration is 6 to 8 weeks
    Peak activity occurs at twilight
    *Note:* A small mayfly, but hatches out in massive clouds. Many fish feed
      actively on spinners as well as ascending nymphs. Look for insects in
      quiet water or rocky eddies.
    Best imitating flies—Male Pale Evening Spinner and Pale Evening
      Spinner or Little Marryatt and Pale Watery Dun, No. 14 & 16

*Stenonema fuscum* (Grey Fox)
    Hatch begins in early June
    Duration is 4 to 6 weeks
    Peak activity occurs at twilight
    Best imitating fly—Ginger Quill Spinner, No. 12

*Ephemera guttulata* (Green Drake)
>    Hatch begins in mid-June
>    Duration is 3 to 4 weeks
>    Peak activity occurs in the evening
>    *Note:* Look for insects in larger streams or pools, especially in rocky
>        areas.
>    Best imitating fly—Coffin, No. 8

*Isonychia bicolor* (Slate Drake or Coachman)
>    Hatch begins in late June
>    Duration is about 8 weeks
>    Peak activity occurs in the late evening
>    *Note:* A good hatch that is productive for anglers.
>    Best imitating flies—Slate Drake and Grey Variant, No. 10 & 12

*Leptophlebia cupida* (Dark Hendrickson)
>    Hatch begins in mid-June
>    Duration is 3 to 4 weeks
>    Peak activity occurs about 2 P.M. on most streams, occasionally later
>    *Note:* A fairly large fly that is common to many Ontario streams.
>    Best imitating flies—Early Brown Spinner and Black Quill Spinner, No.
>        14

*Stenonema vicarium* (March Brown)
>    Hatch beings in mid-June
>    Duration is 3 to 4 weeks
>    Peak activity occurs normally in the afternoon but some hatches come
>        off during early evening
>    *Note:* This hatch of Brown Drakes is often the second most important
>        hatch of Ontario's fishing season.
>    Best imitating flies—Great Red Spinner and American March Brown,
>        No. 10 & 12

*Epeorus vitrea* (Little Marryatt)
>    Hatch begins in late June
>    Duration is about 8 weeks
>    Peak activity occurs in late afternoon to twilight
>    Best imitating fly—Ginger Quill Spinner, No. 16

*Hexagenia recurvata* (Drake)
>    Hatch begins in mid-June
>    Duration is 4 to 8 weeks
>    Peak activity occurs after 11 A.M.
>    *Note:* An important hatch on many streams, especially in the southern
>        zone. It can bring some big fish to the surface.
>    Best imitating fly—Brown Drake, No. 8 & 10

*Ephemerella attenuata* (Blue-Olive Dun)
    Hatch begins in mid-June
    Duration is 6 to 8 weeks
    Peak activity occurs from 11 A.M. to 2 P.M.
    Best imitating fly—Red Quill, No. 16

*Brachycentrus fuliginous* (Grannon)
    Hatch begins in early to mid-June
    Duration is 3 to 4 weeks
    Peak activity occurs at dusk
    Best imitating fly—Cinnamon Sedge, No. 10 & 12

*Ephemerella needhami* (Red Quill)
    Hatch begins in late June
    Duration is 4 to 6 weeks
    Peak activity occurs in the afternoon or early evening
    Best imitating flies—Rusty Spinner or Little Red Spinner, No. 14

*Potamanthus distinctus* (Golden Drake or Cream Dun)
    Hatch begins in late June
    Duration is about 3 weeks
    Peak activity occurs at dusk
    Note: An important Mayfly hatch. Look for insects in quiet water or an
        eddy off faster currents.
    Best imitating flies—Golden Spinner or Cream Variant, No. 10 & 12

*Rhithrogena impersonata* (Brown Dun)
    Hatches occur in early to mid-June
    Duration is 4 weeks
    Peak activity occurs in late afternoon or early evening
    Note: This insect is fairly common to swift-water stretches of some
        northern streams.
    Best imitating flies—Dark Gordon Dun or Dark Gordon Quill, No. 10

Other insects hatch from Ontario waters but these are the most important. Look for good hatches to occur on the Nipigon, Severn, Winisk, Pukuskwa, Harmony, Batchawana, Ganaraska, Greenhill, Magpie rivers and Hay Creek; and Nipigon, Silver, Dickinson, Laveille, Canoe, Kasagami, Kabinakagami, Green, Blacktrout, Wawa, McCrea, Patton, McMahon, Dobson, Hyland, Robb, Seymour, Chipman, Stuart, Trout, Ranger, Quinn, and Cumming lakes.

## PRINCE EDWARD ISLAND

This Maritime province is small, but trout fishing is a way of life for residents and nonresident anglers. Brook trout, sea-run brook, and rainbow are the predominant species although a few Atlantic salmon are taken in some streams during fall months.

*Prosimulium hirtipes* (Black)
    Hatch begins in early May
    Duration is all summer during warm, still weather
    Best imitating fly—Black Midge, No. 20

*Tanyderidae protoplasa* (Crane)
    Hatch begins in early to mid-May
    Duration is all summer
    Peak activity is sporadic
    Best imitating fly—Black Spider, No. 12

*Isonychia bicolor* (Slate Drake)
    Hatch begins in late May
    Duration is 8 to 10 weeks
    Peak activity occurs in late afternoon and early evening
    Best imitating fly—Grey Variant, No. 12

*Hexagenia recurvata* (Lake)
    Hatch begins in early June
    Duration is 6 to 8 weeks
    Peak activity occurs from 11 A.M. until dark
    Best imitating fly—Brown Drake, No. 10

*Stenonema canadense* (Cahill)
    Hatch begins in late June
    Duration is 3 to 4 weeks
    Peak activity occurs at twilight
    Best imitating fly—Light Quill Spinner, No. 16

*Stenonema ithaca* (Small Cahill)
    Hatch begins in late June
    Duration is 3 to 4 weeks
    Peak activity occurs during late afternoon until dusk
    Best imitating fly—Ginger Quill Spinner, No. 14

*Nemouridae nemoura* (Stonefly)
    Hatch begins in early-to-mid June
    Duration is 8 to 10 weeks
    Peak activity is sporadic
    Best imitating fly—Stonefly, No. 14

*Potamanthus distinctus* (Cream Dun)
   Hatch begins in late June
   Duration is 4 weeks
   Peak activity occurs at twilight
   Best imitating fly—Cream Variant, No. 12

*Ephemera varia* (Yellow Drake)
   Hatch begins in late June to early July
   Duration is 4 to 5 weeks
   Peak activity occurs at twilight
   Best imitating fly—Yellow Drake, No. 10 or 12

Almost every river running to the ocean will have some of the above listed hatches. Good bets for fly-fishermen are Black River, Winter River, West River, Cow River, Murray River, Montague River, Johnson's River, French River, Percival River, Goose River, and Carr's Stream. East and North lakes can be good.

## QUEBEC

This is the largest of Canada's provinces with more than one million lakes and thousands of miles of rivers and streams. It is bordered on the southeast by the St. Lawrence River and Gulf of St. Lawrence, on the north by Ungava Bay, and on the northwest by James and Hudson bays. A narrow finger of land borders upstate New York, Vermont, New Hampshire, and Maine.

This province must be broken down into two zones, with the northern zone lying north of an east-west line drawn from Chicoutimi (on the upper St. Lawrence River) to Val-d'Or. The southern zone includes the Gaspe Peninsula.

Name it and Quebec has it—brook, rainbow, some brown, lake trout, splake, and lake whitefish. These are the species most apt to rise to an angler's dry fly. Two to four weeks difference may be noted between hatches in the northern and southern zone. The tables listed below are based on southern zone hatches. Subtract two weeks from these figures if the weather is unusually warm, and add four weeks during a colder year.

*Epeorus pleuralis* (Gordon Quill)
   Hatch begins the end of April
   Duration is 4 to 8 weeks
   Peak activity occurs at 1 to 3 P.M.
   *Note:* A very important early season hatch.
   Best imitating fly—Red Quill Spinner, No. 12

*Iron fraudator* (Sulphur Dun)
 Hatch begins in late April
 Duration is 3 to 4 weeks
 Peak activity occurs at midday
 Best imitating fly—Dark Gordon Quill, No. 14

*Ephemerella subvaria* (Hendrickson)
 Hatch begins in late April
 Duration is 4 to 6 weeks
 Peak activity occurs at midday
 *Note:* One of the best of the early hatches.
 Best imitating fly—Red Quill or Hendrickson, No. 14

*Leptophlebia cupida* (Black Quill)
 Hatch begins in late April
 Duration is 4 weeks
 Peak activity occurs from 2 P.M. until dark
 *Note:* Another important early hatch.
 Best imitating fly—Black Quill, No. 14

*Stenonema vicarium* (March Brown)
 Hatch begins in mid-day
 Duration is about 4 weeks
 Peak activity occurs from noon to 5 P.M.
 Best imitating flies—Great Red Spinner or March Brown, No. 10

*Epeorus vitrea* (Sulphury Dun)
 Hatch begins in mid-May
 Duration is late afternoon
 Peak activity occurs late afternoon or dusk
 *Note:* I've seen some good hatches of this small Mayfly on certain
  southern Quebec streams. Look for emergences from riffles just before
  dark.
 Best imitating flies—Ginger Quill Spinner or Pale Watery Spinner, No.
  16 & 18

*Paraleptophlebia mollis* (Jenny Spinner)
 Hatch begins in late May
 Duration is 4 weeks
 Peak activity occurs about 11 A.M.
 *Note:* Look for this hatch in slow water.
 Best imitating flies—Blue Quill Spinner and Jenny Spinner, No. 18 & 20

*Ephemera guttulata* (Green Drake or Shad Fly)
 Hatch begins in late May
 Duration is 4 to 5 weeks
 Peak activity occurs at dusk

*Note:* Look for shad flies on slow stretches of streams.
Best imitating flies—Green Drake and Coffin, No. 8 & 10

*Isonychia bicolor* (Winged Coachman or Slate Wing)
　　Hatch begins in late May
　　Emergence can continue off and on all summer
　　Peak activity occurs in late afternoon or early evening
　　*Note:* Another important emergence for anglers to cover.
　　Best imitating flies—Grey Variant or White-Gloved Howdy, No. 10 & 12

*Hexagenia recurvata* (Dark Green Drake)
　　Hatch begins in early June
　　Duration is 8 weeks
　　Peak activity occurs in the evening
　　*Note:* A large fly will attract large trout wherever a hatch occurs. Look
　　　　for insects to emerge from slow water over silt beds.
　　Best imitating fly—Brown Drake, No. 10

*Ephemerella needhami* (Red Rusty Spinner)
　　Hatch begins in early June
　　Duration is 4 weeks
　　Peak activity occurs from 11 A.M. until 2 P.M.
　　Best imitating fly—Rusty Spinner, No. 18

*Rhithrogena impersonata* (Olive Quill)
　　Hatch begins in early to mid-June
　　Duration is 4 weeks
　　Activity is sporadic
　　Best imitating fly—Dark Gordon Quill, No. 10 & 12

*Brachycentrus fuliginosus* (Grannon)
　　Hatch begins in early June
　　Duration is about 4 weeks
　　Activity is sporadic
　　Best imitating fly—Male Grannon, No. 14

*Ephemerella attenuata* (Olive Dun or Blue-Winged Olive Dun)
　　Hatch begins in mid-June
　　Duration is 2 to 3 weeks
　　Peak activity usually occurs in late afternoon
　　Best imitating flies—Blue Quill or Blue-Winged Olive Dun, No. 14 &
　　　　16

*Stenonema canadense* (Light Cahill)
　　Hatch begins in late June
　　Duration is 3 to 4 weeks
　　Peak activity normally occurs at dusk

*Note:* One of the most important summer hatches wherever found.
Best imitating flies—Red Ginger Quill, Ginger Quill Spinner, and Little
Salmon Spinner, No. 12 & 14

*Hexagenia limbata* (Caddis)
Hatch begins in late June
Duration is about 4 weeks, less if cold weather is present
Peak activity occurs after dark
*Note:* This is not a Caddis Fly but a large Mayfly. It is a good producer for
big wary fish. Look for activity in slow, quiet stretches near large silt
beds.
Best imitating flies—Light Mayfly, Michigan Spinner, and Dark Michigan
Mayfly, No. 6 & 8

It's been my pleasure to hit a few of the more important Quebec
hatches. They can rival anything I've found elsewhere. One was the
*Hexagenia limbata* hatch on the Matane. It produced four big trout over
16 inches—one measured 19½ inches and weighed nearly 4 pounds.
Good hatches occur on the Paribonka, Croche, Windigo, Gaspe, Cas-
capedia, Eastmain, Metapedia, Trenche, Chandler, Kaniapiskau,
George, Moisie rivers and Lac Clair, Lac Remi, Portage Lake, 31 Mile
Lake, Parent Lake, Lac St. Jean, and Mistassini Lake.

## SASKATCHEWAN

This so-called "western prairie province" may have some prairie,
but it also has a lot of water. Roughly one-eighth of Saskatchewan is
water and literally tens of thousands of lakes, beaver ponds, or potholes
are available to anglers. It has thousands of miles of running water,
ranging from small tributaries to large, roaring rivers in the North.

Trout is a specialty and brook trout is one of the major drawing
cards for nonresident anglers. Rainbow, brown, lake trout, and Arctic
grayling offer an additional challenge for fishermen. Big lake whitefish are considered a bonus fish by many sportsmen, and they deliver
fantastic fly rod sport on calm summer evenings.

It's necessary to divide this province into two zones. The northern
zone is separated from the southern zone by an east-west line running
through La Ronge. Add two weeks to the following tables if the weather
is warm in the north, and three weeks during cool or cold weather. This
should put the hatches in the north just about on schedule.

*Epeorus nitidus* (Big Red)
  Hatch begins in early June
  Duration is 6 to 8 weeks
  Peak activity occurs at midday
  *Note:* A very important early hatch, but one that is difficult to
    distinguish.
  Best imitating fly—Hendrickson, No. 14

*Cinygmula ramaleyi* (Red Fly)
  Hatch begins in early June
  Duration is 6 to 8 weeks
  Peak activity occurs at midday
  Best imitating fly—Red Quill, No. 18

*Trichoptera psilotreta* (Blue Sedge)
  Hatch begins in early June
  Duration is all season
  Activity is sporadic with good hatches on some streams and poor
    emergences on others
  Best imitating fly—Dark Sedge, No. 14

*Petaluridae tanypteryx* (Snakefly or Needle)
  Action begins in early June
  Duration is all season
  Peak activity is sporadic
  Best imitating fly—Dragonfly, No. 12

*Gomphidae ophiogomphus* (Flying Needle)
  Action begins in early June
  Duration is all season
  Activity is sporadic
  Best imitating fly—Black Dragon, No. 12

*Epeorus longimanus* (Spinner)
  Hatch begins in mid-June
  Duration is 4 weeks
  Peak activity occurs from 10 A.M. to 2 P.M.
  *Note:* An important hatch.
  Best imitating fly—Gordon Quill, No. 14

*Filipalpia peltoperlidae* (Stonefly)
  Hatch begins in mid-June
  Duration is 4 weeks
  Peak activity is from 11 A.M. until dark, but sporadic in nature
  Best imitating fly—Little Black Stonefly, No. 16

*Plecoptera capnia* (Snowfly)
    Hatch begins in mid-June
    Duration is 4 weeks
    Peak activity can occur all day
    Best imitating fly—Black Stonefly, No. 14

*Trichoptera arctoecia* (Cinnamon Brown Fly)
    Hatch begins in mid-June
    Duration is 3 to 4 weeks
    Peak activity is from 11 A.M. until dusk
    *Note:* Another important hatch for anglers to zero in on.
    Best imitating fly—Cinnamon Sedge, No. 12

*Chimarra* species (Black Caddis)
    Hatch begins in mid-June
    Duration is 3 to 4 weeks
    Peak activity is from noon until dusk
    Best imitating fly—Black Caddis, No. 16 & 18

*Tanyderidae protoplasa* (Crane)
    Hatch begins in mid-June
    Duration is balance of season
    Peak activity varies; hatches are erratic
    Best imitating fly—Black Spider, No. 14

*Prosimulium hirtipes* (Black Fly)
    Hatches begin in mid-June
    Duration is balance of summer
    Peak activity is sporadic, usually based on warm, windless days
    Best imitating fly—Black Gnat, No. 20 & 22

*Ephemerella infrequens* (Hendrickson)
    Hatch begins in late June
    Duration is 3 to 4 weeks
    Peak activity is from 11 A.M. until 1 P.M.
    *Note:* A very important hatch on many Saskatchewan streams.
    Best imitating fly—Rusty Spinner or Hendrickson, No. 16

*Ephemerella grandis* (Big Mayfly)
    Hatch begins in early July
    Duration is 6 to 7 weeks
    Peak activity occurs from 10 A.M. until 1 P.M.
    *Note:* Another very important hatch.
    Best imitating fly—Big Red Quill, No. 10 or 12